Step by Step

MICROSOFT®

SQL SERVER™ 2000
DTS

STEP BY STEP

Carl Rabeler

PUBLISHED BY
Microsoft Press
A Division of Microsoft Corporation
One Microsoft Way
Redmond, Washington 98052-6399

Library of Congress Cataloging-in-Publication Data
Rabeler, Carl, 1955-
    Microsoft SQL Server 2000 DTS Step by Step / Carl Rabeler.
        p. cm.
    Includes index.
    ISBN 0-7356-1916-6
        1. Client/server computing. 2. SQL server. I. Title.

    QA76.9.C55R32   2003
    005.75'85--dc21   2003051213

Printed and bound in the United States of America.

1 2 3 4 5 6 7 8 9   QWE   8 7 6 5 4 3

Distributed in Canada by H.B. Fenn and Company Ltd.

A CIP catalogue record for this book is available from the British Library.

Microsoft Press books are available through booksellers and distributors worldwide. For further information about international editions, contact your local Microsoft Corporation office or contact Microsoft Press International directly at fax (425) 936-7329. Visit our Web site at www.microsoft.com/mspress. Send comments to *mspinput@microsoft.com*.

Acquisitions Editor: Juliana Aldous Atkinson
Project Editor: Jenny Moss Benson
Technical Editor: Paul Chambre
Copyeditor: Victoria Thulman
Cover Graphic Designer: Methodologie
Principal Compositor: Elizabeth Hansford
Indexer: Richard Shrout

Body Part No. X09-59423

Contents

Introduction

One of the challenges that business executives face today is the need to integrate data from disparate sources, in different locations, and in disparate formats into a single data store to assist them in making business decisions. The developer of the data movement application charged with the task of integrating this disparate data needs a single tool that he or she can use to extract the data from each disparate data source, transform the data in many different ways, and then load the data into the integrated data structure. This tool must be flexible and extensible enough to meet the needs of experienced developers yet be simple enough for beginning developers to use. In addition, the tool must be capable of developing data movement applications that are easy for database administrators to use and manage.

Microsoft SQL Server 2000 Data Transformation Services (DTS) is this tool. Developers can use DTS to create simple or complex data movement applications. These applications can be created using the DTS Import/Export Wizard, DTS Designer, and Microsoft Visual Basic, depending on the complexity required for the data movement application and the skill set of the developer. The data movement application can consist of a single DTS package or can consist of a number of interrelated DTS packages. Each DTS package contains connection objects, tasks, and workflow constraints.

This book teaches you how to use DTS by providing you with step-by-step procedures that let you build an extensible data movement application that periodically moves data from delimited text files, a SQL Server database, and Microsoft Excel spreadsheets into a multidimensional cube in Microsoft Analysis Services. While some knowledge of SQL Server, Analysis Services, and ActiveX is assumed in the design of the data movement application, this knowledge is not required to understand the DTS techniques and best practices encapsulated in the data movement application that you will build.

The first part of this book is written for those readers who are new to DTS, and the remaining chapters are geared to those readers who have some previous exposure to DTS. The packages created in each chapter build upon themselves; it is intended that you complete the procedures in this book in chapter order. However, the files for each chapter also include completed packages from previous chapters and database backup files to allow you to perform the procedures in this book in any order you want.

How This Book Is Organized

This book consists of ten chapters, organized as follows:

- Chapter 1, "Jumping into DTS," provides an introduction to the capabilities of DTS. In this chapter, you learn how to create DTS packages using the DTS Import/Export Wizard that import and export data from heterogeneous data sources. You also learn how to copy objects and data between SQL Server databases.

- Chapter 2, "Using DTS Designer to Build and Extend Packages," teaches you how to modify and extend existing DTS packages using DTS Designer. You learn how to work with connection objects and to work with the Transform Data, Execute SQL, and Bulk Insert tasks. You also learn how to add precedence constraints to package tasks to control their execution order.

- Chapter 3, "Working with DTS Packages," teaches you how to save DTS packages in different formats and to utilize version control. You also learn how to secure and execute DTS packages. Finally, you learn how to enable package execution logging and error logging.

- Chapter 4, "Creating Advanced DTS Tasks," teaches you how to perform lookup queries inside a Transform Data task and to use a Data Driven Query task to determine which of several queries to execute based on the content of the data in each row. You also learn how to access the phases of the multiphase data pump and to call a subpackage using an Execute Package task.

- Chapter 5, "Working with Advanced DTS Options," teaches you how to configure package and task execution properties. You also learn how to enable transactions and join packages and tasks into existing transactions. Finally, you learn how to enable and configure exception files.

- Chapter 6, "Dynamically Configuring DTS Package Objects," teaches you how to use a data link connection to dynamically configure the connection objects in a package. You also learn how to use the Dynamic Properties task to dynamically configure package and task objects at run time through the use of an initialization file and global variables. Finally, you also learn how to change the global variable values in a subpackage from a master package at run time.

- Chapter 7, "Using ActiveX Script Tasks," teaches you how to use ActiveX Script tasks to set global variable values in packages and tasks at run time from a SQL Server table and from the Windows registry. You also learn how to use ActiveX Script tasks to incorporate branching into your DTS packages.

- Chapter 8, "Incorporating Error Handling into DTS Packages," teaches you how to add batch control to a data movement application. You also learn how to create step and package success and error logging tasks. Finally, you also learn to record information about the number of rows transformed and the number of rows with errors in an audit table in SQL Server.

- Chapter 9, "Completing the Data Movement Application," teaches you how to create a starter DTS package as a template for future packages. You then use this starter package to create the final package required to complete the data movement application. Finally, you learn how to restore an Analysis Services cube and then add an Analysis Services Processing task to a package, which updates the data in the Analysis Services cube.

- Chapter 10, "Operating the Data Movement Application," teaches you how to use the data movement application. You learn how to modify the initialization file and configurations of global variable values in a SQL Server table to control the operation of the data movement application. You also learn how to use an audit table in SQL Server and the batch capabilities of the data movement application to easily understand the results of each execution of the data movement application.

What Do I Need to Use This Book?

The following are the basic hardware and software requirements for using *Microsoft SQL Server 2000 DTS Step by Step* and its companion CD:

- PC with 300-megahertz or higher clock speed, 128 megabytes (MB) of RAM or more, at least 500 MB of available hard disk space, super VGA (800 x 600) or higher, CD-ROM or DVD drive, keyboard, and Microsoft Mouse or compatible pointing device.

- Microsoft Windows XP—all procedures in this book assume you are using Windows XP, although you can also use any edition of Windows 2000 or Windows Server 2003.

- Microsoft SQL Server 2000—install a default instance of SQL Server 2000 using the Typical installation option. Do not change any default values.

- Microsoft Analysis Services 2000—install Analysis Services using the default options.

▶ **Important**   The procedures in this book assume that you are a member of the Administrators and OLAP Administrators local group on your computer and that you are a member of the System Administrators server role within SQL Server.

▶ **Note**   An evaluation version of SQL Server 2000 can be obtained at *http://www.microsoft.com/sql/evaluation/trial/default.asp*. The evaluation edition contains 120-day trial versions of both SQL Server 2000 and Analysis Services 2000.

How Do I Install the Practice Files?

The companion CD included in the back of this book contains the practice files that you will use to complete the procedures in this book and the skipped chapter files for each chapter in this book (to allow you to begin this book at the beginning of any chapter). Installing the practice files requires approximately 50 MB of disk space. Follow these steps to install the practice files on your computer's hard disk so that you can use them with the procedures in this book.

1   Insert the CD in your CD-ROM drive. If a menu screen does not appear, double-click StartCD.exe in the root of the CD-ROM.

2   Click the Install Practice Files option, and follow the prompts that appear on the screen.

3   When the files have been installed, remove the CD from your CD-ROM drive and replace it in the package inside the back cover of the book.

A folder named Microsoft Press has been created at the root of your C drive that contains all of the practice files in a subfolder named SQL DTS SBS.

▶ **Important**   Before you begin, you must execute the BeforeYou-Begin.cmd batch file from the C:\Microsoft Press\SQL DTS SBS folder to attach the SBS_OLTP database. This database is a copy of the English version of the Northwind database. This database is the online transactional processing (OLTP) database that you will use as the source for some of the data that the data movement application will move into an online analytical database (OLAP).

How Do I Obtain More Information?

Every effort has been made to ensure the accuracy of this book and the companion CD. Microsoft Press provides corrections for books through the World Wide Web at:

http://www.microsoft.com/mspress/support

To connect directly to the Microsoft Press Knowledge Base and enter a question you may have about this book, go to:

http://www.microsoft.com/mspress/support/search.asp

If you have comments, questions, or ideas regarding this book or the CD-ROM, or questions that are not answered by querying the Knowledge Base, please send them to Microsoft Press via e-mail at:

mspinput@microsoft.com

or via postal mail to:

Microsoft Press
Attn: DTS Step by Step Editor
One Microsoft Way
Redmond, WA 98052-6399

Please note that product support is not offered through the above address. For technical assistance, please try the Microsoft Developer Network library or the Microsoft support Web site at:

http://msdn.microsoft.com/library/

http://support.microsoft.com/directory/

Jumping into DTS

In this chapter, you will learn how to:

- Import data into SQL Server using the DTS Import/Export Wizard

- Export data from SQL Server using the DTS Import/Export Wizard

- Copy objects and data between SQL Server databases using the DTS Import/ Export Wizard

---

One of the challenges business executives face today is the integration of data from disparate sources and formats into a single data store to assist them in making informed business decisions. To populate this integrated data store, the data movement application developer needs a single tool that is flexible and extensible enough to meet the needs of experienced developers, yet simple enough for beginning developers to use. In addition, the data movement application built by the tool must be easy for Database Administrators (DBAs) to manage and control.

Microsoft SQL Server 2000 Data Transformation Services (DTS) is this tool. You can use DTS to create simple data movement applications by using the DTS Import/Export Wizard, which we'll discuss in this chapter. You can create more complex data movement applications by using DTS Designer, which you'll learn about in Chapter 2, or by using Microsoft Visual Basic. The data movement application can range in complexity from a single DTS package to a large set of interrelated DTS packages. Each *DTS package* contains connection objects, tasks, and precedence constraints. *Connection objects* define data sources, data destinations, and data lookup structures. *Tasks* define the actions that will be performed within the DTS package, and they use the connection objects as

12 Select the Save DTS Package check box, click Structured Storage File, and then click Next to provide the details for the save options.

You will save the package to the local file system and use an owner password to secure the package. You will learn about package security in Chapter 3.

13 Type **SQL_DTS_SBS_1.1** in the Name box, type **DTS Step By Step Chapter 1 Package 1** in the Description box, type **mypassword** in the Owner Password box, and type the following in the File Name box:

**C:\Microsoft Press\SQL DTS SBS\Ch1\WorkingFolder\
SQL_DTS_SBS_1.1.dts**

Click Next to review the selections you made in the wizard.

14 Click Finish to save and execute the package. The progress of the
package execution is displayed.

15 Click OK to acknowledge that the package copied one table successfully from Microsoft SQL Server to Microsoft SQL Server.

Notice that the wizard saved the package and then executed three
tasks (also called steps). The first task, *Drop Table
[SBS_OLAP].[dbo].[Sales By Category SBS] Step* (the Drop Table
step), failed. This task failure is expected because this destination
table does not yet exist. The next time the task is executed, the existing table will be dropped. Notice that the failure of the drop table
task did not cause the entire package to fail. (You will learn more
about workflow execution rules between tasks in Chapter 2.) The
next task, *Create Table [SBS_OLAP].[dbo].[Sales By Category SBS]
Step* (the Create Table step), created the *Sales By Category SBS* table.
The final task, *Copy Data From Sales By Category to
[SBS_OLAP].[dbo].[Sales By Category SBS] Step* (the Copy Data
step), populated the *Sales By Category SBS* table in the SBS_OLAP
database.

Notice also that 77 rows were copied to the *Sales By Category SBS*
table. Finally, if you scroll to the right, you can observe the start, finish, and execution times of each step in the package.

▶ **Tip** If a problem is encountered during the execution of any step in the package, you will receive an error. To obtain more details about the error, double-click the task with the error. If the error causes the package to fail, you can click Back and correct the error. However, you will need to rename the package before clicking Finish to save and execute the package again. The DTS Import/Export Wizard created the package containing the error on the first execution attempt, and the wizard will not overwrite an existing package.

16 Click Done.

You have successfully created your first DTS package. In Chapter 2, you will learn how packages function by using DTS Designer to look at the details of each task in this package. You'll also learn how to create more complex packages with additional functionality. In the remainder of this chapter, you will learn how to perform additional tasks using the DTS Import/Export Wizard and how to work with different data sources and destinations.

Copy data between SQL Server databases using a SQL query

In the next procedure, you will learn how to use a SQL query to consolidate and filter data as it is copied between SQL Server databases. DTS is frequently used to assist in preparing a variety of reports by consolidating and filtering data from disparate sources.

1 To launch the DTS Import/Export Wizard, click the Start button, point to All Programs, point to Microsoft SQL Server, and then click Import And Export Data.

2 Click Next to select a data source from which you will copy data.

In this procedure, you will again select the SBS_OLTP database on your local server as your data source.

▶ **Note** DTS can extract data from or copy data to any OLE DB or ODBC data source to which it can establish a connection and to which it has sufficient permissions.

3 Ensure that Use Windows Authentication is selected, and ensure that
(local) appears in the Server list. In the Database list, select
SBS_OLTP, and then click Next to select a data destination.

In this procedure, you will select the SBS_OLAP database on your
local server, the database that you created in the previous procedure,
as the destination for the data you are importing.

4 Ensure that Use Windows Authentication is selected, and ensure that
(local) appears in the Server list. In the Database list, select
SBS_OLAP, and then click Next to specify what DTS will copy from
the data source to the data destination.

In this procedure, you will use a query to consolidate and filter the
data as it is being copied from the SBS_OLTP database to the
SBS_OLAP database.

5 Click Use A Query To Specify The Data To Transfer, and then click
Next to specify the query that DTS will use.

You can type a Transact-SQL query directly into the Query Statement text box, or you can click Browse to locate and load a query
from a script file stored in the file system. If you need help building
basic Transact-SQL queries, a graphical query builder is also available.
In this procedure, you will use the Query Builder to build a simple
query.

6   Click Query Builder. This will bring up an interface in which you can select tables and columns from the data source.

In this procedure, you will select a subset of the columns in the *Customers* and *Orders* tables to retrieve the list of customers with orders that have not been shipped.

7   In the Source Tables list, expand Customers, double-click Company-Name, double-click ContactName, and then double-click Phone. Expand Orders, double-click OrderID, double-click RequiredDate, and then click Next to choose a sort order. You will sort the rows based on the required date of the order.

8 In the Selected Columns list, double-click the RequiredDate column in the Orders table and then click Next to specify the query criteria.

By default, all rows will be returned. In this procedure, you will limit the rows returned to those orders that have not shipped and whose required date is greater than or equal to the current date.

9 Click Only Rows Meeting Criteria. In the Column list, select [Orders].[RequiredDate]; in the Oper. list, select >=; and in the Value/Column list, type **GETDATE()**. In the first column in the second row, select And; from the drop-down list in the Columns list, select [Orders].[ShippedDate]; in the Oper. List, select =; in the Value/Column list, type **NULL**; and then click Next to review the query.

Review the generated query and its syntax. *GETDATE()* is an internal Transact-SQL function that returns the current *Datetime* information at the time that the package's query is executed. Although the Query Builder did a pretty good job of creating this query that joins the *Customers* and *Orders* tables, to achieve the desired results, you need to change this query to use the *IS NULL* clause rather than = *NULL*.

▶ **Important**   The Query Builder is very good at generating the Transact-SQL script for basic queries and joins, but you will sometimes need to modify the generated script to achieve the result set you desire. As you can see in this example, the Query Builder does not know to change *=NULL* to *IS NULL* when performing *NULL* comparisons.

10   In the Transact-SQL statement, replace the = before the NULL clause with **IS**, and add a space between IS and NULL.

▶ **Tip**   To verify that the Transact-SQL syntax for your completed script is valid, click Parse.

11   Click Next to modify the schema or the data as it is copied to the data destination.

Notice that Query is displayed as the source and Results is displayed as the destination. If you click Next, the results of the query you just created will be copied to a new table called *Results* in the SBS_OLAP database. However, you will change this default name to *Unshipped-Orders*, which is a more descriptive name for the new table.

12 In the Destination column, highlight Results, and then type
UnshippedOrders. Do not include a space in the table name.

13 Click the ellipsis in the Transform column to view the details of the
new table that will be created.

In the Mappings box on the Column Mappings tab, notice the mapping between the columns returned by the source query and the columns that will be created in the destination table. Notice also the
data types, the nullable property, and the column size for the columns in the destination table. These properties of the destination
table are generated automatically by DTS based on the properties of
the columns in the result set. You can change these properties in the
Mappings box, or you can click the Edit SQL button and modify the
Transact-SQL script directly.

14 Click Edit SQL to view the Transact-SQL script that DTS will use to create the destination table.

You can change this Transact-SQL statement to change the column names or properties. However, the DTS Import/Export Wizard does not support major changes to the script. In Chapter 2, you will learn how to use the Execute SQL task to write more complex Transact-SQL statements within a package. In this procedure, you will not change the properties of the destination table.

▶ **Tip** If you make a mistake when viewing or modifying the Transact-SQL statement, click Auto Generate to regenerate to the original Transact-SQL statement.

15 Click Cancel to close the Create Table SQL Statement dialog box.

16 Select the Drop And Recreate Destination Table check box.

17 Click the Transformations tab, and then click Transform Information As It Is Copied To The Destination to view the transformation options.

The Visual Basic transformation script copies information from each source column to each destination column without changing any data. You can perform additional transformations by changing this script. In this procedure, you will not perform any script-based transformations.

You will learn to perform transformations using the default scripting language—Visual Basic, Scripting Edition (VBScript)—throughout the course of this book. Microsoft JScript is also available with an installation of SQL Server, and additional programming languages can be installed.

Column Mappings and Transformations

Source: Query
Destination: UnshippedOrders

Column Mappings | Transformations |

○ Copy the source columns directly to the destination columns

◉ Transform information as it is copied to the destination

```
'==========================================
' Visual Basic Transformation Script
' Copy each source column to the destination column
'==========================================
Function Main()
    DTSDestination("CompanyName") = DTSSource("CompanyName")
    DTSDestination("ContactName") = DTSSource("ContactName")
    DTSDestination("Phone") = DTSSource("Phone")
    DTSDestination("OrderID") = DTSSource("OrderID")
    DTSDestination("RequiredDate") = DTSSource("RequiredDate")
    Main = DTSTransformStat_OK
End Function
```

Language: [VB Script Language ▼]   [Browse...]

[OK]   [Cancel]   [Help]

18 Click OK and then click Next to choose whether to execute the package immediately and to save, schedule, or replicate the package.

19 Click Save DTS Package, click Structured Storage File, and then click Next to provide the details for the save options.

20 Type **SQL_DTS_SBS_1.2** in the Name box, type **DTS Step By Step Chapter 1 Package 2** in the Description box, type **mypassword** in the Owner Password box, and type the following in the File Name box:

**C:\Microsoft Press\SQL DTS SBS\Ch1\WorkingFolder\
SQL_DTS_SBS_1.2.dts**

Click Next to review the selections that you made in the wizard.

21 Click Finish to save and execute the package.

22 Click OK to acknowledge that the package copied one table successfully.

The wizard saved the package and then executed three tasks. The first task, the *Drop Table UnshippedOrders Step* task, failed. This task failure was expected because this destination table does not yet exist. The next task created the *UnshippedOrders* table. The final task populated the *UnshippedOrders* table. The next time this package is executed, the existing table will be dropped before the new table is created and populated. No rows are copied to the *Unshipped-Orders* table because there are no orders with a required date equal to or greater than now in the SBS_OLTP database.

23 Click Done.

You have successfully created a package that extracts data from two tables at the data source and creates a new table at the data destination by using a Transact-SQL query containing a multi-table join and a *WHERE* clause. In Chapter 2, you will use DTS Designer to add additional functionality to this package.

Copy data from a Microsoft Access database to a SQL Server database

Businesses frequently store data in a variety of structured formats, such as in Microsoft Access databases or in Microsoft Excel worksheets, and need to consolidate this data for reporting purposes. In the following procedure, you will learn how to copy data from an Access database into the SBS_OLAP database. You will launch the DTS Import/Export Wizard from within the SQL Server Enterprise Manager management console rather than from the Start menu.

1   To launch the DTS Import/Export Wizard from within SQL Server Enterprise Manager, click the Start button, point to All Programs, point to Microsoft SQL Server, and then click Enterprise Manager.

2   In the SQL Server Enterprise Manager console tree, expand Microsoft SQL Servers, expand SQL Server Group, and then click (local) (Windows NT) to establish a connection to the default instance of SQL Server on your local server.

> ▶   **Important**   Most of the SQL Server wizards operate in the context of a connection to a SQL Server instance. If your focus within SQL Server Enterprise Manager is not within a connection to a SQL Server instance (for example, if your focus is at the top of the console tree), most of the SQL Server Enterprise Manager wizards will be grayed out.

3   On the Tools menu, point to Data Transformation Services, and then click Import Data to launch the DTS Import/Export Wizard.

4   Click Next to select a data source from which you will copy data.

In this procedure, you will change the default data source and select an Access database as your data source.

5   In the Data Source list, select Microsoft Access.

Notice the extensive list of data sources from which DTS can import data. After you select Microsoft Access as your data source, the page changes to reflect the connection information required to connect to an Access database. You do not need to have Access installed to connect to an Access database, but you must be able to connect to the Access .mdb file using its file name. Based on the security set for the Access file, you might have to provide a user name and password. In this procedure, you will connect to the AccessPubsDB database.

> ▶ **Important**   When you save a DTS package that includes user names and passwords, you will have to edit the connection object or objects in the package to reflect any changes to this information that occur in the future. This task can become quite time consuming in large data movement applications because the number of connection objects increases in more complex packages. Chapter 3 discusses the security implications of embedding authentication information in packages.

6 In the File Name box, type **C:\Microsoft Press\SQL DTS SBS\Ch1\ ChapterFiles\AccessPubsDB.mdb** and then click Next to select a data destination. You will leave the Username and Password boxes empty because this database file does not have any security restrictions.

7 Verify that Microsoft OLE DB Provider For SQL Server appears as the data destination, ensure that Windows Authentication is selected, and ensure that (local) appears in the Server list. In the Database list, select SBS_OLAP and then click Next to specify what DTS will copy from the data source to the data destination.

Notice that the Copy Objects And Data Between SQL Server Databases option is grayed out because the data source is not a SQL Server database. In this procedure, you will copy entire tables from the AccessPubsDB database into the SBS_OLAP database rather than use a query to filter or consolidate the data being imported.

8 Click Next. This will bring you to the page in which you can select which tables in the Access database to copy.

In this procedure, you will select all the tables in AccessPubsDB to copy, with their data, to the SBS_OLAP database. When the package is executed, DTS will create destination tables with the same names as the source tables and populate them with all the data from the source tables.

9 Click Select All and then click Next to choose whether to execute the package immediately and to save, schedule, or replicate the package.

10 Click Save DTS Package, click Structured Storage File, and then click Next to provide the details for the save options.

11 Type **SQL_DTS_SBS_1.3** in the Name box, type **DTS Step By Step Chapter 1 Package 3** in the Description box, type **mypassword** in the Owner Password box, and type the following in the File Name box:

C:\Microsoft Press\SQL DTS SBS\Ch1\WorkingFolder\ SQL_DTS_SBS_1.3.dts

Click Next to review the selections that you made in the wizard.

12 Click Finish to save and execute the package.

13 Click OK to acknowledge that the package copied 10 tables successfully from Microsoft Access to Microsoft SQL Server.

The wizard saved the package and then created and populated a table for each table in the source database, using separate steps for each of these tasks.

14 Click Done.

You have successfully imported the tables and data from an Access database to a SQL Server database with very little effort.

▶   **Note**   For more information on using DTS to convert or transform data between heterogeneous data sources and destinations, see "Data Conversion and Transformation Considerations" in SQL Server Books Online. There are important variations in the way that different programs, providers, and drivers support data types and SQL statements, and you must be aware of them when working with heterogeneous data sources.

Copy data from a text file to a SQL Server database

In the next procedure, you will learn how to import data from a structured text file to a SQL Server database. Because the large majority of structured data sources have tools to export data to or import data from structured text files, you will frequently use DTS to either import data from text files or export data to text files. Moving data from a mainframe application into a text file and then from the text file into SQL Server is often the easiest way to interface with mainframe applications. Importing data from a text file is easy with DTS because DTS assists you with determining the file properties for the text file and creating format files (if format files are required).

1   To launch the DTS Import/Export Wizard from within SQL Server Enterprise Manager, ensure that your focus is within your local SQL Server instance. On the Tools menu, point to Data Transformation Services, and then click Import Data.

2   Click Next to select a data source from which you will copy data.

    In this procedure, you will use a semicolon-delimited text file as your data source.

3   In the Data Source list, select Text File.

The page changes to reflect the only connection information required to connect to a text file: the name and path of the text file.

4   In the File Name box, type **C:\Microsoft Press\SQL DTS SBS\Ch1\ ChapterFiles\PotentialCustomers.txt** and then click Next to select the file format.

When DTS imports data from a text file, DTS attempts to determine the properties of the text file. For more information on file formats, see "Select File Format" in SQL Server Books Online. Notice that the wizard provides you with a preview of the text file to help you specify the appropriate format properties for the source file. You can also choose to skip a specified number of rows at the beginning of a text file, which enables you to import only part of a large text file during development, or to avoid header information that might precede the formatted rows.

The Customer.txt file contains semicolon-delimited columns, contains ANSI data, uses a vertical bar as a row delimiter, does not use a text qualifier, and has column names in the first row.

5   In the Row Delimiter box, select Vertical Bar. In the Text Qualifier box, select <none>. Select the First Row Has Column Names check box, and then click Next to specify the column delimiter. The Customer.txt file uses a semicolon as a column delimiter.

6   Click Semicolon. Notice that the preview pane properly displays a preview of the source file after you specify a semicolon as the delimiter type.

7   Click Next to select a data destination. In this procedure, you will import the data from the text file into the SBS_OLAP database.

8   Verify that Microsoft OLE DB Provider For SQL Server appears as the data destination, ensure that Windows Authentication is selected, and ensure that (local) appears in the Server list. In the Database list, select SBS_OLAP, and then click Next to modify the schema or the data as it is copied to the data destination.

The text file appears as the source, and a new table called *Potential-Customers* appears as the destination table in the SBS_OLAP database. You can transform the source data as it is being imported using ActiveX scripts or edit the Transact-SQL that will be used to create this new table by clicking the ellipsis in the Transform column. In this procedure, you will modify the Transact-SQL script.

9   Click the ellipsis in the Transform column to view the column mappings and transformations that DTS will perform.

In the Mappings box on the Column Mappings tab, notice the mapping of columns between the columns in the text file and the columns in the destination table that will be created. The name for each column in the new table is determined by the names specified in the first row of information in the text file. DTS uses *varchar* (8000) as the default data type for all data when importing data from a text file.

In this procedure, you will add a column constraint, change column data types, and change column data lengths so that the formatting is more appropriate for the data being imported from the text file.

10 In the Mappings box, modify the data types, null constraints, and data sizes using the information in the following table:

Column name	Data type	Nullable	Size
Customer Name	Varchar	Not nullable	50
Street Address	Varchar	Nullable	50
City	Varchar	Nullable	30
State	Char	Nullable	2
Zip Code	Char	Nullable	10
Telephone Number	Char	Nullable	14

11 Click OK and then click Next to choose whether to execute the package immediately and to save, schedule, or replicate the package.

12 Click Save DTS Package, click Structured Storage File, and then click Next to provide the details for the save options.

13 Type **SQL_DTS_SBS_1.4** in the Name box, type **DTS Step By Step Chapter 1 Package 4** in the Description box, type **mypassword** in the Owner Password box, and type the following in the File Name box:

C:\Microsoft Press\SQL DTS SBS\Ch1\WorkingFolder\ SQL_DTS_SBS_1.4.dts

14 Click Next to review the selections that you made in the wizard.

15 Click Finish to save and execute the package.

16 Click OK to acknowledge that the package copied one table successfully from Flat File to Microsoft SQL Server.

The wizard saved the package, created the *PotentialCustomers* table,
and then copied the data from the text file into the *PotentialCustomers*
table.

17 Click Done.

You have successfully imported data from a text file into a table in a SQL Server
database. This simple example shows how easy it is to use DTS to import data
from a structured text file.

Exporting Data Using the DTS Import/Export Wizard

DTS can export data from SQL Server to a variety of data stores as easily as it
can import data into SQL Server from a variety of data stores. Although exporting data using the DTS Import/Export Wizard is frequently thought of as
exporting data from a SQL Server database into another data format, from the
perspective of DTS, exporting is simply copying data from one data source to
another data source. In this section, you will export data from a SQL Server
database to an Excel worksheet (which is the same as importing to an Excel
worksheet from a SQL Server database). You could just as easily export data
from an Excel worksheet to a text file, or from a text file to an Access database.
The data source and the data destination can be any data structure to which
DTS can connect. Neither the data source nor the data destination need be a
SQL Server database.

Copy data from a SQL Server database to an Excel worksheet

In the following procedure, you will learn how to export data to an Excel worksheet from a SQL Server database. Business executives are familiar with Excel
and often use it to work with summarized data, such as weekly or monthly
reports.

1 To launch the DTS Import/Export Wizard from within SQL Server
Enterprise Manager, right-click the (local) (Windows NT) server
icon, point to All Tasks, and then click Export Data.

The wizard that appears when you click Export Data is the same
wizard that appears when you click Import Data—there are two
menu items, but only one wizard.

2   Click Next to select a data source from which you will copy data.

In this procedure, you will use the SBS_OLTP database on your local server as your data source.

3   Verify that Microsoft OLE DB Provider For SQL Server appears as the data source, ensure that Windows Authentication is selected, and ensure that (local) appears in the Server list. In the Database list, select SBS_OLTP, and then click Next to select a data destination.

In this procedure, you will use an Excel worksheet as your data destination. Notice that the list of data destinations is the same as the list of data sources.

4   In the Destination list, select Microsoft Excel 97-2000.

The page changes to reflect the information required to connect to or create an Excel worksheet.

5   In the File Name box, type **C:\Microsoft Press\SQL DTS SBS\Ch1\ WorkingFolder\UnshippedOrders.xls** and then click Next to specify what DTS will copy from the data source to the data destination.

In this procedure, you will use a query to consolidate and filter data as it is being copied from the SBS_OLTP database to an Excel worksheet.

6   Click Use A Query To Specify The Data To Transfer, and then click Next to specify the query DTS will use.

In this procedure, you will use the same query that you used in the "Copy data between SQL Server databases using a SQL query" procedure. However, you will paste this query from a saved script file rather than use the Query Builder to create the query.

7   Click Browse, navigate to C:\Microsoft Press\SQL DTS SBS\Ch1\ ChapterFiles in the Look In list, and then double-click Unshipped-Orders.sql.

The saved query is pasted into the Query Statement box.

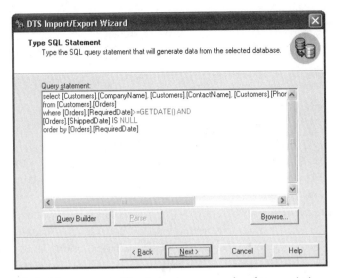

8   Click Next to modify the schema or the data as it is copied to the data destination.

9   Click the ellipsis in the Transform column, verify the Create Destination Table option button is selected, select the Drop And Recreate Destination Table check box, and then click OK.

10   Click Next to choose whether to execute the package immediately and to save, schedule, or replicate the package.

11   Click Save DTS Package, click Structured Storage File, and then click Next to provide the details for the save options.

12   Type **SQL_DTS_SBS_1.5** in the Name box, type **DTS Step By Step Chapter 1 Package 5** in the Description box, type **mypassword** in the Owner Password box, and type the following in the File Name box:

C:\Microsoft Press\SQL DTS SBS\Ch1\WorkingFolder\ SQL_DTS_SBS_1.5.dts

Click Next to review the selections that you made in the wizard.

13   Click Finish to save and execute the package.

14   Click OK to acknowledge that the package copied one table successfully from Microsoft SQL Server to Microsoft Excel 97-2000.

Notice that the wizard saved the package, attempted to drop the Results table (this step failed because the *Results* table does not yet exist), created the *Results* table, and then copied the data from the *Results* table into an Excel worksheet. Again, since there are no orders with a *RequiredDate* greater than or equal to now, the results show that zero rows of data were copied.

15   Click Done.

You have successfully exported data to an Excel worksheet from a SQL Server database using a SQL query. You have learned that it is as simple to export data to an OLE DB or ODBC data destination as it is to import data from an OLE DB or ODBC data source.

Copying Objects and Data Using the DTS Import/Export Wizard

Now that you have learned how to import and export data using the DTS Import/Export Wizard, you are ready to learn how to copy database objects and data between SQL Servers. The ability to copy SQL Server objects and data between SQL databases in different SQL instances is one of the most powerful capabilities of the DTS Import/Export Wizard. The objects you can transfer include tables, views, stored procedures, defaults, rules, constraints, user-defined data types, logins, users, roles, and indexes. When transferring objects between SQL Server instances, some version restrictions apply. You can transfer objects only between multiple instances of SQL Server 2000, from an instance of SQL Server 7 to an instance of SQL Server 2000, and between multiple instances of SQL Server 7. Copying objects is useful for many purposes, including migrating an existing database to a secondary server without taking the database offline, converting a database from one collation sequence to another, and copying logins from a primary server to a standby server.

Copy objects and data between SQL Server 2000 databases

In the next procedure, you will learn how to copy all the database objects and data from one SQL Server 2000 database into another.

1 To launch the DTS Import/Export Wizard from within SQL Server Enterprise Manager, right-click the (local) (Windows NT) server icon, point to All Tasks, and then click Export Data.

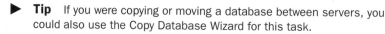

> ▶ **Tip**   If you were copying or moving a database between servers, you could also use the Copy Database Wizard for this task.

2 Click Next to select a data source from which you will copy objects and data. You will select the SBS_OLTP database on your local server (or you can select a remote server if you have one available).

3   Verify that Microsoft OLE DB Provider For SQL Server appears as the data destination, ensure that Windows Authentication is selected, and ensure that (local) appears in the Server list. In the Database list, select SBS_OLTP, and then click Next to select a data destination. You will create the SBS_OLTP_Copy database as your data destination.

4   Verify that Microsoft OLE DB Provider For SQL Server appears as the data destination, ensure that Windows Authentication is selected, and ensure that (local) appears in the Server list. In the Database list, select New.

5   Type **SBS_OLTP_Copy** in the Name box and then click OK. Click Next to specify what DTS will copy from the data source to the data destination. You will copy objects and data between SQL Server databases.

6   Click Copy Objects And Data Between SQL Server Databases, and then click Next to specify the objects to copy.

By default, all objects and all data in the source database are copied to the destination database, and if identically named destination objects already exist, they are dropped along with all dependent objects. However, the default settings do not copy extended properties that have been defined on various objects in the database. You must specifically choose to copy extended properties when you copy database objects. If you do not specify the dropping and recreating of existing destination objects, data is appended to the existing data.

> ▶ **Important**   If you are copying objects and data between SQL Server 2000 databases with differing collations using the DTS Import/Export Wizard, you must select the Use Collation check box to ensure no data is lost. A collation encodes the rules governing the proper use of characters for either a language, such as Arabic or Polish, or an alphabet, such as Latin1_General (the Latin alphabet used by western European languages). For more information on collations, see "SQL Server Collation Fundamentals" in SQL Server Books Online. For more information on using DTS to copy data between databases with differing collations, see "Data Conversion and Transformation Considerations" in SQL Server Books Online.

Finally, notice the Script File Directory text box. This text box specifies the location in which SQL Server stores the script files used to create the objects in the destination database, the data files used to populate the objects in the destination database, and the log files associated with the object creation and file copy process.

7   Clear the Copy All Objects check box and then click Select Objects
to display the Select Objects dialog box.

In this dialog box, you can view and then select specific tables, views,
stored procedures, user-defined functions, defaults, rules, and user-
defined data types. This enables you to copy or skip specific objects
when copying database objects in the package. In this procedure, you
will copy all objects.

8   Click Cancel and then re-select the Copy All Objects check box.

9 Clear the Use Default Options check box and then click Options to view the default options in the Advanced Copy Options dialog box. In this procedure, you will use the default settings.

By default, all security settings, indexes, triggers, and primary and foreign keys are copied. However, SQL Server logins are not copied and the scripts are not generated in Unicode.

▶ **Important** You should generate scripts in Unicode when the source data contains *nchar*, *nvarchar*, or *ntext* data types or double-byte character set (DBCS) data. For more information on Unicode data, see "Unicode Data" in SQL Server Books Online.

Quoted identifiers are used when copying objects. This setting encloses all object names in the generated script in quotation marks to delimit an identifier. For more information on quoted identifiers, see "System Configuration" in SQL Server Books Online.

10 Click Cancel, re-select the Use Default Options check box, and then click Next to choose whether to execute the package immediately and to save, schedule, or replicate the package.

11 Click Save DTS Package, click Structured Storage File, and then click Next to provide the details for the save options.

Jumping into DTS

12 Type **SQL_DTS_SBS_1.6** in the Name box, type **DTS Step By Step Chapter 1 Package 6** in the Description box, type **mypassword** in the Owner Password box, and type the following in the File Name box:

C:\Microsoft Press\SQL DTS SBS\Ch1\WorkingFolder\ SQL_DTS_SBS_1.6.dts

13 Click Next to review the selections that you made in the wizard.

14 Click Finish to save and execute the package.

15 Click OK to acknowledge that objects were successfully copied from Microsoft SQL Server to Microsoft SQL Server.

16 Click Done.

You have successfully copied objects and data to a new database. This is one of the simplest methods for copying the data and objects in an existing database to a new database without taking the database offline.

Chapter Summary

The DTS Import/Export Wizard is an excellent tool for quickly copying data between disparate data sources, and it is a powerful tool for migrating database objects and data between instances of SQL Server. It is also a good place for beginning developers to start when creating more complex data movement applications using DTS Designer. In Chapter 2, you will learn how the packages you created in this chapter actually work, and you will begin to extend their functionality.

Using DTS Designer to Build and Extend Packages

In this chapter, you will learn how to:

■ Create and edit package connection objects

■ Create and edit Transform Data, Execute *SQL*, and Bulk Insert tasks

■ Create and edit precedence constraints between package tasks

---

DTS Designer is a graphical application available from within SQL Server Enterprise Manager that enables you to build and edit packages containing one or more connections to homogenous or heterogeneous data sources, simple or complex workflows between and among multiple types of tasks, and event-driven logic. In Chapter 1, you created six different data movement packages using the DTS Import/Export Wizard. In this chapter, you will use DTS Designer to open, review, and edit the components of these packages and learn how these packages perform the tasks you configured in Chapter 1. You will also create the first of many packages that you will build as part of a complex data movement application, which will teach you how to use DTS to solve real-world problems.

> ▶ **Note**   If you skipped Chapter 1, execute the IfYouSkippedChapter1.cmd
> batch file. This batch file restores the SBS_OLTP and SBS_OLAP databases
> that were created in Chapter 1 and copies the DTS packages that would have
> been created in Chapter 1 into the WorkingFolder for Chapter 1. If you do not
> want this batch file to overwrite any packages that you saved to the Working-
> Folder for Chapter 1, you must move them or rename them before you execute
> this batch file.

Opening and Editing Existing Packages

The packages you created in Chapter 1 contain the connection objects, tasks, and precedence constraints necessary to perform the data movement tasks you specified in the DTS Import/Export Wizard. The quickest and easiest way to learn about these package components is to open several of the packages in DTS Designer and review them.

Connection Objects

The packages you created in Chapter 1 contain different types of connection objects. As you learned in Chapter 1, connection objects are used by package tasks to connect to various data sources. In Chapter 1, these data sources included SQL Server databases, a Microsoft Access database, a delimited text file, and a Microsoft Excel worksheet.

View and modify SQL Server connection objects

A *connection object* defines the connection parameters that enable a task to connect to a data store. A connection object in a package can represent a separate connection to a data store or the reuse of an existing connection to a data store. The data stores to which DTS can connect include relational database management systems (such as SQL Server and Oracle), file system databases (such as Access, dBase, or Paradox), applications (such as Excel), text files (such as comma-delimited or HTML files), and any other structured data source that has an OLE DB provider or ODBC driver (such as Sybase, DB2, Microsoft Exchange Server, and Active Directory).

In the following procedure, you will learn about SQL Server connection objects by opening and modifying those created by the DTS Import/Export Wizard in the *SQL_DTS_SBS_1.1* package. This package copies the data as seen through a view from the SBS_OLTP database to a newly created table in the SBS_OLAP database.

1   In Microsoft Windows, click the Start button, point to All Programs, point to Microsoft SQL Server, and then click Enterprise Manager.

> ▶ **Tip**   DTS Designer is available only from within SQL Server Enterprise Manager and cannot be started as a stand-alone application.

2   In the SQL Server Enterprise Manager console tree, expand Microsoft SQL Servers, expand SQL Server Group, expand your local SQL Server instance, right-click Data Transformation Services, and then click Open Package.

3   Navigate to C:\Microsoft Press\SQL DTS SBS\Ch1\WorkingFolder in the Look In list, and then double-click SQL_DTS_SBS_1.1.dts.

You are prompted to select the package and package version that you want to load. Structured storage files can contain multiple packages and multiple versions of each package. (See Chapter 3 for more information about package formats and version control.)

4   In the Select Package dialog box, click SQL_DTS_SBS_1.1 and then click OK.

Only users who know the owner password can view or edit a package that is secured with an owner password. If you also provide a user password, users who know it can execute a secured package (but not view or edit it). (See Chapter 3 for more information about package security.)

5   In the Password box, type **mypassword** and then click OK.

This package contains a number of different icons representing types of objects in the package, including two connection objects, three tasks, and two precedence constraints. The connection icons are labeled *Connection 1* and *Connection 2*. The DTS Import/Export Wizard does not generate descriptive names for connection objects in the packages that it creates. In this procedure, you will learn how to edit the properties of the connection objects in this package.

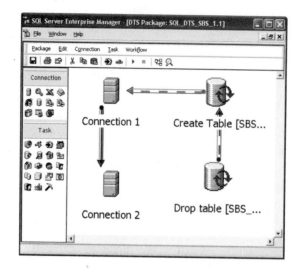

> ▶ **Tip**   When there are many objects in a package, for easier viewing, you can use the Zoom icon on the DTS Designer toolbar to resize the objects that appear on the design sheet. You can also click and drag objects on the design sheet to rearrange them for easier viewing or to better represent task or data flow within a package.

6   On the design sheet, double-click Connection 1.

This connection object defines the connection properties to the SBS_OLTP database on your local server, which you configured in the DTS Import/Export Wizard. The properties do not define how the connection is used; as mentioned earlier, connection objects merely define how to connect to a data source and can be used by different tasks. You can easily change most of the properties except the connection name of an existing connection object. For example, you can change its security context, or you can configure it to access a completely different data source or database.

> ▶ **Tip**   You must take great care when modifying a connection object that is referenced by an existing task because changing a connection on which a task is dependent can cause that task to fail or execute in unforeseen ways. In this procedure, you will not make any changes to this connection object using this interface.

2

Using DTS Designer

7   Click Cancel and then double-click Connection 2 on the design sheet. This connection object defines the connection properties to the SBS_OLAP database on your local server, which you configured in the DTS Import/Export Wizard. The only differences between *Connection 1* and *Connection 2* are the name of the connection and the database to which the object connects. In this procedure, you will not make any changes to this connection object using this interface.

8   Click Cancel and then click Disconnected Edit on the Package menu to display the Edit All Package Properties dialog box, which shows the properties and values of every object in this package.

Using this interface, you can directly edit package properties. In this procedure, you will use the Disconnected Edit feature of DTS Designer to change the names of the connection objects in this package.

▶   **Important**   You should modify a package property using the Disconnected Edit feature of DTS Designer only when you cannot modify the package property using another method, such as through an object's Properties dialog box. The reason for this is that when you edit the properties of an object in DTS Designer using one of the property sheets for the object, DTS validates the property value change and will invalidate an invalid change. However, if you make changes using the Disconnected Edit feature of DTS Designer, no validation of the change occurs and you can make an invalid change that will break the package. Editing a package using this feature is similar to editing the Windows registry using the Registry Editor rather than using one of the icons in Control Panel.

9 In the left pane, expand the Connections property node and then click the Connection 1 property group to display the Connection 1 property names and values in the right pane. The value for the *Name* property is Connection 1.

10 In the right pane, double-click the Name property so that you can enter a more descriptive name for this connection object.

The *Name* property is a string value that you can edit. In this procedure, you will provide a more descriptive name for this connection object.

Edit Property

Enter a new value for the property you selected to edit.

Name: Name

Type: String

Value:

DataSource

OK   Cancel   Help

11 In the Value box, select Connection 1, type **DataSource**, and then click OK to display the changed value for the *Name* property.

Notice that the change also applies to the name of the property collection in the left pane.

12 In the left pane, click the Connection 2 property group to display the Connection 2 property names and values in the right pane.

13 In the right pane, double-click the Name property.

14 In the Value box, select Connection 2, type **DataDestination**, and then click OK.

Once again, the changed value for the *Name* property appears in both the left and the right panes.

15 Click Close.

The connection object names have not been updated on the design sheet because you used the Disconnected Edit feature. To update the display of the package on the design sheet, you must open each connection object to update the connection object and its dependent objects.

16 On the design sheet, double-click Connection 1.

The renaming of *Connection 1* to *DataSource* is now reflected in the Connection Properties dialog box.

17 Click OK.

The Task References dialog box appears because DTS detects that the *Copy Data From Sales By Category To [SBS_OLAP].[dbo].[Sales By Category]* task (the Copy Data step) references this connection object and that the connection object has been modified.

Since a modification to a connection object can invalidate transformation tasks that reference the connection object, you must tell DTS whether to keep or delete the existing transformations in the task. For example, if a connection object is modified to point to a different database with a different schema, you would delete and then create new transformations in the tasks that were using the modified connection object to reflect the schema of the new data source. However, since you changed only the name of the connection object, do not delete any transformations in this task.

Task references

The following tasks reference the connection that you just modified. Please select the tasks for which the transformations should be deleted.

Tasks:

Task Name	Clear Transformations
Copy Data from Sales by Category to [S...	☐

Select All   Deselect All

OK   Cancel   Help

18 Click OK.

The design sheet displays the new descriptive name for this connection object.

19 On the design sheet, double-click Connection 2.

The renaming of *Connection 2* to *DataDestination* is now reflected in the Connection Properties dialog box.

20 Click OK, and then click OK again to retain all existing transformations.

The design sheet now displays the descriptive names for both connection objects in the package.

21 On the toolbar, click Save. Do not close this package.

▶ **Tip**   Use a descriptive name for each connection object to enable you to easily determine its properties and function. As you add tasks to packages and increase their complexity, using descriptive names will make it easier to reference the appropriate connection object in each task. You can provide these descriptive names when you create the connection objects using DTS Designer rather than rename them later, as you have done here.

You have successfully viewed and modified your first package in DTS Designer and used two different interfaces to look at the properties of a connection object. This simple package required only one data source connection object and one data destination connection object to serially perform the three tasks in the package. Before you learn about these tasks and how to control the order of their execution, however, you need to learn about using multiple connection objects in a package to support the execution of multiple tasks in parallel.

Work with an Access connection object

In this procedure, you will open and review the SQL_DTS_SBS_1.3 package that you created in Chapter 1 to learn how it uses multiple connection objects to execute some tasks serially and some in parallel. This package creates 10 tables in the SBS_OLAP database in SQL Server based on the schema of these same tables in the AccessPubsDB database in Access. This package then copies data unchanged from the tables in the Access database into the newly created tables in the SQL Server database.

1 On the Window menu in SQL Server Enterprise Manager, click Console Root\Microsoft SQL Servers to display the SQL Server Enterprise Manager console root.

▶ **Tip**   You cannot open a second package from within DTS Designer while you are viewing an existing package. You must first return your focus to the SQL Server Enterprise Manager console root to open a second package.

2   In the SQL Server Enterprise Manager console tree, right-click Data Transformation Services in your local SQL Server instance, and then click Open Package.

3   Navigate to C:\Microsoft Press\SQL DTS SBS\Ch1\WorkingFolder in the Look In list, and then double-click SQL_DTS_SBS_1.3 to display the Select Package dialog box.

4   In the Select Package dialog box, click SQL_DTS_SBS_1.3, and then click OK.

5   In the Password box, type **mypassword**, and then click OK.

In the initial view of this package in DTS Designer, the icons are too small to see, even when you maximize DTS Designer on your computer screen.

6   On the toolbar, click Zoom, and then click 75% to increase the size of the icons so that you can more easily see the objects in the package. You can use the scroll bar to see the icons that appear to the left and right of the current focus on the design sheet. (If your monitor still doesn't show the icons clearly with the 75 percent setting, increase the zoom percentage further.)

You can also rearrange the icons to fit within the display window of the design sheet. There are five *Connection 1*, five *Connection 2*, five *Connection 3*, and five *Connection 4* connection objects in this package.

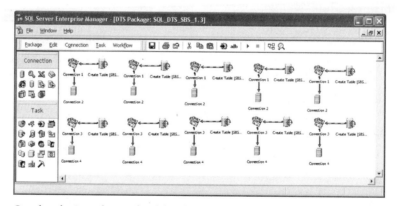

7   On the design sheet, double-click one of the Connection 1 connection objects.

This connection object defines connection properties to the Access-PubsDB.mdb database file in the file system. Do not make any changes to this connection object.

8 Click Cancel and then double-click another Connection 1 connection object on the design sheet.

   You'll see that this *Connection 1* object displays identical connection information. Each of the *Connection 1* objects in this package represents a shared connection to the AccessPubsDB database; *Connection 1* is shared by five tasks. Do not make any changes to this connection object.

9 Click Cancel and then double-click one of the Connection 3 connection objects on the design sheet.

   This connection object is a different object from *Connection 1*, but both objects define a connection to the same AccessPubsDB.mdb database file. In this package, *Connection 3* is shared by five separate tasks.

If you open the *Connection 2* and *Connection 4* connection objects, you will see that these connection objects define connections to the SBS_OLAP database in SQL Server. *Connection 2* is shared by five tasks and *Connection 4* is shared by five tasks. Do not make any changes to these connection objects.

▶ **Important**   Tasks that share the same connection object execute serially and can block one another. Tasks with separate connection objects execute in parallel and cannot block one another (unless they cause a lock on the same resource in the underlying data store). In a package, you need to determine how many tasks you want DTS to execute in parallel versus how many tasks you want DTS to execute serially. Each connection object must be maintained separately, and each separate connection consumes resources when opened. However, separate connections can yield superior performance in situations that benefit from parallel processing. Shared connections do not require separate maintenance and do not consume additional resources, but a task that shares a connection can be blocked by another task sharing the same connection.

The prototype of a data movement application that you will build during the course of this book illustrates how to create a complete data movement application using multiple packages and multiple connections to eliminate blocking and take advantage of parallel processing.

10 Click Cancel.

In these two packages, you looked at connection objects that connect to a SQL Server database and to an Access database. Open the *SQL_DTS_SBS_1.4 DTS* package to view a Text File (Source) connection object and open the *SQL_DTS_SBS_1.5 DTS* package to view an Excel 97-2000 connection object. Now that you understand connection objects, you are ready to learn about the tasks that the DTS Import/Export Wizard created in the packages you built in Chapter 1.

Tasks

Tasks perform the real work of a package and divide that work into discrete units. This enables the package to be more easily understood and extended. DTS ships with many predefined tasks, but you can also create your own custom tasks using scripting. The packages you created in Chapter 1 contain simple Transform Data tasks and Execute SQL tasks that use connection objects to extract, query, and save data. In this chapter, you will look at these tasks and also learn how to use the Bulk Insert task to import data from a structured text file. You will learn about other tasks throughout the remaining chapters in this book.

The Transform Data task

The Transform Data task is an implementation of a DTS COM component called the *data pump*. The Transform Data task moves data between a data source and a data destination, mapping columns in the data source to columns in the data destination. This task supports the use of a query that uses set-based logic to limit and filter the source data before it is copied or transformed by the data pump.

This task also supports the use of complex scripting to change the data on a row-by-row basis as it is being copied from the data source to the data destination. Although row-by-row transformation offers additional functionality not easily provided by using queries, it comes at the cost of slower performance. The Transform Data task can also be customized to fire events before and after the transformation.

View a Transform Data task

In this procedure, you will learn about the Transform Data task by reviewing one in the *SQL_DTS_SBS_1.1* package. This Transform Data task copies data as seen through a view from the SBS_OLTP database to a newly created table in the SBS_OLAP database.

1   On the Window menu in SQL Server Enterprise Manager, click DTS Package: SQL_DTS_SBS_1.1 to switch to this package in DTS Designer.

2   Position your cursor over the black directional arrow that points from the DataSource connection object to the DataDestination connection object.

This black arrow represents a Transform Data task and indicates the direction of the data flow between two connection objects. Positioning your cursor over the black arrow enables you to read the description of the Transform Data task that transforms data between the *DataSource* and the *DataDestination* connection objects. You can also see the task description by viewing the properties of the task.

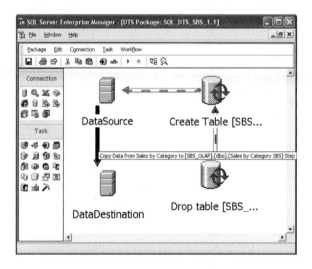

3 Double-click the Transform Data task in this package to view or edit its properties.

The data source is the *DataSource* connection object, and the data retrieved from this data source is determined by a SQL query.

4 Click the Destination tab.

The data destination is the *DataDestination* connection object, and the schema of the destination table created by this package is displayed. You cannot change the schema of the destination table for this task without creating a new table. If you create a new table from within this task, the Create Table task in this package will simply recreate the original table the next time the package is executed. If you want to change the schema for the *Sales By Category SBS* table, you should modify the Create Table task and then modify the transformations in this task to match the new schema.

Transform Data Task Properties

Source | Destination | Transformations | Lookups | Options

Store the results for this transformation.

Connection: DataDestination

Table name: [SBS_OLAP].[dbo].[Sales ▼]   Create...

Name	Type	Nullability	Size	Precision	Scale
CategoryID	int	☐			
CategoryName	nvarchar	☐	15		
ProductName	nvarchar	☐	40		
ProductSales	money	☑			

OK   Cancel   Help

5   Click the Transformations tab to show the data transformation properties. The transformation name, *DirectCopyXform*, indicates that
the column data are copied, without any modification, from the data
source to the data destination. This Transform Data task is merely
used to insert the rows retrieved by the SQL query into the appropriate columns in the destination table.

The four columns in the source and the four columns in the destination are linked through a single multi-headed arrow. This indicates
that a single COM object is used to perform this transformation
operation. Multiple arrows indicate that multiple COM objects are
used.

▶ **Tip**   When you are transforming 20 or more columns in a Transform
Data task, you can obtain a performance increase of up to approximately
15 percent through the use of a single COM object.

▶ **Tip**   Lookups are discussed in Chapter 4.

6   Click the Options tab. The default Max Error Count value is 0,
which means that the task will terminate if any errors are detected in
the transformation (such as an invalid data type or a referential
integrity violation). A higher value will permit a specified number of
errors before the task will terminate. In Chapter 5 you will learn
about using the exception file to capture error rows.

Notice that the Use Fast Load check box is selected by default, which
means that this task will use high-speed, bulk-copy processing for
better insert performance. This option is automatically selected and
is available only when the data destination is the Microsoft OLE DB
Provider for SQL Server. When this option is selected, you can use
the Insert Batch Size text box to specify the loading of data in
batches. A value of 0 indicates that the entire insert operation is performed using a single batch.

2

Using DTS Designer

When the Use Fast Load option is selected, you also have the option to ignore constraints on the relational tables during data loading (which you should use only when you know the data is clean) and enable table-level locking rather than row-level locking. These options can increase data throughput during data loading.

7   Click Cancel.

You have learned how a simple Transform Data task copies data unchanged from a data source to a data destination, and you've looked at some of the options you can set for the Transform Data task to improve its performance and control its operation. You are now ready to learn about the other two tasks in this package.

The Execute SQL Task

The Execute SQL task is a programming task that enables you to use Transact-SQL code to access data stored within a SQL Server database from within a package. This task also enables you to create objects in a SQL Server database before a transformation process commences or to update objects in a SQL Server database after a transformation process has completed. For example, you can run maintenance procedures after an import, such as rebuilding indexes or updating statistics. You can also store the results of an Execute SQL task into a global variable for use in another task, or pass values into an Execute SQL task from another task to control how the Execute SQL task functions.

View an Execute SQL task

In this procedure, you will learn about the Execute SQL task by reviewing the two Execute SQL tasks in the *SQL_DTS_SBS_1.1* package. One of these tasks creates a table in the SBS_OLAP database, and the other deletes the same table.

1   On the design sheet for the SQL_DTS_SBS_1.1 package in DTS Designer, position your cursor over the Create Table [SBS_OLAP].[dbo].[Sales By Category SBS] Step task (the Create Table step). This enables you to read the description of this Execute SQL task. Take note of the icon that represents an Execute SQL task.

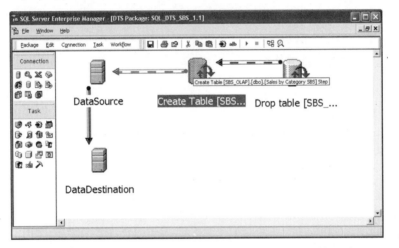

2   Double-click the Create Table step to view its properties.

This task is using the *DataDestination* connection object and executes a *CREATE TABLE* statement to create the *Sales By Category SBS* table. The table created by this task is used by the *Copy Data* step. If you make any schema changes to the *Sales By Category SBS* table in this task, you will need to modify the Transform Data task to incorporate these changes; if you do not, the package will either fail or execute in an unexpected manner. In this procedure, you will not change the *Create Table* step.

3   Click Cancel and then double-click the Drop Table
[SBS_OLAP].[dbo].[Sales By Category SBS] Step task (the Drop
Table step) to view its properties.

This task is using the *DataDestination* connection object and executes a *DROP TABLE* statement to drop the destination table each
time the package is executed. In this procedure, you will not change
the *Drop Table* step.

4   Click Cancel.

You have learned how this package uses one Execute SQL task to drop a table and another Execute SQL task to create a table in a SQL Server database. You are now ready to learn about how this package uses precedence constraints to ensure that the *Drop Table* step executes and completes before the *Create Table* step executes, and to ensure that the *Create Table* step completes successfully before the Transform Data task executes.

Precedence Constraints

Precedence constraints enable you to control workflow in a package. A precedence constraint between two tasks links the tasks in a sequential order. There are three types of precedence constraints:

- **On Completion**   An *On Completion* precedence constraint (which is labeled as a *Completion* constraint on the design sheet) is represented by a blue and white directional arrow between two tasks (Task A and Task B) and specifies that Task B wait until Task A completes before Task B executes. As long as Task A completes, Task B will execute, regardless of the success or failure of Task A.

- **On Success**   An *On Success* precedence constraint (which is labeled as a *Success* constraint) is represented by a green and white directional arrow between two tasks and specifies that Task B will execute only after Task A completes successfully. If Task A never completes successfully, Task B will never execute.

- **On Failure**   An *On Failure* precedence constraint (which is labeled as a *Failure* constraint) is represented by a red and white directional arrow between two tasks and specifies that Task B will execute only after Task A fails to complete successfully. If Task A never fails, Task B will never execute.

In the absence of precedence constraints that limit when tasks can execute, tasks in a package execute without regard to the execution of any other task. As discussed previously, tasks that share a connection object execute serially through the connection object and tasks that have their own connections execute in parallel to each other. Without precedence constraints, the sequence of execution for serial tasks is based on the order in which the tasks request use of the connection object. This sequence can vary from execution to execution of the package, depending on how quickly any pre-connection processing occurs within the tasks before they request the use of the connection object.

View and modify precedence constraints

In this procedure, you will learn about precedence constraints by reviewing and modifying them in the *SQL_DTS_SBS_1.1* package, and then executing the package with and without them. This package contains both *On Completion* and *On Success* precedence constraints.

1   On the design sheet for the SQL_DTS_SBS_1.1 package in DTS Designer, position your cursor over the blue and white directional arrow between the Drop Table step and the Create Table step (the *Completion* constraint).

The *Completion* constraint dictates that when the *Drop Table* step completes; regardless of its success or failure, the *Create Table* step will execute.

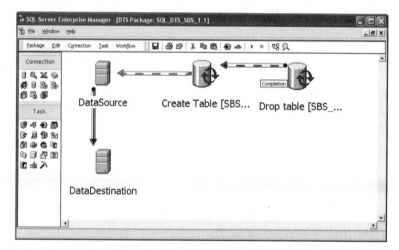

2   On the design sheet for the SQL_DTS_SBS_1.1 package in DTS Designer, position your cursor over the green and white directional arrow between the Create Table step and the DataSource connection object (the *Success* constraint).

The *Success* constraint dictates that when the *Create Table* step completes successfully, the *Copy Data* step will execute. If the creation of the destination table in the destination database fails for any reason, the Transform Data task will not execute and data will not be copied into the destination table.

▶ **Important**   By default, the failure of a step in a package does not stop other steps in a package from executing unless the steps are linked by a precedence constraint or the step is configured to cause the entire package to fail when the step fails.

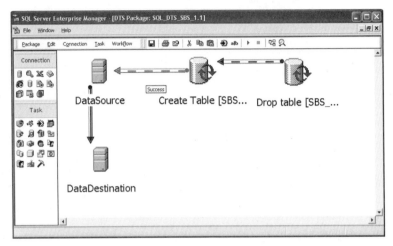

3   On the toolbar, click Execute (the green arrowhead).

The *Sales By Category SBS* table is dropped, recreated, and then populated with data.

4   Click OK to close the Package Execution Results message box. Click Done to close the Executing DTS Package: SQL_DTS_SBS_1.1 dialog box.

To learn more about how precedence constraints function, you will delete the *Completion* constraint and then re-execute the package.

5   On the design sheet, right-click the Completion constraint between the Drop Table step and the Create Table step and then click Delete.

6   On the design sheet, right-click the Success constraint between the Create Table step and the DataSource connection object and then click Delete.

7   On the toolbar, click Execute and then click OK when the Package Execute Results message box appears.

Without the *Completion* and *Success* constraints, one or two of the three tasks might fail because of out-of-order task execution. For the package to execute successfully, the *Drop Table* step must execute first, followed by the *Create Table* step and then the *Copy Data* step. Execution of the steps without precedence constraints can fail for the following reasons:

- If the *Copy Data* step fails, the *Create Table* step executed first and then the *Drop Table* step immediately deleted the destination table before the *Copy Data* step could populate it, or the *Drop Table* step dropped the table and the *Copy Data* step tried to execute before the *Create Table* step had re-created it.

- If the *Create Table* step fails, the *Create Table* step executed before the *Drop Table* step had completed its task.

- If the *Drop Table* step fails, the *Drop Table* step task executed first and the *Sales By Category SBS* table did not exist in the database.

▶ **Tip** To determine why a particular step failed, double-click the failed step in the Executing DTS Package dialog box.

8 Click Done.

You might be able to see more than one of these failure patterns by executing the package several times. The pattern of task failures and successes will depend upon the speed of your computer. Some computers will demonstrate all three failure patterns, and others will never demonstrate a failure.

You have now learned how precedence constraints control workflow and ensure that tasks execute in a predictable and repeatable manner.

Create a precedence constraint

In this procedure, you will learn three ways to create a precedence constraint.

1 Simultaneously select both of the tasks that will be related by the precedence constraint. To do this, on the design sheet, click the Drop Table step, hold down the Ctrl key, and then click the Create Table step.

▶ **Tip** You can select multiple items on the design sheet by holding down the Ctrl key while selecting them or by using your mouse to draw a box around them.

2 Right-click the Create Table step, point to Workflow, and then click On Success. The *On Success* constraint is created with the arrow pointing from the Drop Table step to the Create Table step (this is the order in which you want them to execute).

If you had right-clicked the Drop Table step rather than the Create Table step when defining the precedence constraint, the arrow would be pointing from the Create Table step to the Drop Table step (and the tasks would execute in the wrong order).

> ▶ **Tip**   You can also create a precedence constraint by selecting the tasks and then selecting the precedence constraint from the Workflow menu. If you use this approach, the order in which you select the tasks on the design sheet will determine the direction of the precedence constraint arrow.

3   Double-click the On Success precedence constraint to show a dialog box that displays steps that must be completed for the constraint to be exercised. In this package, the Drop Table step must be completed for the *On Success* constraint to be exercised. In this procedure, you will change the *On Success* constraint to an *On Completion* precedence constraint.

4   In the Precedence list box, select Completion and then click OK to change the *On Success* precedence constraint between the Drop Table step and the Create Table step to an *On Completion* precedence constraint.

5   On the design sheet, select the Create Table step and the DataSource connection object by drawing a rectangle around them.

6   Right-click DataSource, point to Workflow, and then click On Success.

7   On the toolbar, click Execute.

The Package Execution Results message box appears telling you that the DTS Designer successfully completed the execution of the package.

8   Click OK to close the message box.

The Status box in the Executing DTS Package dialog box shows that all three steps completed successfully because they executed in the required order.

9   Click Done.

10   On the toolbar, click Save and then close the SQL_DTS_SBS_1.1 package in DTS Designer. Do not close SQL Server Enterprise Manager.

Now that you have learned about precedence constraints, connection objects, and simple tasks—the building blocks of a data movement application—you are ready to create your first package from scratch using DTS Designer.

Creating a New Package in DTS Designer

In the next set of procedures, you will build the first package that you will use in the data movement application. This package loads and updates the SBS_OLAP data warehouse. First, you will execute a script that adds tables to the SBS_OLAP database. Then you will create a package containing an Execute SQL task that populates the *TimeDim* table in the SBS_OLAP database with time data for a specified date range.

Add tables to the SBS_OLAP database

In this procedure, you will add dimension, fact, and staging tables to the SBS_OLAP database using a Transact-SQL script. The prototype of the data movement application you are building throughout the course of this book will populate these staging tables from a number of different data sources, transform this data into the dimension and fact tables, and then process the data in these dimension and staging tables into the Analysis Services cube that you will build in Chapter 9.

1   In Microsoft Windows, click the Start button, point to All Programs, point to Microsoft SQL Server, and then click Query Analyzer.

2   Ensure that your SQL Server default instance is selected, ensure that Windows Authentication is selected, and then click OK to connect to your default instance.

3   On the toolbar, click Load SQL Script.

4   In the Look In list, navigate to C:\Microsoft Press\SQL DTS SBS\Ch2\ChapterFiles and then double-click AddTablesToSBS_OLAP.sql.

   This script adds three dimension tables, one fact table, and three staging tables to the SBS_OLAP database. The staging tables will be used to stage data before the data is transformed and added to the dimension and fact tables. No staging table is created for the Time dimension because you will populate the table storing Time dimension members directly using the SQL Server DATEPART function. The IDENTITY property is used to populate the key value in each of the dimension tables. A PRIMARY KEY constraint enforces uniqueness in each of the dimension tables and FOREIGN KEY constraints enforce the relationship between the fact table and each dimension table.

5   On the toolbar, click Execute to add these tables to the SBS_OLAP database.

Now that you have added these tables to the SBS_OLAP database, you are ready to begin creating the packages that will populate these tables with both historical data and incremental data.

Create a connection object to the SBS_OLAP database

In this procedure, you will create a connection object to the SBS_OLAP database that will be used by an Execute SQL task, which you will create in the next procedure.

1   Switch to SQL Server Enterprise Manager.

2   In the console tree, right-click Data Transformation Services in your local SQL Server instance and then click New Package to open a blank design sheet in DTS Designer.

3   On the Connection menu, click Microsoft OLE DB Provider For SQL Server to begin creating a new connection object to a SQL Server database.

The text in the New Connection text box is selected so that you can easily change the name of this connection to a descriptive name. In this procedure, you will configure a connection to the SBS_OLAP database called SBS_OLAPDestination.

▶   **Tip**   In addition to selecting new connection objects and tasks for your package from the menu, you can use the undockable Connection and Task toolbars provided by DTS Designer.

4   Type **SBS_OLAPDestination** in the New Connection text box, ensure that (local) appears in the Server list, ensure that Windows Authentication is selected, select SBS_OLAP in the Database list, and then click OK.

The *SBS_OLAPDestination* connection object appears on the design sheet.

▶   **Important**   Using (local) for the server name ensures that this package can be easily migrated from a development computer to a production computer without editing the package, because this connection object will always attempt to connect to the default SQL Server instance on the computer on which the package is executed.

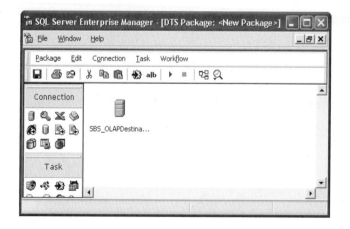

5   On the toolbar, click Save to display the Save DTS Package dialog
box.
You will save all packages that you will use in the prototype of the
data movement application in the Data Movement Application
folder.

6   Type **PopulateTimeDimension** in the Package Name box, type
mypassword in the Owner password box, select Structured Storage
File in the location list, type **C:\Microsoft Press\SQL DTS SBS\Data-
MovementApplication\PopulateTimeDimension.dts** in the File Name
box, and then click OK to save this package.

7   In the Password box, type **mypassword** again to confirm the owner
password and then click OK.

8   Click OK to acknowledge that the package cannot be executed without the owner password.

Now that you have created a connection object to the SBS_OLAP database, you
are ready to create a task that uses this connection object. But first, you will create a stored procedure that will be used by the task.

Create a stored procedure that populates the *TimeDim* table

In this procedure, you will execute a SQL script that creates the *TimeDimBuild*
stored procedure that will be used by the Execute SQL task that you will create
in the next procedure. The *TimeDimBuild* stored procedure requires two input
parameters, a start date and an end date, that determine the range of the Time
members added to the *TimeDim* table in the SBS_OLAP database.

1   Switch to SQL Query Analyzer and then click Load SQL Script on
the toolbar.

2   In the Look In list, navigate to C:\Microsoft Press\SQL DTS
SBS\Ch2\ChapterFiles and then double-click CreateTimeDim-
Build.sql.
This script creates the *TimeDimBuild* stored procedure that adds
time records to the *TimeDim* table for the time period specified by
two input parameters.

```
CREATE PROCEDURE dbo.TimeDimBuild
           @p_start_date DATETIME, @p_end_date DATETIME
AS
   DECLARE @full_date DATETIME
         ,@day_of_month INTEGER
         ,@day_of_year INTEGER
         ,@day_full_name VARCHAR(30)
         ,@week_number  INTEGER
         ,@week_full_name VARCHAR(30)
         ,@month_full_name VARCHAR(10)
         ,@month_number INTEGER
         ,@calendar_year  INTEGER
         ,@quarter INTEGER
WHILE @p_start_date < @p_end_date
   BEGIN
      SELECT
             @full_date = @p_start_date
            ,@day_of_month = DATEPART(DD, @p_start_date)
            ,@day_of_year = DATEPART(DY, @p_start_date)
            ,@day_full_name = UPPER(DATENAME(weekday, @p_start_date))
            ,@week_number = DATEPART(WK, @p_start_date)
            ,@month_full_name = UPPER(DATENAME(month, @p_start_date))
            ,@month_number = DATEPART(M, @p_start_date)
            ,@calendar_year = DATEPART(YYYY, @p_start_date)
            ,@quarter = DATEPART(QQ, @p_start_date)
      INSERT INTO dbo.TimeDim
             (FullDateCode, DayOfMonth, DayOfYear, DayFullName
             ,WeekNumber, MonthFullName, MonthNumber, Quarter
             ,CalendarYear )
      VALUES
             (@full_date, @day_of_month, @day_of_year, @day_full_name
             ,@week_number, @month_full_name, @month_number,@quarter
             ,@calendar_year )
      SELECT @p_start_date = @p_start_date+1
   END
```

3 On the toolbar, click Execute to create this stored procedure.

Now that you have created this stored procedure, you are ready to create the Execute SQL task that uses it.

Create an Execute SQL task that populates the *TimeDim* table

In this procedure, you will create an Execute SQL task that calls the *TimeDim-Build* stored procedure to add time records to the *TimeDim* table in the SBS_OLAP database based on the values passed to the stored procedure by the Execute SQL task. The *TimeDimBuild* stored procedure requires two input parameters, a start date and an end date. You will create two global variables and define default values for these global variables. The default value for a global variable can be changed at run time or during package execution. The Execute SQL task will retrieve these variable values and pass them as parameters to the *TimeDimBuild* stored procedure. Using the input parameters that are passed by the Execute SQL task, the stored procedure will generate time members for the Time dimension and add these records to the *TimeDim* table in the SBS_OLAP database. Passing these input parameters through global variables enables you to pass different global variable values at run time to add additional Time dimension members without opening and modifying the package each time. You will learn methods for modifying global variables at run time in Chapter 3, Chapter 6, and Chapter 7.

1. Switch to the PopulateTimeDimension package in DTS Designer.

2. On the Task menu, click Execute SQL Task.

    Notice that the *SBS_OLAPDestination* connection object is already selected as the connection that will be used by this task. In this procedure, you will provide a descriptive name for this task and then provide the SQL code that this task will execute.

3. Type **Load Time Dimension** in the Description box and then type **EXEC TimeDimBuild ?, ?** in the SQL Statement window.

    The two question marks are placeholders for the parameters required by this stored procedure. In this procedure, you will define these global variables from within the Execute SQL task.

4. Click Parameters to define the parameters for the stored procedure executed by this Execute SQL task.

▶ **Tip**   If you receive an error when you click Parameters, verify that you have selected the SBS_OLAP database in the *SBS_OLAPDestination* connection object.

Since you have not yet created any global variables for this package, you must first create the global variables required for this stored procedure. If the appropriate global variables had already been created, you could have mapped them to the parameters.

5   Click Create Global Variables, which opens the Global Variables dialog box. Here you can add, edit, or delete global variables that can be accessed from any task or script in this package.

In this procedure, you will define the *StartDate* and *EndDate* global variables. Since the input parameters in the stored procedure are defined using the SQL Server *datetime* data type, you will select a type *Date* in DTS. You will also specify July 1, 1996, as the initial start date, and December 31, 1997, as the initial end date.

6   Type **StartDate** in the Name field, select Date in the Type list, and then type **7/1/1996** in the Value field.

DTS anticipates that you will add another global variable on the second line.

7 On the second line, type **EndDate** in the Name field, select Date in the Type list, and then type **1/1/1998** in the Value field.

> ▶ **Tip**   To include December 31, 1997, as the last value populated, you need to specify January 1, 1998, as the end point.

You have now defined two global variables that can be used by any task or script in this package.

8 Click OK, which returns you to the Parameter Mapping dialog box. You can now map the global variables that you just created as input global variables for the parameters that you defined earlier in the SQL statement.

> ▶ **Important**   You must assign the global variables that will provide the input values for the stored procedure in the order required by the stored procedure. In this case, the *TimeDimBuild* stored procedure uses the first parameter passed as the start date and the second parameter passed as the end date.

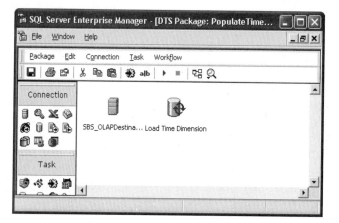

9   Select StartDate in the Input Global Variables list for Parameter 1, select EndDate in the Input Global Variables list for Parameter 2, and then click OK.

10 Click Parse Query to verify that the SQL statement can be successfully parsed, and then click OK. (The statement parses successfully.)

    When the syntax is incorrect or the parameters are not assigned to global variables, the statement will not parse successfully.

11 Click OK to complete the configuration of the Execute SQL task.

12 On the toolbar, click Save.

You have now successfully created your first package using DTS Designer.

Execute the *PopulateTimeDimension* package and verify results

In this procedure, you will execute the *PopulateTimeDimension* package from within DTS Designer and then ensure the results are correct using SQL Query Analyzer.

1 Switch to SQL Query Analyzer, and then click Clear Window on the toolbar to clear the query pane.

2 In the query pane, type **SELECT * FROM SBS_OLAP.dbo.TimeDim,** and then click Execute on the toolbar.

   No rows are displayed in the results pane because you have not yet populated the *TimeDim* table. Do not close this query in SQL Query Analyzer.

3 Switch to SQL Server Enterprise Manager to return to the Populate-TimeDimension package in DTS Designer.

4 Right-click an open area of the design sheet and then click Package Properties so that you can review the general properties of the package. You will learn about these properties in Chapter 3.

5 Click the Global Variables tab to review the global variables that you created while configuring the Load Time Dimension step.

   When the Load Time Dimension step in this package executes, it will use the default values for these global variables unless you override them at run time. You can also create new global variables for the package on the Global Variables tab of the DTS Package Properties dialog box.

6 Click Cancel and then click Execute on the toolbar.

7 When the package finishes, click OK in the Package Execution Results message box and then click Done to close the Executing DTS Package: PopulateTimeDimension dialog box.

The *TimeDim* table in the SBS_OLAP database was successfully populated with time values from July 1, 1996, through December 31, 1997.

8 Switch to SQL Query Analyzer and click Execute on the toolbar to re-execute the query in the query pane.

Notice that the *TimeDim* table was populated with 549 rows, one row for every day in the time range specified by the *StartDate* and *EndDate* global variables used by the Execute SQL task in the package. Ensure that the first date is July 1, 1996, and the last date is December 31, 1997.

9 Close SQL Query Analyzer and then switch to the PopulateTime-Dimension package in DTS Designer.

10 On the toolbar, click Save and then close the PopulateTimeDimension package in DTS Designer.

Now that you have successfully populated the time dimension table for the SBS_OLAP data warehouse, you are ready to build a more complex package with multiple connections, tasks, and precedence constraints.

Creating a Data Load Package in DTS Designer

The next step in building your data movement application is to load historical data into the dimension and fact tables that will constitute the data warehouse. Some of the information required to populate data warehouse tables can simply be copied from the production database or from historical data archived to delimited text files. Information such as certain dimension data will frequently have to be imported from secondary data stores such as Excel spreadsheets. Other information for dimension and fact tables will have to be derived from existing tables using ActiveX transformations and table lookups. In addition, to assure that you have clean data, you need to perform error-checking and data validation as part of the data load process. DTS can perform all these tasks for you. You have already learned how to perform basic data imports and transformations. In later chapters, you will learn how to perform the more complex tasks required for this application.

In the procedures in this section, you will create a package that contains the necessary tasks to load data into the *CustomerDim*, *ProductDim*, and *SalesFact* tables. The data for the *CustomerDim* and *ProductDim* tables will be loaded directly from tables in the SBS_OLTP database. The data for the *SalesFact* table will first be loaded into the *SalesStage* table from delimited text files containing sales data that has been extracted from the SBS_OLTP database for 1996 and 1997. (This simulates a data feed from a heterogeneous data store.) This data will then be loaded into the *SalesFact* table using a multiple table join with the *CustomerDim*, *ProductDim*, and *TimeDim* tables. The multiple table join is needed to link each row in the *SalesFact* table with a row in each of these three tables.

▶ **Important**   In a production environment, the data warehouse tables and its staging tables are generally placed on a separate computer from the computer used for the production database (for performance reasons). You should design your data movement application to minimize the effect on the production system when extracting data from the production system. In general, this means performing all data transformations on either the data warehouse computer or a staging computer, and extracting the data from the production system using a method that consumes the fewest resources on the production system. Typically, such a method would be copying the data unchanged directly to staging tables or to text files that are then loaded into staging tables.

Create a new package and then save it

In this procedure, you will create a new package for the connection objects, tasks, and precedence constraints required to load the historical data, and then you will save it.

1 In the console tree, right-click Data Transformation Services in your local SQL Server instance and then click New Package.

2 On the toolbar, click Save.

3 Type **LoadHistoricalData** in the Package Name box, type **mypassword** in the Owner Password box, select Structured Storage File in the location list, type **C:\Microsoft Press\SQL DTS SBS\ DataMovementApplication\LoadHistoricalData.dts** in the File Name box, and then click OK to save this package.

4 In the Password box, type **mypassword** again to confirm the owner password and then click OK.

5 Click OK to acknowledge that the package cannot be executed without the owner password.

Your first step in configuring the *LoadHistoricalData* package will be to create connection objects for the tasks that you will add to this package.

Create connection objects to the SBS_OLTP database

In this procedure, you will create two connection objects to the SBS_OLTP database. These connection objects will be used by two separate tasks that extract data from the *Products* and *Customers* tables. Because there are no dependencies between these tasks, performance will be enhanced if these tasks execute in parallel. To enable parallel processing of these tasks, you will create two separate connection objects to the SBS_OLTP database.

1 On the Connection menu, click Microsoft OLE DB Provider For SQL Server.

2 Type **ProductsSource** in the New Connection text box, ensure that (local) appears in the Server list, ensure that Windows Authentication is selected, select SBS_OLTP in the Database list, and then click OK.

3 On the Connection menu, click Microsoft OLE DB Provider For SQL Server.

4 Type **CustomersSource** in the New Connection text box, ensure that (local) appears in the Server list, ensure that Windows Authentication is selected, select SBS_OLTP in the Database list, and then click OK.

Create connection objects to the SBS_OLAP database

In this procedure, you will create six connection objects to the SBS_OLAP database. The first three connection objects will be used initially by three separate tasks that load data into the *ProductDim*, *CustomerDim*, and *SalesFact* tables. This package will also contain a task that loads data into the *SalesStage* table, but since the data that will populate the *SalesStage* table is being extracted from two text files, you will create two separate connection objects to the SBS_OLAP database to enable the loading of this data in parallel.

Finally, you will create an additional connection object that will be used for two separate tasks that do not execute at the same time. A Transform Data task will use this connection object to extract data from the *SalesStage* table and load the *SalesFact* table. Another task will use the same connection object to delete all data from the *ProductDim*, *CustomerDim*, *SalesStage*, and *SalesFact* tables. This task will enable you to re-execute this package multiple times during development without duplicating data. These two tasks can share one connection object because they will never be running at the same time.

1   On the Connection menu, click Microsoft OLE DB Provider For SQL Server.

2   Type **ProductsDestination** in the New Connection text box, ensure that (local) appears in the Server list, ensure that Windows Authentication is selected, select SBS_OLAP in the Database list, and then click OK.

3   On the Connection menu, click Microsoft OLE DB Provider For SQL Server.

4   Type **CustomersDestination** in the New Connection text box, ensure that (local) appears in the Server list, ensure that Windows Authentication is selected, select SBS_OLAP in the Database list, and then click OK.

5   On the Connection menu, click Microsoft OLE DB Provider For SQL Server.

6   Type **SalesFactDataDestination** in the New Connection text box, ensure that (local) appears in the Server list, ensure that Windows Authentication is selected, select SBS_OLAP in the Database list, and then click OK.

7   On the Connection menu, click Microsoft OLE DB Provider For SQL Server.

8   Type **1996DataDestination** in the New Connection text box, ensure that (local) appears in the Server list, ensure that Windows Authentication is selected, select SBS_OLAP in the Database list, and then click OK.

9   On the Connection menu, click Microsoft OLE DB Provider For SQL Server.

2

Using DTS Designer

10 Type **1997DataDestination** in the New Connection text box, ensure that (local) appears in the Server list, ensure that Windows Authentication is selected, select SBS_OLAP in the Database list, and then click OK.

11 On the Connection menu, click Microsoft OLE DB Provider For SQL Server.

12 Type **SBS_OLAPAdditionalConnection** in the New Connection text box, ensure that (local) appears in the Server list, ensure that Windows Authentication is selected, select SBS_OLAP in the Database list, and then click OK.

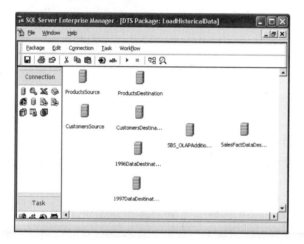

▶ **Tip**   When you create multiple objects on the design sheet, these objects might appear one on top of the other. Use your cursor to drag each icon to a separate location on the design sheet to ensure each is visible. You will also find it useful to arrange the icons to represent the flow of data between the connection objects.

13 On the toolbar, click Save.

Now that you have created all the required connection objects, you are ready to create the tasks to load the historical data into the SBS_OLAP database.

Create the *Load CustomerDim Table* Transform Data task

In this procedure, you will create a Transform Data task that uses a query to extract data from the *Customers* and *Orders* tables in the SBS_OLTP database. This task will then insert these results into the *CustomerDim* table in the SBS_OLAP database.

1   On the Task menu, click Transform Data task.

You are prompted to choose the connection object that this Transform Data task will use to obtain the source data for the transformation. In this procedure, you will query the SBS_OLTP database using the dedicated connection object you previously created for this purpose.

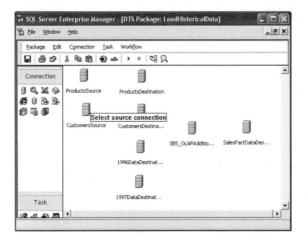

2   Click the CustomersSource connection object.

You are prompted to choose the connection object that this Transform Data task will use as the destination for the extracted data. In this procedure, you will copy the results of the query to the SBS_OLAP database using the dedicated connection object you previously created for this purpose.

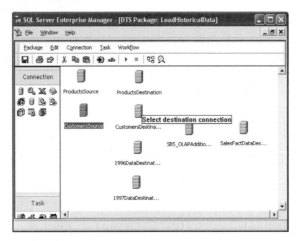

3   Click the CustomersDestination connection object.

An undefined Transform Data task appears on the design sheet between these two connection objects, represented by a black directional arrow.

4   Double-click this new Transform Data task to begin defining its properties.

5   In the Description box, type **Load CustomerDim Table,** click SQL Query, and then click Browse to load a query from an existing script file to use for this Transform Data task.

6   Navigate to C:\Microsoft Press\SQL DTS SBS\Ch2\ChapterFiles in the Look In list, and then double-click LoadCustomers.sql.

This query performs an *INNER JOIN* between the *Customers* table and the *Orders* table in the SBS_OLTP database to retrieve a distinct list of all customers that ordered products between July 1, 1996, and December 31, 1997. This task will use the result of this query to populate the *CustomerDim* table in the SBS_OLAP database.

7   Click the Destination tab and then select [SBS_OLAP].[dbo]. [CustomerDim] in the Table Name list.

The schema for the *CustomerDim* table is displayed.

8   Click the Transformations tab.

DTS attempts to map the columns generated by the source query to the columns in the destination table, beginning with the first column in each. However, the mapping is inappropriate for this transformation. The first column in the destination table is defined using the

IDENTITY property (which generates an integer surrogate key) and should not have any column mapped to it.

The first column in the source query should be mapped to the second column in the destination table, the second column in the source query should be mapped to the third column in the destination table, and so on. In addition, notice that DTS has configured each column transformation to use separate COM objects. As discussed previously, when transforming many columns, DTS executes faster if a single COM object is used rather than a separate COM object for each transformation. In this procedure, you will delete all existing transformations and then create the appropriate transformations using a single COM object.

9 Click Delete All, click Select All, and then click New to specify a transformation type.

The predefined transformation types enable you to copy columns unchanged, convert dates from a *datetime* format into a different format, convert strings in a number of ways, extract a substring, read a file, or write a file. You can also use an ActiveX script to create a custom transformation. (You will begin learning about using ActiveX transformations in Chapter 4.)

Because you will not be changing any data as it is copied from the source query to the destination table, you will use the Copy Column transformation option.

10 Click Copy Column and then click OK.

11 In the Name box, type **Copy Column** and then click the Source Columns tab.

The list of columns from the source query appears in the Available Columns list as well as in the Selected Columns list because you clicked Select All for this transformation. In this procedure, you will map all the columns generated by the source query to columns in the destination table.

12 Click the Destination Columns tab.

The list of all available columns in the destination table appears in the Available Columns list as well as in the Selected Columns list because you clicked Select All for this transformation. In this procedure, you will map all the columns in the destination table except for the *CustomerKey* column.

Transformation Options

General | Source Columns | Destination Columns

Select the destination table columns you want to use in the transformation.

Available columns

CustomerKey
CustomerCode
CustomerName
BillAddress
BillCity
BillRegion
BillPostalCode
BillCountry
ShipAddress
ShipCity
ShipRegion
ShipPostalCode
ShipCountry

Selected columns

CustomerCode
CustomerName
BillAddress
BillCity
BillRegion
BillPostalCode
BillCountry
ShipAddress
ShipCity
ShipRegion
ShipPostalCode
ShipCountry

OK   Cancel   Help

13 In the Selected Columns list, click the CustomerKey column, click the left angle bracket (<) to remove this column, and then click OK.

The Transform Data Task Properties dialog box reappears displaying the new transformation on the Transformations tab. All the column transformations use only a single COM object, and the first column in the destination table is not mapped to any column in the source query.

Transform Data Task Properties

Source | Destination | Transformations | Lookups | Options

Define the transformations between the source and destination.

Name: Copy Column
Type: Copy Column

New   Edit   Delete   Test

Source

CustomerID
CompanyName
Address
City
Region
PostalCode
Country
ShipAddress
ShipCity
ShipRegion

Destination

CustomerKey
CustomerCode
CustomerName
BillAddress
BillCity
BillRegion
BillPostalCode
BillCountry
ShipAddress
ShipCity

Select All   Delete All

OK   Cancel   Help

14 Click OK to save this transformation.

You have successfully created your first Transform Data task using DTS Designer.

Create the *Load ProductDim Table* **Transform Data task**

In this procedure, you will create a Transform Data task that extracts data from the *Products* and *Categories* tables in the SBS_OLTP database using a source query and inserts the results into the *ProductDim* table in the SBS_OLAP database.

1   On the Task menu, click Transform Data Task.

2   Click the ProductsSource connection object.

3   Click the ProductsDestination connection object.

4   Double-click this new Transform Data task to begin defining its properties.

5   In the Description box, type **Load ProductDim Table**, click SQL Query, and then click Browse.

6   Navigate to C:\Microsoft Press\SQL DTS SBS\Ch2\ChapterFiles in the Look In list, and then double-click LoadProducts.sql.

7   Click the Destination tab and then select [SBS_OLAP].[dbo].[ProductDim] in the Table Name list.

8   Click the Transformations tab.

The automatic mapping needs to be fixed for this task as well.

9   Click Delete All, click Select All, and then click New.

10 Click Copy Column and then click OK.

11 In the Name box, type **Copy Column** and then click the Source Columns tab.

12 Ensure that the Selected Columns list includes all the columns in the Available Columns list and then click Destination Columns.

13 In the Selected Columns list, click the ProductKey column, click < to remove this column, and then click OK.

14 Review the mappings and then click OK.

You have successfully created your second Transform Data task. You are now ready to extract data from the delimited text files containing the 1996 and 1997 sales data.

Create the *Load 1996 Sales Data* and the *Load 1997 Sales Data* tasks

In this procedure, you will create the two Bulk Insert tasks that load data from delimited text files into the *SalesStage* table in the SBS_OLAP database. Two separate tasks are used to enable the table to be loaded in parallel from two separate text files. The Bulk Insert task does not require a separate connection object for its source data. You actually create the connection to the text file as part of the configuration of the Bulk Insert task.

▶ **Important**   The Bulk Insert task is the fastest way to import data from delimited text files into SQL Server using DTS because it just generates an *OLEDBCommand* object with the Transact-SQL *BULK INSERT* statement in it, and it runs in the same process space as SQL Server. The Transform Data task with the Fastload option uses the *IRowsetFastLoad* OLEDB interface from inside in the DTS process space, which means that there is context switching between DTS and SQL Server. However, the Bulk Insert task works only with delimited text files as the data source and SQL Server as the destination, whereas the Transform Data task works with a wide range of data sources and destinations.

On a related note, the Execute SQL task is faster than the Transform Data task for the same reason (namely that no context switching is required).

1   On the Task menu, click Bulk Insert Task.

2   In the Description box, type **Load 1996 Sales Data**.

3   In the Existing Connection list, select 1996DataDestination.

4   In the Destination Table list, select [SBS_OLAP].[dbo].[SalesStage].

5   In the Source Data File box, type **C:\Microsoft Press\SQL DTS SBS\DataMovementApplication\1996SalesData.txt**.

6   Click Use Format File and then type **C:\Microsoft Press\SQL DTS SBS\DataMovementApplication\SalesData.fmt** in the Select Format File box.

2

Using DTS Designer

Bulk Insert Task Properties

General | Options |

Import text files into SQL Server. You cannot validate, scrub, or transform data using this task.

Description: Load 1996 Sales Data

Existing connection: 1996DataDestination ▼

Destination table: [SBS_OLAP].[dbo].[Sal ▼]   Refresh

Source data file: C:\Microsoft Press\SQL DTS SBS\Da   ...

(•) Use format file: ntApplication\SalesData.fmt   ...   Generate

( ) Specify format: Row delimiter: (LF)   ▼
                                Column delimiter: Tab   ▼

                    OK   Cancel   Help

7   Click the Options tab, select the Insert Batch Size check box, type 500 in the list box, and then click OK.

Bulk Insert Task Properties

General | Options |

☐ Check constraints   ☐ Keep Nulls
☐ Enable identity insert   ☐ Table Lock
☐ Sorted data: [   ]

Advanced options
Code page: OEM   ▼
Data file type: char   ▼
☑ Insert batch size: 500 ⇅
☐ Only copy selected rows:
    First row: 0   ⇅
    Last row: 0   ⇅

                    OK   Cancel   Help

▶   **Tip**   When you use the Bulk Insert task, you can use a variety of data insertion options provided by DTS so that you can control functionality. Specifying a batch size allows you to control the number of records committed at one time at the destination (an error in a batch rolls back the entire batch, not the entire insert). To maximize performance, constraints on the destination table are not checked unless you select the Check Constraints check box. If the data in the data source has been sorted on a particular column, identifying this to DTS (by selecting the Sorted Data check box and specifying the sort column) can increase the insert performance when the destination table has an index on the same column. Specifying a table lock can increase performance, but at the expense of other users if they will be accessing the destination table during the insert operation. Selecting the Enable Identity Insert check box allows inserts into a column with identities. Selecting the Keep Nulls check box retains nulls in the source data when a default value has been defined on the column in the destination table.

8 On the Task menu, click Bulk Insert Task.

9 In the Description box, type **Load 1997 Sales Data**.

10 In the Existing Connection list, select 1997DataDestination.

11 In the Destination Table list, select [SBS_OLAP].[dbo].[SalesStage].

12 In the Source Data File box, type **C:\Microsoft Press\SQL DTS SBS\DataMovementApplication\1997SalesData.txt**.

13 Click Use Format File. In the Select Format File box, type **C:\Microsoft Press\SQL DTS SBS\DataMovementApplication\SalesData.fmt**.

14 Click the Options tab, select the Insert Batch Size check box, type 500 in the list box, and then click OK.

You have successfully created two Bulk Insert tasks that will load the *SalesStage* table in parallel from structured text files. You are now ready to create the Transform Data task that loads the *SalesFact* table using the data in the *SalesStage*, *TimeDim*, *CustomerDim*, and *ProductDim* tables.

Create the *Load Sales Fact Table* task

In this procedure, you will create a Transform Data task that extracts sales data from the *SalesStage* table, joins that data with key values from the *TimeDim*, *ProductDim*, and *CustomerDim* tables, and then inserts the result into the *SalesFact* table.

1 On the Task menu, click Transform Data Task.

2 Click the SBS_OLAPAdditionalConnection connection object to select it as the data source.

3 Click the SalesFactDataDestination connection object to select it as the data destination.

4 Double-click this new Transform Data task to begin defining its properties.

5 In the Description box, type **Load SalesFact Table**, click SQL Query, and then click Browse.

6 Navigate to C:\Microsoft Press\SQL DTS SBS\Ch2\ChapterFiles in the Look In list, and then double-click LoadSalesFact.sql.

This SQL query performs inner joins among the *TimeDim*, *Product-Dim*, *CustomerDim*, and *SalesStage* tables to generate the result set that DTS will use to populate the *SalesFact* table.

Transform Data Task Properties

| Source | Destination | Transformations | Lookups | Options |

Enter a table name or the results of a query as a data source.

Description: Load Sales Fact Table

Connection: SBS_OLAPAdditionalConnection

○ Table / View: [SBS_OLAP].[dbo].[authors]

● SQL query:

```
SELECT p.ProductKey, c.CustomerKey, t.TimeKey ,s.QuantitySales ,s.A
FROM TimeDim t INNER JOIN ProductDim p
   INNER JOIN CustomerDim c
   INNER JOIN SalesStage s
   ON c.CustomerCode = s.CustomerCode
   ON p.ProductCode = s.ProductCode
   ON t.FullDateCode = s.OrderDate
```

| Parameters... | Preview... | Build Query... |
| Browse... | Parse Query |

| OK | Cancel | Help |

7 Click the Destination tab and then select [SBS_OLAP].[dbo].[SalesFact] in the Table Name list.

8 Click the Transformations tab and review the auto-mapped transformations.

The auto-mapping is correct, and, since only five columns are involved, you will not change this transformation to use a single COM object.

9 Click OK to save this transformation task.

> ▶ **Tip** Because this Transform Data task actually makes no transforma-
> tions, the data source is a SQL Server database, and the data destina-
> tion is a SQL Server database on the same instance, this task could also
> have been configured as an Execute SQL task. Furthermore, an Execute
> SQL task will generally perform better than a Transform Data task. How-
> ever, as you will discover in Chapter 8, the Transform Data task has some
> benefits in terms of error handling and execution reporting.

You have now added each of the Transform Data tasks required by this package. However, before you add the precedence constraints required by this package, you will add an Execute SQL task that enables this package to be executed
repeatedly without duplicating data in the SBS_OLAP database.

Create the *Truncate Tables* task

In this procedure, you will create an Execute SQL task that truncates all data in
the dimension and fact tables before data is loaded into them. Without this
task, each time you executed this package, you would reload the same data

(generating duplicate data). In addition, by using the *TRUNCATE TABLE* statement, the *IDENTITY* property in each table is also reset.

1   On the Task menu, click Execute SQL Task.

2   In the Description box, type **Truncate Data**.

3   In the Existing Connection list, click SBS_OLAPAdditionalConnection.

   Any connection object that defines a connection to the SBS_OLAP database could be used because this task will become the first task that executes in this package and it will complete before any other task requires the use of this connection object.

4   Click Browse.

5   Navigate to C:\Microsoft Press\SQL DTS SBS\Ch2\ChapterFiles in the Look In list and then double-click TruncateTables.sql.

   This SQL query truncates the *ProductDim*, *CustomerDim*, *SalesStage*, and *SalesFact* tables. To do so, it first drops the foreign key constraints on the *SalesFact* table using an *ALTER TABLE* statement. After the *TRUNCATE TABLE* statements have completed, the script adds these foreign key constraints back to the *SalesFact* table.

6   Click OK to save the configuration of this Execute SQL task.

You have successfully added the final task required by this package. You are now ready to add the precedence constraints necessary to enable the tasks in this package to execute in the proper order.

Create the precedence constraints

In this procedure, you will use *On Success* constraints to ensure that the first step that executes is the *Truncate Data* step, and that the *Load SalesFact Table* step executes after all other steps have completed successfully. The intermediate steps will execute in parallel.

1   On the design sheet, click the Truncate Data step, and then hold down the Ctrl key while you click the CustomersSource connection object.

2   Right-click the CustomersSource connection object, point to Workflow, and then click On Success.

3   On the design sheet, click the Truncate Data step, and then hold down the Ctrl key while you click the ProductsSource connection object.

4   Right-click the ProductsSource connection object, point to Workflow, and then click On Success.

5   On the design sheet, click the Truncate Data step, and then hold down the Ctrl key while you click the Load 1996 Sales Data step.

6   Right-click the Load 1996 Sales Data step, point to Workflow, and then click On Success.

7   On the design sheet, click the Truncate Data step, and then hold down the Ctrl key while you click the Load 1997 Sales Data step.

8   Right-click the Load 1997 Sales Data step, point to Workflow, and then click On Success.

9   On the design sheet, click the CustomersDestination connection object and hold down the Ctrl key while you click the SBS_OLAPAdditionalConnection connection object.

10   Right-click the SBS_OLAPAdditionalConnection connection object, point to Workflow, and then click On Success.

11   On the design sheet, click the ProductsDestination connection object, and then hold down the Ctrl key while you click the SBS_OLAPAdditionalConnection connection object.

12   Right-click the SBS_OLAPAdditionalConnection connection object, point to Workflow, and then click On Success.

13   On the design sheet, click the Load 1996 Sales Data step, and then hold down the Ctrl key while you click the SBS_OLAPAdditionalConnection connection object.

14 Right-click the SBS_OLAPAdditionalConnection connection object, point to Workflow, and then click On Success.

15 On the design sheet, click the Load 1997 Sales Data step, and then hold down the Ctrl key while you click the SBS_OLAPAdditionalConnection connection object.

16 Right-click the SBS_OLAPAdditionalConnection connection object, point to Workflow, and then click On Success.

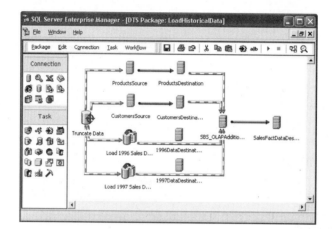

17 On the toolbar, click Save.

You have now completed the package that populates the *CustomerDim* and *ProductDim* tables, loads historical sales data into the *SalesStage* table, and then populates the *SalesFact* table by joining the data in the first three tables with the data in the *TimeDim* table. You are now ready to execute this package.

Executing the *LoadHistoricalData* package

In this procedure you will execute the *LoadHistoricalData* package.

1 On the toolbar, click Execute.

2 Click OK.

This package added 88 rows to the *CustomerDim* table, 77 rows to the *ProductDim* table, and 1464 rows to the *SalesFact* table.

3 Close SQL Server Enterprise Manager.

You have successfully executed the *LoadHistoricalData* package. Before you learn how to add additional functionality to the data movement application that you are building, you will learn about saving, securing, executing, and scheduling packages.

Chapter Summary

In this chapter, you learned how to use DTS Designer to view, edit, and create the building blocks of DTS packages: connections, tasks, and precedence constraints. You also learned about the difference between dedicated and shared connection objects, and about the most commonly used tasks in a data movement application: the Transform Data, the Execute SQL, and the Bulk Insert tasks. You learned that tasks execute in parallel unless you use precedence constraints to control the order of task execution in a package. Finally, you created the first two packages that will become a prototype of a data movement application. In the next chapter, you will learn how to work with the packages you have created.

Chapter

3

Working with DTS Packages

In this chapter, you will learn how to:

- Save packages to SQL Server, Meta Data Services, structured storage files, and Microsoft Visual Basic files, and utilize version control

- Secure packages in Microsoft SQL Server and in the file system

- Execute packages using DTS Designer, SQL Server Enterprise Manager, a scheduled SQL Server Agent job, the DTSRunUI graphical utility, the DTSRun command prompt utility, and the *Execute* method

- Enable package execution logging and error logging

Before you add functionality to your DTS packages and continue building your data movement application, you need to learn how to work with these packages. Packages can be saved in several different formats, most of which utilize a form of version control. Each format has functionality and security advantages and disadvantages. You need to understand the differences between the formats before you build the rest of your data movement application, so you will work with each in this chapter.

You also need to ensure that the packages you create are secure—DTS packages can perform a variety of powerful tasks, but only authorized users should be able to view, modify, or execute these packages. The packages that you created in Chapter 1 and Chapter 2 have been created as secure packages. However, you need to consider additional security and backup issues before you continue developing your data movement application.

Finally, understanding how packages are executed is important to the design of your packages. In this chapter, you will learn how to pass global variable values at run time to control the execution of a package. You will also learn how to enable execution logging and error logging to assist in package debugging and auditing.

Saving Packages

You saved the packages that you created in Chapter 1 and Chapter 2 to the Microsoft Windows operating system as structured storage files. As you will see, saving packages to the file system increases the portability of the packages and enables you to have different versions of packages with identical names in the same system. You can save a DTS package in one of the following four package formats:

- **SQL Server**   Packages saved to SQL Server are saved to the *sysdtspackages* table in the msdb database in an instance of SQL Server. Packages saved to SQL Server are faster to load and save than packages saved to Meta Data Services, but not as fast to load or save as packages saved to a structured storage file. Saving large packages or a large number of packages to SQL Server can cause the msdb database to become quite large.

- **Meta Data Services**   Packages saved to Meta Data Services are saved to a repository stored in the msdb database. The Meta Data Services repository uses the Open Information Model (OIM) and the Universal Modeling Language (UML). Meta Data Services stores package meta data and execution information, database schemas, data transformation details, data analysis descriptions, and COM objects. The package execution information stored can include data lineage information; this lineage information enables you to track the original source of each row of transformed data and provides an execution audit trail. However, these additional features make packages stored in Meta Data Services slower to save, load, and execute than packages stored in SQL Server or in a structured storage file. Saving packages to Meta Data Services can also cause the msdb database to become quite large—even larger than packages stored to SQL Server.

- **Structured storage file**   Packages saved as structured storage files are saved to the file system as .dts files using COM-structured storage. Packages stored in the file system are faster to save and load than packages stored in SQL Server or Meta Data Services. Packages saved as structured storage files are easier to move, both individually and as a group, across the network than packages saved to SQL Server or Meta Data Services. Saving packages to the file system makes it easy to migrate an entire data movement application from the development computer to a production computer by simply copying all the .dts files. To move packages saved to SQL Server or Meta Data Services, you must open them individually and then save them to another location. In addition, when you store packages as structured storage files, you can use a folder structure to save different packages with identical names, enabling you to easily maintain different generations of the same data movement application on the same computer. Packages saved in the msdb database must have unique names due to the flat name space used by SQL Server.

- **Microsoft Visual Basic file**   Packages saved as Visual Basic files are saved to the file system as .bas files for editing in Visual Basic and the Microsoft Visual Studio development environment. Once a package has been saved as a Visual Basic file, the package cannot be edited or executed through SQL Server. Saving packages as Visual Basic files is particularly useful for learning the syntax of the DTS objects that can be programmed.

When you save a package, DTS assigns a Globally Unique Identifier (GUID) to identify it. When you save a package to SQL Server, Meta Data Services, or a structured storage file, DTS employs a form of version control to assist the developer as changes are made to a package. Each time a package is saved, a GUID is assigned to the version being saved, and each version is saved within the same package. Saving multiple versions of each package enables you to load an older version in case you need to roll a package back to an earlier version because of a programming error, or because you need to determine how a package changed over time. However, this save feature can cause a package to eventually become quite large; packages saved to SQL Server or Meta Data Services can also cause the msdb database to become quite large.

▶ **Important**   If you save a package to SQL Server, you can directly delete older versions of it when these versions become obsolete. If you save a package to Meta Data Services or a structured storage file, the only way to delete older versions within the package is to save the updated package as a new package and then delete the old package and rename the new one to the original name.

▶ **Note**   If you skipped Chapter 2, execute the IfYouSkippedChapter2.cmd batch file. This batch file restores the SBS_OLTP and SBS_OLAP databases and copies the DTS packages that would have been created in Chapters 1 and 2 into the appropriate folders. If you do not want this batch file to overwrite any packages that you created in Chapters 1 and 2, you must move them or rename them before you execute this batch file.

Work with version control in a structured storage file

In this procedure, you will learn how to load a particular version of a package stored in a structured storage file, and how to delete obsolete versions of a package to reduce the size of a structured storage file.

1 In Microsoft Windows, click the Start button, point to All Programs, point to Microsoft SQL Server, and then click Enterprise Manager.

2 In the SQL Server Enterprise Manager console tree, expand Microsoft SQL Servers, expand SQL Server Group, expand your local SQL Server instance, right-click Data Transformation Services, and then click Open Package.

3 Navigate to C:\Microsoft Press\SQL DTS SBS\DataMovementApplication in the Look In list, and then double-click LoadHistorical-Data.dts.

You are prompted to select a package to load from within this file. You can store multiple packages in a single structured storage file.

4 Expand LoadHistoricalData in the Select Package dialog box.

This file contains three versions of the *LoadHistoricalData* package that are sorted by date, with the most recent version at the top of the list.

5 Double-click the second package in the list, type **mypassword** in the Password box, and then click OK.

This version of the *LoadHistoricalData* package contains the connection objects but doesn't have any tasks or precedence constraints because they were not added at the time this version of the package was saved.

6 Close this package in DTS Designer, right-click Data Transformation Services in the SQL Server Enterprise Manager console tree, and click Open Package.

7   Double-click LoadHistoricalData.dts, double-click LoadHistorical-
Data in the Select Package dialog box, type **mypassword** in the Pass-
word box, and then click OK to open the most recent version of the
LoadHistoricalData package in DTS Designer.

> ▶ **Important**   When you open or execute a package without specifying a
> particular version, the most recent version is always used. This feature
> enables you to create batch scripts that always execute the most recent
> version of a DTS package without having to edit the batch script.

8   On the Package menu, click Save As.

9   Type **mypassword** in the Owner Password box, change the file name
to **C:\Microsoft Press\SQL DTS SBS\Ch3\WorkingFolder\
LoadHistoricalData.dts** in the File Name box, and then click OK.

10   Type **mypassword** in the Password box, and then click OK. Click OK
to acknowledge that the package cannot be executed without the
owner password.

11   Close this package in DTS Designer, right-click Data Transformation
Services in the SQL Server Enterprise Manager console tree, and click
Open Package.

12   Navigate to C:\Microsoft Press\SQL DTS SBS\Ch3\WorkingFolder in
the Look In list, and then double-click LoadHistoricalData.dts.

13   Expand LoadHistoricalData in the Select Package dialog box.

Only one version of this package appears in the list. When you use
Save As to save an existing package to the file system, only the
most recent version of the package is saved in the new structured
storage file.

> ▶ **Tip**   Saving an existing package that is stored as a structured storage
> file to a new location or using a new file name enables you to eliminate
> all previous versions of the package and reduce the size of a structured
> storage file.

14   Double-click LoadHistoricalData, type **mypassword** in the Password
box, and then click OK to open the LoadHistoricalData package in
DTS Designer.

Now that you have learned how to work with package versions stored in a
structured storage file, let's look at how to work with package versions stored
in SQL Server.

Work with version control in packages saved to SQL Server

In this procedure, you will learn how to load a particular version of a package stored in SQL Server and how to delete obsolete versions of a package.

1 On the Package menu, click Save As.

2 Type **mypassword** in the Owner Password box, select SQL Server in the Location list, ensure that (local) appears in the Server list, ensure that Windows Authentication is selected, and then click OK to save this package to your local SQL Server instance.

3 Type **mypassword** in the Confirm Package Owner Password dialog box, and then click OK.

4 Click OK to acknowledge that the package cannot be executed without the owner password.

5 On the design sheet, click Truncate Data and then press the Delete key.

6 On the toolbar, click Save and then close the package in DTS Designer.

7 In the SQL Server Enterprise Manager console tree, expand Data Transformation Services, and then click Local Packages.

The *LoadHistoricalData* package that you saved appears in the details pane.

8 In the details pane, right-click LoadHistoricalData and then click Versions.

Both the original version that you saved and the most recent version appear in the version list.

DTS Package Versions	
Select the version of the DTS package that you want to edit/delete.	

Package name: LoadHistoricalData

Versions:

Create date	Description
2003-05-27 12:28:45.367	
2003-05-27 12:28:25.617	

    Edit   Delete   Close   Help

9 Click the most recent version of the package (the top one in the list) and then click Delete.

10 Click Edit to open the original version of the LoadHistoricalData package, type **mypassword** in the Password box, and then click OK to display it.

> ▶ **Tip** When you save packages to SQL Server, the only way you can save two versions of a package with the same name is to use version control. You cannot save separately two identically named packages.

Now that you understand how to save a package to a structured storage file and to SQL Server, and use version control with each of these storage methods, let's briefly look at saving a package as a Visual Basic file. Then we'll discuss Meta Data Services.

Save a package as a Visual Basic file

In this procedure, you will save a package as a Visual Basic file and look at its contents.

1 On the Package menu, click Save As.

2 Select Visual Basic File in the Location list, type **C:\Microsoft Press\SQL DTS SBS\Ch3\WorkingFolder\LoadHistoricalData.bas** in the File Name box, and then click OK to save the LoadHistorical-Data package as a Visual Basic file.

3   Open Notepad.

4   On the File menu, click Open.

5   In the Files Of Type list, select All Files.

6   Navigate to C:\Microsoft Press\SQL DTS SBS\Ch3\WorkingFolder, and then double-click LoadHistoricalData.bas.

The Visual Basic file generated for *LoadHistoricalData* appears in Microsoft Notepad. You could extend or modify this package using your preferred development environment.

```
LoadHistoricalData.bas - Notepad
File  Edit  Format  View  Help

Dim oConnection as DTS.Connection2

'------------- a new connection defined below.
'For security purposes, the password is never scripted

Set oConnection = goPackage.Connections.New("SQLOLEDB")

        oConnection.ConnectionProperties("Integrated Security") = "SSPI"
        oConnection.ConnectionProperties("Persist Security Info") = True
        oConnection.ConnectionProperties("Initial Catalog") = "SBS_OLTP"
        oConnection.ConnectionProperties("Data Source") = "(local)"
        oConnection.ConnectionProperties("Application Name") = "DTS Designer"

        oConnection.Name = "ProductsSource"
        oConnection.ID = 1
        oConnection.Reusable = True
        oConnection.ConnectImmediate = False
        oConnection.DataSource = "(local)"
        oConnection.ConnectionTimeout = 60
        oConnection.Catalog = "SBS_OLTP"
        oConnection.UseTrustedConnection = True
        oConnection.UseDSL = False

        'If you have a password for this connection, please uncomment and add your password below.
        'oConnection.Password = "<put the password here>"

goPackage.Connections.Add oConnection
Set oConnection = Nothing

'------------- a new connection defined below.
'For security purposes, the password is never scripted

Set oConnection = goPackage.Connections.New("SQLOLEDB")

        oConnection.ConnectionProperties("Integrated Security") = "SSPI"
        oConnection.ConnectionProperties("Persist Security Info") = True
        oConnection.ConnectionProperties("Initial Catalog") = "SBS_OLTP"
        oConnection.ConnectionProperties("Data Source") = "(local)"
```

▶   **Tip**   Most developers use the Visual Basic file generated by DTS as example code only. The code generated by DTS is not necessarily modular, variables are not always initialized, and the generated transformations are not particularly effective. In addition, the Visual Basic generating tool in DTS Designer does not reverse engineer symbolic offsets; you must do this yourself to see the constant as well as the parameter.

7   Close Notepad.

Now that you have learned how to save packages to a structured storage file, SQL Server, and a Visual Basic file, you are ready to learn about the additional features available to you when you save your packages to Meta Data Services.

Save a package to Meta Data Services and link its meta data

In this procedure, you will learn how to save a package to Meta Data Services and link the package's meta data to meta data in Meta Data Services. Linking package meta data enables you to browse packages and package versions that use a specific column as a source or destination. It also lets you determine whether that specific column is used as a source or destination in any packages saved to Meta Data Services. This linking of columns to a package is called *column-level data lineage*.

▶ **Important** Saving packages to Meta Data Services is an advanced option. By default, SQL Server Service Pack 3 (SP3) disables the option to store DTS packages to Meta Data Services because packages saved to Meta Data Services are not as secure as packages saved to SQL Server or to a structured storage file. Furthermore, Meta Data Services is a relatively new feature that is not used extensively in production environments due to performance problems with large systems.

1 On the Window menu in SQL Server Enterprise Manager, click Console Root\Microsoft SQL Servers\SQL Server Group\(local) (Windows NT)\ DataTransformationServices\LocalPackages.

2 In the SQL Server Enterprise Manager console tree, right-click Data Transformation Services and then click Properties.

3 In the Package Properties dialog box, select the Enable Save To Meta Data Services check box and then click OK.

4 Click Yes to acknowledge that packages saved to Meta Data Services should not be considered secure.

5 On the SQL Server Enterprise Manager Window menu, click DTS Package: LoadHistoricalData.

6 On the Package menu, click Save As.

7 In the Location list, select Meta Data Services to display the scanning option.

When you save a package to Meta Data Services, you cannot save the package using an owner or a user password. (For more information about securing packages saved to Meta Data Services, see the section titled "Securing Packages Stored in Meta Data Services" later in this chapter.)

8   Click Scanning.

Scanning enables you to access the SQL Server 2000 OLE DB Scanner and specify how the data schema is recorded to Meta Data Services as meta data. By default, package meta data is not scanned to Meta Data Services.

▶   **Tip**   Package meta data must be scanned into Meta Data Services to track lineage.

9 Select the Resolve Package References To Scanned Catalog Meta Data check box, which links the package to meta data stored in Meta Data Services.

10 After you link the package to stored meta data, you must specify settings for scanning package meta data into Meta Data Services and for keeping that information current. By default, catalogs that were previously scanned into Meta Data Services are used, and these catalogs are not refreshed each time you save a package. This default saves time when a package is saved but will cause problems when the underlying meta data has changed. With a new package, you should scan all information into Meta Data Services.

11 Click Scan All Referenced Catalogs Into Repository, click Scan Catalog Always, and then click OK.

12 Click OK to save the package to Meta Data Services. Saving this small package will take about 15–30 seconds. (Saving and scanning a large package will take more time.)

Now that you have linked the package to Meta Data Services, recorded meta data into Meta Data Services, and saved the package to Meta Data Services, you are ready to learn how to implement row-level data lineage to track data transformations.

Enable row-level data lineage

In this procedure, you will learn how to enable row-level data auditing and write data lineage information to Meta Data Services. Row-level lineage also enables you to track changes to package meta data across package versions, determine which package version produced a particular set of transformations, and track package execution information.

1 Right-click an open area on the LoadHistoricalData design sheet and then click Package Properties.

2 Click the Advanced tab to display two lineage options.

3   Select the Show Lineage Variables As Source Columns check box, select the Write Lineage To Repository check box, and then click OK.

These options enable the generation of lineage information at package run time. DTS supplies two types of column identifiers when you move data from a data source to a destination table: a short identifier called *DTSLineage_Short*, and a long identifier called *DTSLineage_Full*. The long identifier is a GUID, and the short identifier is a checksum of the package version. The checksum value uses less space but is not guaranteed to be unique, though duplicates are unlikely. To take advantage of this generated lineage information, you must store these variables in columns in your destination table while a column in each row of data is transformed and stored in the destination table.

▶ **Tip** Although the ability of Meta Data Services to track data lineage is very useful, it comes at the cost of considerable performance overhead. You might want to use this feature for testing and debugging only, or for situations in which row-level lineage is an absolute requirement.

Now that you have enabled row-level data lineage in the *LoadHistoricalData* package, you are ready to add the columns to hold this data lineage information and configure the *Load SalesFact Table* task to use these columns.

Configure the *Load SalesFact Table* task to use lineage columns

1 On the Windows menu in SQL Server Enterprise Manager, click Console Root\Microsoft SQL Servers\SQL Server Group\(LOCAL)(Windows NT)\Data Transformation Services\Local Packages.

2 On the Tools menu, click SQL Query Analyzer.

3 On the SQL Query Analyzer toolbar, click Load SQL Script.

4 In the Look In list, navigate to C:\Microsoft Press\SQL DTS SBS\Ch3\ChapterFiles and then double-click AddColumnsToSales-FactTable.sql.

   This script adds the two columns to the *SalesFact* table in the SBS_OLAP database that are required to demonstrate the data lineage feature.

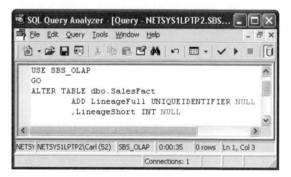

5 On the toolbar, click Execute to add these two columns.

6 Switch to the LoadHistoricalData package in DTS Designer.

7 On the design sheet, double-click the Load SalesFact Table task and then click the Destination tab.

   The schema for the *SalesFact* table in the SBS_OLAP database now contains two lineage columns: *LineageFull* and *LineageShort*.

8 Click the Transformations tab to display the Source column list, which includes columns called *DTSLineage_Full* and *DTSLineage_Short*.

   You can map these columns to the destination columns you created in the destination table. The values for these columns are generated by DTS at run time.

9 Click Delete All and then click Select All.

10 Click New, select Copy Column, and then click OK.

11 Click OK to create the default copy column transformations.
The data lineage columns have now been correctly mapped.

12 Click OK to close the Transform Data Task Properties dialog box and save the transformation changes.

13 On the toolbar, click Save.

You have successfully implemented both column-level and row-level data lineage for the *LoadHistoricalData* package that you stored in Meta Data Services. You are now ready to test this feature and browse the meta data stored in Meta Data Services.

Test the data lineage feature and use the Metadata Browser

In this procedure, you will execute the *LoadHistoricalData* package stored in Meta Data Services, view the data lineage information recorded in the *SalesFact* table when the package executed, and use the Metadata Browser to view the package meta data stored in the Meta Data Services repository.

1 On the DTS Designer toolbar, click Execute.

2 When the package completes, click OK to close the Package Execution Results message box, and then click Done to close the Executing DTS Package: LoadHistoricalData dialog box.

3 Close the LoadHistoricalData package in DTS Designer.

4 In the SQL Server Enterprise Manager console tree, expand Databases, expand SBS_OLAP, and then click Tables.

5 In the details pane, right-click SalesFact, point to Open Table, and then click Return All Rows.

The *LineageFull* and *LineageShort* columns for all rows in this table have been populated with lineage variable values that identify the package that populated them. If you take advantage of this Row Level Lineage feature, when the data is modified by subsequent package executions, the lineage column can track the packages that modified each particular row.

6   Select and copy the checksum value displayed in the LineageShort
    column. (You will enter this value into the Metadata Browser in the
    next procedure.)

7   Close the SQL Server Enterprise Manager – [Data in Table 'Sales-
    Fact' in 'SBS_OLAP' on '(local)'] window.

8   In the console tree, expand Data Transformation Services and then
    click Meta Data to display the Metadata Browser in the details pane.

    Depending upon your security settings in Microsoft Internet
    Explorer, you might receive a prompt informing you that an ActiveX
    control in SQL Server Enterprise Manager is attempting to interact
    with other parts of the page. If so, click Yes. Notice that meta data
    about the SBS_OLAP database appears on the Browse tab.

    ▶   **Tip**   If the Metadata Browser does not appear, click the View menu and
        then click Metadata Browser. To hide the console tree so that you see only
        the details pane, click the Show/Hide Console Tree icon on the toolbar.

9   On the Browse tab in the Metadata Browser, expand the SBS_OLAP
    database, expand dbo, and then expand SalesFact to display meta
    data about this user table.

10 Hover your cursor over the yellow circle containing the black trian-
    gle next to the ProductKey column in the SalesFact table on the
    Browse tab to display the Packages and Source/Destination links.

These links enable you to display information about packages affecting this column, the sources of data used to populate this column, and the destinations that get data from this column.

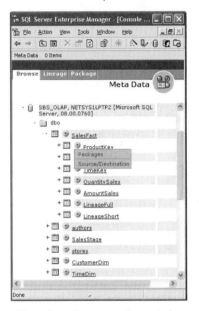

11 Click the Lineage tab and then paste the copied value from the LineageShort column into the Lineage Short text box.

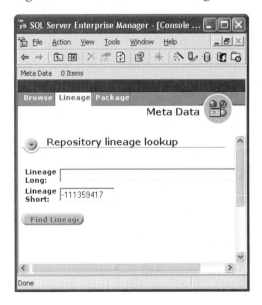

12 Click Find Lineage to display details about the package version responsible for generating this lineage value in the details pane.

Details include the package creation date, package version creation time, modification time, exception log (if any), the system the package was executed on, the user who executed to the package, and the time the package was executed.

13 Click the Package tab to display each package stored in Meta Data Services.

You can expand each version of a package to obtain the following: details about when the package was created and by whom, a description of the package, comments about the package, details about when the package was last executed and by whom, and the location of the exception log (if any) for the package.

Now that you have learned how to save a package using each of the available formats, you are ready to learn how to keep your packages secure and how to prevent unauthorized users from creating packages.

Securing Packages

Securing packages in DTS involves controlling access to them—wherever they are stored—and ensuring that they are regularly backed up to protect against disaster. Specifically, you must limit the ability of unauthorized users to edit, execute, create, or delete packages in any storage location. For packages stored in SQL Server or in Meta Data Services, a user must have a login account to even attempt to access a package. This login account is your first line of defense for packages stored in the msdb database. You can use passwords to protect packages stored in SQL Server or in a structured storage file. Packages stored in the file system should also be protected using NTFS permissions.

Securing Packages Stored to SQL Server

Packages saved to SQL Server are stored in the *sysdtspackages* table in the msdb database, and only members of the sysadmin server role can modify or delete existing packages. The *sp_add_dtspackage* system stored procedure in the msdb database is used to create new packages, and the *sp_get_dtspackage* system stored procedure is used to view existing packages. By default, the public role has *EXECUTE* permission on each of these stored procedures, which means that any user with a valid login can create a new package or view an existing package (including all its details). You should revoke *EXECUTE* permission on these stored procedures from the public role to limit who has permission to save or view DTS packages in SQL Server. To prevent unauthorized users from even seeing the list of packages stored in SQL Server, you should also revoke *EXECUTE* permission on the *sp_enum_dtspackages* stored procedure from the public role in the msdb database. Grant *EXECUTE* permission on these three stored procedures only to those users who should be creating new packages or viewing existing packages.

 Note A package stored in SQL Server can also be secured with an owner password to further restrict access to the package.

Securing Packages Stored in Meta Data Services

DTS packages saved to Meta Data Services are stored in tables whose names begin with *Rtbl* using stored procedures whose names begin with *R_i*. By default, only members of the sysadmin server role or the RepositoryUser fixed database role in the msdb database can create, view, modify, or delete packages stored in Meta Data Services.

 Note A package stored in Meta Data Services cannot be secured with an owner password, but it can be viewed or modified only by members of the sysadmin server role or the msdb database RepositoryUser fixed database role.

DTS Packages

3

Securing Packages Stored in the File System

Because packages stored as structured storage files or as Visual Basic files are not protected by SQL Server, you must use NTFS permissions to prevent unauthorized users from gaining access to these packages. A recommended best practice is to place all packages in a common folder structure, place the desired NTFS permissions on the top-level folder, and use inherited permissions to automatically restrict access to the subfolders.

▶ **Note**   A package stored as a structured storage file can also be secured with an owner password to further restrict access to the package. However, a package stored as a Visual Basic file cannot be secured with an owner password. Any user who can access a Visual Basic file can read or modify the file.

Securing Packages Using Passwords

When you save a package to SQL Server or as a structured storage file, you can use an owner password to limit who can open, edit, and execute the package. You cannot use passwords to secure packages saved to Meta Data Services or as Visual Basic files. When a package is saved with an owner password, only users who know the owner password can open or edit a package. When a package is saved with an owner password and a user password, users who know only the user password can execute the package, but they will not have permission to open or edit the package.

Backing Up Packages

Packages saved to SQL Server or Meta Data Services should be regularly backed up as part of your backup of SQL Server system databases. Since these packages are stored in the msdb database, backing up the msdb database automatically backs up these packages. Packages saved to structured storage files should be regularly backed up as part of your backup of the file system. Packages saved as Visual Basic files are not as critical to back up because they are generally used only as code examples and are relatively easy to regenerate.

Executing Packages

You can execute packages in the following ways:

- Clicking Execute in DTS Designer on the toolbar or the Package menu
- Right-clicking a package in SQL Server Enterprise Manager and clicking Execute Package
- Right-clicking a package in SQL Server Enterprise Manager and clicking Schedule Package to create a scheduled SQL Server Agent job

- Using the DTSRunUI utility
- Using the DTSRun command prompt utility, either directly or through a batch file
- Using the *Execute* method in the DTS package object in a custom application

> ▶ **Tip** For debugging purposes, you can also individually execute each task in a package by right-clicking the task and then clicking Execute Step.

When you execute a package directly, it executes in the security context of the Windows user account that you used to log in to the computer that is executing the package. If you are at the server (either physically or through remote access software), the package executes on the server. If you are seated at a workstation, the package executes on the workstation. When the package is run as a scheduled job, the package always executes on the server and generally runs in the security context of the owner of the job. However, if the owner of the job executing the package is not a member of the System Administrator server role, the package executes in the security context of the SQL Server Agent Proxy Account. (For more information about running a package as a scheduled job, see the Microsoft Knowledge Base Article 269074 at *http://support.microsoft.com /default.aspx?scid=kb;%5bLN%5d;269074.*)

> ▶ **Important** Developers commonly run into issues when executing through scheduled jobs packages that they created and tested interactively on their workstations using DTS Designer. Since executing a package in the context of a job changes the execution location of the package from the developer's work-station to the server, problems frequently occur. Packages fail because text files that were local to the developer's workstation are not local to the server. Packages also fail because connections to data sources or destinations that succeeded for the developer fail for the owner of a job.

Use DTSRunUI to generate a DTSRun statement

The parameters you must pass to execute a package with a number of global variables are difficult to generate manually. However, the DTSRunUI makes this task easy. In this procedure, you will learn how to use the DTSRunUI graphical utility to generate a DTSRun statement. In the next procedure, you will save this generated DTSRun statement into a batch file.

1 Click Start, and then click Run.
2 In the Open box, type **DTSRunUI** and click OK to display the DTS Run dialog box, in which you specify the package format using the Location list and also specify where the package is located.

You must specify the package location information before you can browse to and select the name of the package you want to execute. In this procedure, you will specify the *PopulateTimeDimension* package that you created in Chapter 2.

3   In the Location list, select Structured Storage File and then type **C:\Microsoft Press\SQL DTS SBS\DataMovementApplication\ PopulateTimeDimension.dts** in the File Name box.

4   Click the ellipsis next to the Package Name text box to browse the list of packages stored in that structured storage file.

Since only one package (*PopulateTimeDimension*) is stored in this file and you want to execute the most recent version of it, you do not need to select a particular version.

5 Click PopulateTimeDimension and then click OK to display the DTS
Run dialog box, which shows the package ID along with the date of
the most recent package.

If you click Run at this point, this package will execute using the
start date and end date values stored in the package's global variables. However, because you have already executed this package with
these values and populated the *TimeDim* values based on them, you
need to learn how to pass different global variable values at run time
to control the package's functionality. You can also click Schedule to
create a job that executes this package.

▶   **Tip**   If you had selected a specific version of this package, the version
ID would be displayed rather than the package ID. When creating a batch
file that will execute a package, you frequently want the batch to always
execute the most recent version of the package. Using the package ID
rather than the version ID will accomplish this.

6 Click Advanced, type **mypassword** in the Password box, and then
click OK to display the Advanced DTS Run dialog box, which
enables you to select global variables that are defined in this package
and provide run time values for them.

7   Click the first row in the Name column, and then select StartDate.
    Click the second row in the Name column, and then select EndDate.

    The stored values for these variables are displayed. However, since
    you have already executed this package once using these variable val-
    ues, you need to pass new values to this package at run time.

8 In the Value column for the StartDate global variable, type **1/1/1998**, and then in the Value column for the EndDate global variable, type **3/1/1998**.

▶ **Important**   Specifying a value for a global variable at run time does not affect the value of that global variable stored in the package. Rather, the new global variable value is used only at run time.

9 Click Generate to generate a DTSRun statement with a number of parameters. (You will learn about these parameters in the next procedure.)

You can also choose to encrypt this command. It is useful to hide parameters, such as password values, when you schedule the execution of the package. However, if you encrypt the command, you will not be able to modify global variable parameter values in the batch file for different executions of the package.

10 Copy the generated DTSRun statement with all its parameters to the clipboard and then click OK.

> ▶ **Tip** Highlight the complete DTSRun statement and then press Ctrl+C to copy the generated DTSRun statement.

11 Click Cancel, and then click Cancel again.

Although you could click Run to execute this package with these parameters, it is more useful to create a batch file that you can modify and run periodically with new global variable values whenever your data warehouse needs newer time values.

Now that you have generated the most difficult part of the DTSRun statement using DTSRunUI, you are ready to create the batch file that utilizes the statement parameters that you copied to the clipboard.

Use a batch file to execute the *PopulateTimeDimension* package

In this procedure, you will learn how to create a batch file that executes the DTSRun command line utility. You will then execute this batch file to execute the *PopulateTimeDimension* package from a command prompt using specific global variable values.

1 Open Notepad.

2 To make it easier to work with the DTSRun statement in Notepad, click Word Wrap on the Format menu.

3   On the Edit menu, click Paste.

The generated DTSRun statement appears in Notepad and contains the following parameters:

- The /N parameter specifies the package name.

- The /M parameter specifies the password required to execute the package—either the owner or the user password.

- The /G parameter specifies the GUID that identifies the package. If you do not specify a particular version of the package using the /V parameter, the most recent version of the package will be executed. Omitting the /V parameter enables you to update a package and have the most recent version execute without having to update your batch file or scheduled job.

- The /F parameter specifies the file path and name for the package.

- Each /A parameter specifies a global variable and its values. You can have multiple /A parameters.

- The /W parameter specifies the Windows Event Log completion status.

```
UpdateTimeDim.cmd - Notepad
File  Edit  Format  View  Help
DTSRun /N "PopulateTimeDimension" /M "mypassword" /G "{9FC82619-702A-4D08-B9D7-55B0C6EB660C}"
/F "C:\Microsoft Press\SQL DTS SBS\DataMovementApplication\PopulateTimeDimension.dts" /A
"StartDate":"7"="1/1/1998" /A "EndDate":"7"="3/1/1998" /w "0"
```

▶ **Important**   Since this batch file contains the GUID that identifies the package, you will need to change the GUID in this file if you save this package with a different GUID. For example, if you save this package to a different location to eliminate earlier versions and then replace the original package with the newly saved package, the newly saved package will have a different GUID.

4   On the File menu, click Save As.

5   Navigate to C:\Microsoft Press\SQL DTS SBS\DataMovementApplication in the Save In list, type **UpdateTimeDim.cmd** in the File Name box, click All Files in the Save As Type list, and then click Save. Do not close Notepad.

6   Click Start and then click Run.

7   In the Run box, type **cmd** and then click OK.

8   In the command prompt window, type **cd \Microsoft Press\SQL DTS SBS\DataMovementApplication** and then press Enter.

9   At the C:\Microsoft Press\SQL DTS SBS\DataMovementApplication
    command prompt, type **UpdateTimeDim.cmd** and then press Enter.
    DTSRun loads and executes the package, adding two months of new
    date values to the *TimeDim* table in the SBS_OLAP database. Do not
    close the command prompt window.

10   Switch to SQL Query Analyzer.

11   On the toolbar, click Clear Window.

12   In the query pane, type **SELECT * FROM SBS_OLAP.dbo.TimeDim
     WHERE CalendarYear = 1998** and then click Execute on the toolbar.

13   The results pane displays the 59 rows that were added to the
     TimeDim table for the time members for the first two months of
     1998.

You have successfully created a batch file that will enable you to easily add new
time values to the *TimeDim* table as you add new monthly sales data to the
SBS_OLAP database. Before you learn to add functionality to your data movement application, you need to learn about one more package feature—package
logging.

Enabling Package Logging

Logging of DTS package activity, by default, is not enabled. Logging records the time a package executes and the success or failure of each step. You can use DTS Designer to enable logging of all executions of a package to the msdb database in SQL Server. You can use the /L parameter in DTSRun to enable logging of an execution of a package to a text file. Because package logging incurs some performance overhead, to maximize performance in the production environment, you can choose to enable logging of package activity only during the development phase.

In addition to the logging of package activity, you can also enable the creation of an error file at execution time that records the status and error information for each step in a package. For information on enabling and configuring exception files to capture the actual data causing package or task failures, see Chapter 5. For information on adding error handling routines into your data movement application, see Chapter 8.

Use DTSRun to enable logging of package execution to a text file

In this procedure, you will learn how to enable package logging to a text file. You will use the UpdateTimeDim.cmd batch file, add the /L parameter, add an additional month of time values to the *TimeDim* table, and view the package execution log.

1 Switch to the UpdateTimeDim.cmd file in Notepad.

2 Add the following parameter and value to the UpdateTimeDim.cmd batch file (as a single line—do not add a carriage return):

```
/L "C:\Microsoft Press\SQL DTS SBS\DataMovementApplication\
LoadHistoricalDataExecutionLog.txt"
```

3 Change the StartDate parameter in this batch file to **3/1/1998**, change the EndDate parameter to **4/1/1998**, and then save the UpdateTimeDim.cmd batch file.

▶ **Tip** If you do not save the changes that you make to this file, you will re-enter the time members for January and February of 1998. This duplicate data will cause the Sales cube to fail when you get to Chapter 9.

DTS Packages

3

4   Switch to the command prompt window, press F3 to retrieve the last command you executed (the UpdateTimeDim.cmd command), and press Enter to execute this command.

5   Close the command prompt window.

6   Switch to SQL Query Analyzer and re-execute the query in the query pane.

The results pane displays the time members for the first three months of 1998.

7   Close SQL Query Analyzer without saving the changes to the script and then switch to Notepad.

8   On the File menu, click Open.

The focus of Notepad should be C:\Microsoft Press\SQL DTS SBS\DataMovementApplication.

9   Double-click LoadHistoricalDataExecutionLog.txt to review the package execution log created in the file system.

Details about the package execution along with details about the execution of each step are recorded. This log is very short because the *PopulateTimeDimension* package contains only a single step, named *DTSStep_DTSExecuteSQLTask_1*. Do not close Notepad.

Now you are ready to learn how to enable a package to log its execution details to SQL Server.

Enable package logging and error handling in DTS Designer

In this procedure, you will learn how to enable package logging to SQL Server and create an error file. You will use the *LoadHistoricalData* package that you saved as a structured storage file to enable you to see a more substantial error log. (The *LoadHistoricalData* package contains many more steps than the *PopulateTimeDimension* package.)

1   Switch to SQL Server Enterprise Manager.

2   In the SQL Server Enterprise Manager console tree, right-click Data Transformation Services and then click Open Package.

3   Navigate to C:\Microsoft Press\SQL DTS SBS\DataMovementAppli-cation in the Look In list, and then double-click LoadHistorical-Data.dts.

4   Double-click LoadHistoricalData, type **mypassword** in the Password box, and then click OK.

5   On the Package menu, click Properties, and then click the Logging tab.

6   Select the Log Package Execution To SQL Server check box, type **C:\Microsoft Press\SQL DTS SBS\DataMovementApplication\ LoadHistoricalDataErrorLog.txt** in the Error File text box, and then click OK.

You can also choose to have the package fail if any step fails. The default package behavior allows a package to continue if a step fails, which is generally desired unless you are using transactions (see Chapter 5). This default behavior enables you to use On Failure constraints to define the action you want to occur when a step fails. (Chapter 8 discusses the use of error handling routines.)

▶ **Tip** If errors are logged to an existing text file, error information is appended to the existing file.

7 On the toolbar, click Save.

8 Click Execute on the Package menu.

9 Click OK, and then click Done.

10 Close the LoadHistoricalData package in DTS Designer.

Review SQL Server package logs and error files

In this procedure, you will review the *LoadHistoricalData* package log in SQL Server, and then review the LoadHistoricalDataErrorLog.txt error file.

1 In the SQL Server console tree, expand Data Transformation Services, right-click Local Packages, and then click Package Logs.

Each package that has logged its execution details to this SQL Server instance appears, regardless of where the package was stored.

2 Expand the log tree and then double-click Log 1 to display each step of the LoadHistoricalData package, along with step execution details.

Notice that the step names are somewhat cryptic. In Chapter 7, you will learn about changing step names to more user-friendly names.

Log Detail ✕

Step Detail

Status	Step Name	Run...	Start T...	End ...	Elapsed...	Error ...	Error De
✓	DTSStep_DTSExecuteSQLTask_1	4	2003...	200...	0.691	0	
✓	DTSStep_DTSDataPumpTask_1	4	2003...	200...	3.695	0	
✓	DTSStep_DTSBulkInsertTask_1	4	2003...	200...	2.013	0	
✓	DTSStep_DTSBulkInsertTask_2	4	2003...	200...	2.835	0	
✓	DTSStep_DTSDataPumpTask_2	4	2003...	200...	3.265	0	
✓	DTSStep_DTSDataPumpTask_3	4	2003...	200...	1.582	0	

[More Info >>>]   [View error]   [Close]   [Help]

▶ **Tip**   To view details about a step that failed, click the step, or click the step and then click More Info>>>.

3   Click Close and then click Close again.

4   Close SQL Server Enterprise Manager.

5   Switch to Notepad.

6   On the File menu, click Open, and then double-click LoadHistorical-DataErrorLog.txt.

Notice the step execution details recorded in this text file.

LoadHistoricalDataErrorLog.txt - Notepad

File Edit Format View Help

```
The execution of the following DTS Package succeeded:

Package Name: LoadHistoricalData
Package Description: (null)
Package ID: {09358E4F-9287-4FCF-A780-EAB28B6AE294}
Package Version: {6DE77E07-7081-4BB2-8D9D-ADB303A09DD2}
Package Execution Lineage:
{AB48462B-86AE-4457-A254-A7419DA48418}
Executed On: NETSYS1LPTP2
Executed By: Carl
Execution Started: 5/27/2003 4:45:52 PM
Execution Completed: 5/27/2003 4:45:59 PM
Total Execution Time: 7.301 seconds

Package Steps execution information:

Step 'DTSStep_DTSDataPumpTask_1' succeeded
Step Execution Started: 5/27/2003 4:45:54 PM
Step Execution Completed: 5/27/2003 4:45:57 PM
Total Step Execution Time: 3.695 seconds
Progress count in Step: 88

Step 'DTSStep_DTSDataPumpTask_2' succeeded
Step Execution Started: 5/27/2003 4:45:54 PM
Step Execution Completed: 5/27/2003 4:45:57 PM
Total Step Execution Time: 3.265 seconds
Progress count in Step: 77

Step 'DTSStep_DTSBulkInsertTask_1' succeeded
Step Execution Started: 5/27/2003 4:45:54 PM
Step Execution Completed: 5/27/2003 4:45:56 PM
Total Step Execution Time: 2.013 seconds
Progress count in Step: 0

Step 'DTSStep_DTSBulkInsertTask_2' succeeded
Step Execution Started: 5/27/2003 4:45:54 PM
Step Execution Completed: 5/27/2003 4:45:57 PM
Total Step Execution Time: 2.835 seconds
Progress count in Step: 0
```

3

DTS Packages

▶ **Tip**   Package error files record execution details for all steps in a package, whereas the package execution log records only information about steps that were actually executed. In Chapter 7, you will learn to use ActiveX Script tasks to add branching to the packages of the data movement application. With branching, the package error log can be useful for creating a log that keeps an audit trail of which steps executed each time a package was executed.

7   Close Notepad.

You have now learned about how to enable and use SQL Server and text file package execution logs and how to record error logs in the file system.

Chapter Summary

In this chapter, you learned that the format in which a package is saved determines whether certain features are available, affects the performance of a package, determines the options you have to secure the package, and determines the type of backup required to protect the package against disaster. You also learned a number of approaches you can use to execute a package, as well as how to pass a specific global variable value to a package to control its execution at run time. Finally, you learned how to use package execution logs and error files for tracking package activity and recording errors. Now you are ready to begin adding functionality and flexibility to your packages and continue building your data movement application.

Chapter

4

Creating Advanced DTS Tasks

In this chapter, you will learn how to:

■ Perform lookup queries inside a Transform Data task

■ Use a Data Driven Query task to determine which of several queries is used to insert, update, or delete data at the destination data store

■ Access the phases of the multiphase data pump

■ Call a subpackage using an Execute Package task

In Chapter 1 and Chapter 2, you learned how to use a number of tasks, including the Transform Data, Execute SQL, the Bulk Insert, and the Transfer SQL Server Objects tasks. In this and the next few chapters, you will learn how to extend these tasks and how to use additional tasks to work toward completing the prototype of a data movement application.

 Note In Chapter 1, though you worked with them, you didn't get to see several of these task types by name. This is because they were created and used through the DTS Import/Export Wizard. In Chapter 2, using DTS Designer, you were able to see the wizard-created Transform Data tasks, and you also directly created your own Transform Data tasks in the *PopulateTimeDimension* package.

The following list describes the 19 pre-built tasks that ship with DTS that you can use to build data movement applications. You've already learned about a few of these and you'll learn about many of these throughout the remainder of this book as you build a prototype of a data movement application.

Task	Description
Data movement tasks	
Transform Data task	This task enables a DTS package to transform data during insert operations between one or more OLE DB–compliant data sources and destinations. You learned about this task in Chapters 1 and 2, and you added this task to the *LoadHistoricalData* package in Chapter 2. You will use this task again in this chapter in the *UpdateCustomerDim* package and again in Chapter 9 in the *UpdateSalesFacts* package.
Data Driven Query task	This task scans through data in a source rowset one row at a time and then executes a particular SQL statement based on the data in that row. This task can be slow but is very powerful. You will learn how to use this task in this chapter as you add it to the *UpdateProductDim* package.
Bulk Insert task	This task copies data at high speed from a text file to SQL Server using the Transact-SQL *BULK INSERT* statement. You learned about this task in Chapter 2 when you added it to the *LoadHistoricalData* package.
Programming tasks	
Execute SQL task	This task executes any Transact-SQL statement inside a package. You learned about this task in Chapters 1 and 2 and will incorporate it into every package you build throughout this book to perform a variety of functions.
ActiveX Script task	This task executes any ActiveX script inside a package. You will learn about using the ActiveX Script task in Chapter 7 as you add functionality to each package you have previously built.
Execute Package task	This task enables you to divide a package into logical components for ease of programming. You will learn about this task in this chapter and use it in the *MasterUpdate* package to execute the *UpdateCustomerDim* and *UpdateProductDim* packages. You will use it again in Chapter 9 to execute the *UpdateSalesFacts* package from the *MasterUpdate* package.
Execute Process task	This task executes any Windows-compatible program or batch file. This task is discussed in Chapter 5 of this book but is not incorporated into any of the packages you will build.

Task	Description
Dynamic Properties task	This task sets DTS object property values at run time. The values can be retrieved from a number of different sources. You will learn how to use this task in Chapter 6, and you'll add this task to every package in the data movement application.
Specialized tasks	
Send Mail task	This task sends e-mail to a recipient from within a DTS package. This task is not covered in this book.
File Transfer Protocol task	This task receives files from an FTP server from within a package using the File Transfer Protocol (FTP). This task is not covered in this book.
Message Queue task	This task communicates asynchronously with applications (including other packages) through Microsoft Message Queuing Services from within a package. This task enables a package to send or receive messages, or to send files between packages and pause until they are received. This task is not covered in this book.
Database maintenance tasks	
Copy SQL Server Objects task	This task copies SQL Server objects, such as views, stored procedures, defaults, and user-defined functions, between SQL Server databases. You learned about this task in Chapter 1. This task is not incorporated into the packages that comprise the prototype of a data movement application.
Transfer Databases task	This task transfers an entire database between SQL Server instances and is used by the Copy Database Wizard. This task is not covered in this book.
Transfer Logins task	This task copies logins between SQL Server instances and is used by the Copy Database Wizard. This task is not covered in this book.
Transfer Master Stored Procedures task	This task copies stored procedures stored in the master database to another SQL Server instance and is used by the Copy Database Wizard. This task is not covered in this book.
Transfer Jobs task	This task copies jobs between SQL Server instances and is used by the Copy Database Wizard. This task is not covered in this book.
Transfer Error Messages task	This task copies user-defined error messages between SQL Server instances and is used by the Copy Database Wizard. This task is not covered in this book.

Task	Description
Data warehouse tasks	
Analysis Services Processing task	This task processes objects within Analysis Services. You will learn about this task in Chapter 9 and add this task to the *MasterUpdate* package.
Data Mining Prediction task	This task runs prediction queries in data mining models within Analysis Services. This task is not covered in this book.

As you will see throughout the remaining chapters, these built-in tasks can be used to solve most of the problems you will face in building a data movement application.

▶ **Important**   If the built-in tasks do not provide the functionality you require, you can build your own custom tasks using Microsoft Visual Basic or C++. Building a custom task requires knowledge of one of these programming languages along with an understanding of the DTS Custom Task object model. Building a custom task is beyond the scope of this book. For more information about building a DTS custom task, see Building a DTS Custom Task at *http://msdn.microsoft.com /library/default.asp?url=/library/en-us/dtsprog/dtspcust_5kc3.asp*.

In this chapter, you will learn to extend the Transform Data task to perform lookup queries so that you can include data from a second data store during a transformation. Lookup queries are similar to Transact-SQL joins and can be performed in both the Transform Data task and the Data Driven Query (DDQ) task. A lookup query is particularly useful when it is not practical to perform a Transact-SQL join with the second data store using a distributed query. For best performance, however, you should use a distributed query whenever possible.

The DDQ task enables DTS to evaluate each row in a rowset and execute one of several different SQL statements based on the content of each row. The DDQ task provides great flexibility, but it can be costly in terms of performance. However, if used properly, the performance penalty can be minimized.

The engine that handles the movement and transformation of data for the Transform Data and Data Driven Query tasks is the multiphase data pump. In the tasks you have learned about so far, you have been using the default entry point to access the DTS data pump. There are additional entry points to the data pump that enable you to customize the behavior of the data pump engine and provide increased functionality to your packages, including customized error handling, data aggregation, and row-level restartability. You will use this functionality in the Data Driven Query task that you will add to the *UpdateProductDim* package in this chapter and also in Chapter 8.

The final task you will learn to use in this chapter is the Execute Package task. This task enables one package to call another package (called a subpackage) and send parameters to the subpackage to control its execution. The Execute Package task enables you to modularize the components of your data movement application so that a master package begins the execution of the data movement application and each subpackage performs a specific function within the data movement application and is executed when it is needed. For example, in the prototype you are building, you will create a separate package for each dimension and each fact table. Each package will perform all tasks related to its corresponding dimension or fact table, including updates of staging and dimension tables and deletes from the staging tables. You will also create a master package that will execute each subpackage at the appropriate time. This modular design makes it easier to understand the function of each package and also makes it easier to extend the data movement application by simply adding a new dimension update package when a new dimension is added to the Sales cube.

Performing Lookup Queries in a Transform Data Task

Lookup queries enable DTS to query rows of data from an initial data source, query the same or an additional data source (the lookup query) to add to or modify some or all the rows retrieved from the original data source, and then write the combined rowset to the data destination. The lookup query can be a *SELECT, INSERT, UPDATE,* or *DELETE* statement; or it can be a stored procedure invocation. For example, suppose you have a column in your destination data source that stores each customer's country as part of his or her address, but the data source from which you are loading the new data stores the value for each customer's country in an inconsistent manner (using a variety of abbreviations for a particular country). You can solve this problem using a DTS lookup query. This lookup query matches inconsistent values with corrected values in a lookup table and ensures that the value for each country is stored consistently. If additional values in each row need to be resolved to a consistent state, or if additional rows need to be added, you can create additional lookup queries that perform these tasks during the same transformation operation. For example, your queries can add contact names or phone numbers.

As mentioned earlier in this chapter, a lookup query is very similar to a Transact-SQL *JOIN* statement. When you can accomplish the same task using a lookup query or a Transact-SQL join, use the Transact-SQL join whenever practical for better performance. For example, a Transform Data task that joins two tables using a Transact-SQL *JOIN* statement to generate the source dataset runs faster than a Transform Data task that reads data from the first table and performs a lookup to include data from the second table to generate the rowset that is inserted into the data destination.

However, a lookup query is appropriate when your source join is not practical to perform because the source data resides in a non–SQL Server database, or because the volume of data generated by a source join would exceed system capacity. A lookup query is also appropriate in cases in which it updates or deletes data in the data destination based on information it retrieves from the secondary source. Finally, use a lookup query when the need for clarity in your code outweighs performance issues.

When DTS performs a lookup query in a Transform Data or Data Driven Query task, it keeps the connection to the data source, lookup table, and data destination open for the duration of the transformation. Keeping these connections open is more efficient than closing the connection to the lookup table after each lookup. If this type of lookup was done using a COM object and global variables in an ActiveX or custom task, the connection to the lookup table would be closed as soon as the lookup values had been retrieved. Closing the lookup connection after each lookup is very inefficient if many lookups must be performed. DTS can also cache the lookup data retrieved during a lookup query for reuse during the transformation. Setting a cache value is useful when the number of rows being transformed is large and the number of rows in the lookup table is small. These optimization techniques increase the performance of lookup queries over most other lookup methods.

▶ **Note**   If you skipped Chapter 3, execute the IfYouSkippedChapter3.cmd batch file. This batch file restores the SBS_OLTP and SBS_OLAP databases and copies the DTS packages that would have been created in Chapters 1 through 3 into the appropriate folders. If you do not want this batch file to overwrite any packages that you created in Chapters 1 through 3, you must move them or rename them before you execute this batch file.

In the following procedures, you will add to an existing package a lookup query that imports a list of new customers from a delimited text file to the *Customer-Stage* table in the SBS_OLAP database. This lookup query will modify the data being imported from the text file using the values in the *CountryCodes* lookup table to ensure the country of each customer is stored in a consistent manner. You will begin by creating the *CountryCodes* lookup table in the SBS_OLAP database.

Create the *CountryCodes* lookup table

1 Connect to your local SQL Server instance as a system administrator using SQL Query Analyzer.

2 On the toolbar, click Load SQL Script.

3 In the Look In list, navigate to C:\Microsoft Press\SQL DTS SBS\ Ch4\ChapterFiles and then double-click CountryCodes.sql.

This script file creates the *CountryCodes* table that the Transform Data task will use as a lookup table to ensure that country names are stored consistently in the *CustomerStage* table in the SBS_OLAP database. The *CountryCodes* table contains two columns for each row. The first column contains an abbreviated value for a country, and the second column contains the value for that country in the desired form for use in the data destination.

4 On the toolbar, click Execute to create this table in the SBS_OLAP database.

Now that you have created the *CountryCodes* lookup table, you are ready to create a lookup query that will use this table.

Create a lookup query in a Transform Data task

1   Open SQL Server Enterprise Manager and, in the console tree, expand Microsoft SQL Servers, expand SQL Server Group, and expand your local SQL Server instance.

2   Right-click Data Transformation Services and click Open Package.

3   Navigate to C:\Microsoft Press\SQL DTS SBS\Ch4\ChapterFiles in the Look In list, and then double-click UpdateCustomerDim.dts.

4   Double-click UpdateCustomerDim in the Select Package dialog box, type **mypassword** in the Password box, and then click OK.

This package uses a Transform Data task to copy data from the NewCustomers.txt delimited text file to the *CustomerStage* table in the SBS_OLAP database. Notice that an additional connection object has already been created to the SBS_OLAP database. You will use this connection object for the lookup query in the Transform Data task.

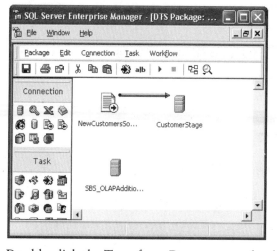

5   Double-click the Transform Data step on the design sheet, verify that C:\Microsoft Press\SQL DTS SBS\Ch4\ChapterFiles\NewCustomers.txt appears in the Table / View list, and then click Preview to view the data in the NewCustomers.txt file.

Notice that the country names are abbreviated inconsistently. In this procedure, you will create a lookup query that uses the *Country-Codes* lookup table that you created in the previous procedure to transform these country values as they are copied to the *Customer-Stage* table.

6   Click OK to close the View Data dialog box and then click the Destination tab.

The destination for the transformed data is the *CustomerStage* table using the *CustomerStage* connection.

7   Click the Transformations tab.

The data is currently being copied directly from the data source to the data destination without any changes.

8   Click the Lookups tab.

On this tab, you will create a lookup query and use a separate connection for it. Although you could use the same connection for the lookup query and the destination, the task will perform better if the lookup query is given its own connection. Doing so avoids serializing the commands across a single shared connection. You will also define a value for the number of lookup values stored in cache. This will improve performance if there are a large number of rows being transformed compared to the number of rows in the lookup table.

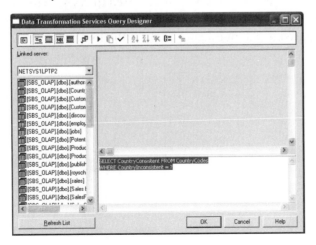

9   Type **CountryCodes** in the Name box, select
SBS_OLAPAdditionalConnection in the Connection list, type **20** in
the Cache box, and then click the ellipsis in the Query box to define
the lookup query.

You can use the DTS Query Designer to help you build the lookup
query, or you can simply type (or paste) your own query into the
query window. For this lookup you will type a parameterized query
into the query window that selects the value in the *CountryConsistent* column for each row that contains a value in the corresponding
CountryInconsistent column.

10 In the query window, delete the partial query, type **SELECT CountryConsistent FROM CountryCodes WHERE CountryInconsistent = ?** and then click OK to save the query.

The **?** is a placeholder for the parameter that will be passed into this query by the transformation script.

Now that you have created this lookup query, you must modify the existing transformation in this Transform Data task in order for this task to use this lookup query. You will change the default transformation from a copy column transformation to an ActiveX script transformation.

Modify the transformation script to use the lookup query

1 Click the Transformations tab, click Delete All, click Select All, and then click New to create an ActiveX script transformation.

To execute the parameterized lookup query that you just created, you need to create an ActiveX transformation script that calls the lookup query for each row that is being transformed.

2 Select ActiveX Script, click OK, type **CountryCodeLookup** in the Name box, and then click Properties.

The default transformation script copies each column, unchanged, from the data source to the data destination. In this procedure, you will modify this script for the *BillCountry* column to call the parameterized lookup query that you created in the previous procedure.

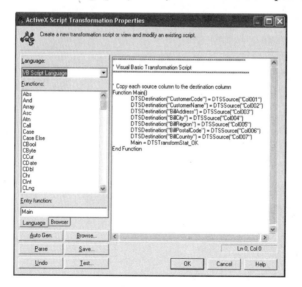

The ActiveX script that you will use to call the lookup query uses the following format to pass a value from a column in the data source to the lookup query and accept the return value from the lookup query:

```
return value = DTSLookups("query name").Execute(argument list)
```

3   Click Browse, navigate to C:\Microsoft Press\SQL DTS SBS\ Ch4\ChapterFiles in the Look In list, and then double-click Lookup.bas.

This ActiveX script is changed in three ways. First, a *CountryCode* variable is declared as an intermediate variable. An *intermediate variable* is used to prevent type mismatches that can occur when you directly map lookup query outputs to destination columns. Second, the value for *Col007* for each row is passed to the *CountryCode-Lookup* query as its input parameter, and the intermediate variable is configured to hold the value returned from this query. Third, the results of the lookup query stored in the *CountryCode* variable are used to populate the *BillCountry* destination column. This ActiveX script and the lookup script execute for each row being transformed.

4   Click OK and then click OK again.

You have now configured the transformation script to use the lookup query.

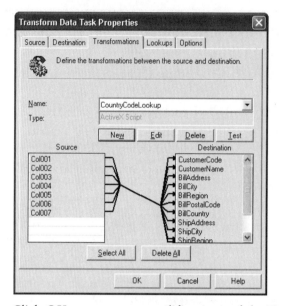

5 Click OK to save your modifications of the Transform Data task.

6 On the Package menu, click Save As.

You will save this package to the DataMovementApplication folder, where you are saving all of the components of the data movement application.

7 Type **mypassword** in the Owner Password box, type **C:\Microsoft Press\SQL DTS SBS\DataMovementApplication\ UpdateCustomerDim.dts** in the File Name box, and then click OK to save the UpdateCustomerDim package with the new lookup query into the folder for the data movement application.

8 Type **mypassword** in the Password box, click OK, and then click OK again to acknowledge that you cannot execute the package without the owner password.

Now that you have added this lookup query to the *UpdateCustomerDim* package and saved this package to the data movement application folder, you are ready to test its execution.

Test the lookup query in the *UpdateCustomerDim* package

1 On the toolbar, click Execute.

2 Click OK to acknowledge that the package executed successfully, and then click Done.

3 Close the UpdateCustomerDim package in DTS Designer.

4 In the SQL Server Enterprise Manager console tree, expand SBS_OLAP in the Databases node, and then click Tables.

5 In the details pane, right-click CustomerStage, point to Open Table, and then click Return All Rows.

The inconsistently stored country names in the NewCustomers.txt file were transformed through the use of a lookup query and a lookup table before they were stored in the *CustomerStage* table. Each county name is now entered consistently in the *CustomerStage* table.

6 Close the [Data in Table 'CustomerStage' in 'SBS_OLAP' on '(Local)'] window in SQL Server Enterprise Manager.

You have successfully configured and executed a lookup query from within a Transform Data task. In the process, you have begun to learn a little about ActiveX transformation scripts. You will learn about the use of ActiveX transformation scripts using Microsoft Visual Basic Script in much more detail in

Chapter 7, but you can already begin to see that some ActiveX scripting is required to take full advantage of the capabilities of DTS.

Using Parameterized Queries in a Data Driven Query Task

The Data Driven Query task enables DTS to read each row of data from a data source and determine the action it should take based on the row contents. Whereas the Transform Data task supports the execution of only a single query in response to the data lookup, the DDQ task enables DTS to look at the data in a row and then select a particular query to execute based on the content of the row of data. The data source for a DDQ task can be a table, view, file, SQL query, or stored procedure. Although the DDQ task provides great flexibility and functionality, it performs more slowly than the Transform Data task because it does not use the Fast Load option. As a result, always try to use the Transform Data task rather than the DDQ task, unless you need the flexibility of the DDQ task.

When you perform a lookup query or a DDQ task, you are performing row-by-row processing rather than set-oriented processing. This means that DTS retrieves a single row, performs the transformation on that row, adds that row to the destination rowset, and then repeats this process for each row in the data source. If the data source supports the use of stored procedures, you can use a stored procedure to generate the rowset from the data source and store that result set in memory. The stored procedure uses set-oriented processing to generate the entire rowset. In this case, when DTS queries the data source for each row, it is querying a rowset stored in memory rather than retrieving rows one by one from the data source. Using set-oriented processing to generate the source rowset reduces the performance impact of row-oriented processing and enables you to increase the flexibility of your data movement application.

In the following procedures, you will learn how the DDQ task operates by creating one that updates the *ProductDim* table with information from the *ProductStage* table. You will begin with an existing package that loads new and updated data into the *ProductStage* table from the NewProducts.txt structured text file. This text file contains a column with a value that indicates whether the product information in the text file updates information about an existing product or contains information about a new product. To store this value for each row in the *ProductStage* table, you will add an *InsertOrUpdate* column to the *ProductStage* table. You will then add a DDQ task that contains two queries. You will create an insert query that inserts new product information into the

ProductDim table from the *ProductStage* table if the value in the *InsertOr-Update* column indicates that the product does not already exist in the *Product-Dim* table. You will also create an update query in the DDQ task that updates existing product information in the *ProductDim* table using the updated product information in the *ProductStage* table if the value in the *InsertOrUpdate* column indicates that the product already exists in the *ProductDim* table. Finally, after you test this DDQ task, you will create a stored procedure that generates the source rowset rather than having the DDQ task retrieve one row at a time from the *ProductStage* table.

▶ **Tip**   Although this DDQ task relies on a value in an indicator column to determine whether to execute an insert or an update query, you could also use a script to compare each row in the data source with the rows in the data destination to determine whether to execute an insert or an update query. You could compare it based on the value of a particular column or you could use a row-sum to compare the rows across all columns. Determining whether a row in the data source contains new data or updated data at execution time can be significantly slower than using an indicator column.

Add the *InsertOrUpdate* column to the *ProductStage* table

1   Switch to SQL Query Analyzer and then click Load SQL Script on the toolbar.

2   In the Look In list, navigate to C:\Microsoft Press\SQL DTS SBS\ Ch4\ChapterFiles and then double-click AddInsertOrUpdateColumn.sql.

This script file adds the *InsertOrUpdate* column to the *ProductStage* table.

3   On the toolbar, click Execute to add this column to the ProductStage table in the SBS_OLAP database.

Now that you have added this column to this table, you are ready to create the DDQ task that will load data into this table.

Create a DDQ task

1   Switch to SQL Server Enterprise Manager.

2   In the SQL Server Enterprise Manager console tree, right-click Data Transformation Services in your local instance and then click Open Package.

3   Navigate to C:\Microsoft Press\SQL DTS SBS\Ch4\ChapterFiles in the Look In list, and then double-click UpdateProductDim.dts.

4   Double-click UpdateProductDim in the Select Package dialog box, type **mypassword** in the Password box, and then click OK.

This package loads new and updated product information from the NewProducts.txt file into the *ProductStage* table. This package also contains an unused connection to the SBS_OLAP database, called *SBS_OLAPAdditionalConnection*, that the DDQ task will use.

5   On the Task menu, click Data Driven Query Task.

6   Type **Insert or Update ProductDim Table** in the Description box, select ProductStage in the Connection list, select [SBS_OLAP].[dbo].[ProductStage] in the Table / View list, and then click the Bindings tab.

In this procedure, you will select the *ProductStage* table as the binding table for the DDQ task to use.

▶ **Important**   A binding table defines the schema for the data that the DDQ task will hold in memory during the execution of its queries; binding tables never store any actual data. You can use any table as the binding table, provided the table has the appropriate schema to work with the queries in the DDQ task. Because the data source can be a stored procedure or a SQL query that generates the source rowset by combining data from multiple tables, you might not be able to use a source table as the binding table. You might not be able to use the destination table as the binding table if the destination table does not contain all the columns in the source rowset. The destination table might not contain columns to store all the columns in the source rowset because some of the columns might be used by the DDQ task only to determine which of several queries are actually executed for each row. As a result, in some cases you might need to create a binding table that maps to the schema of the rowset generated for the DDQ task and that is used only to define the schema for the DDQ task.

DTS uses the columns in the binding table as placeholders for the transformed data; DTS does not actually insert data into the binding table. The binding table can be any table that contains the appropriate schema for the data being received from the data source by the DDQ task. The actual destination for the transformed data is specified by the query in the DDQ task. The connection object used to connect to the binding table must be a different connection object than DTS uses to connect to the data source.

7   Select SBS_OLAPAdditionalConnection in the Connection list, select [SBS_OLAP].[dbo].[ProductStage] in the Table Name list, and then click the Transformations tab.

In this procedure, you will delete the default transformation and then create a transformation using an ActiveX script. This ActiveX transformation script will determine which of two separate Transact-SQL statements the DDQ task executes for each row of data retrieved from the *ProductStage* table. If a row in the *ProductStage* table contains an "I" (denoting an insert record) in the *InsertOrUpdate* column, the ActiveX transformation script will call an insert query. If a row in the *ProductStage* table contains a "U" (denoting an update record) in the *InsertOrUpdate* column, the ActiveX transformation script will call an update query.

8   Click Delete All, click Select All, and then click New.

9   Select ActiveX Script, click OK, type **DDQ** in the Name box, and then click Properties.

The default transformation script copies all data, unchanged, from the data source to the data destination and passes these values to the insert query that it calls. However, in this case, the data destination is merely a location in memory. The final destination is specified by the queries that you will write for this DDQ task. In this procedure, you will replace this transformation script with a script that evaluates the value of the *InsertOrUpdate* column and tells the data pump to execute either the insert query or the update query for a particular row.

10   Click Browse, navigate to C:\Microsoft Press\SQL DTS SBS\ Ch4\ChapterFiles in the Look In list, and then double-click DDQ.bas.

This ActiveX transformation script still copies all data, other than the data in the *InsertOrUpdate* column, unchanged from the data source to the data destination. It uses a *SELECT CASE* statement to pass these values to either an insert or an update query based on the value of the *InsertOrUpdate* column in the data source. If neither an "I" nor a "U" is present in this column, the row is skipped entirely.

11 Click Parse, click OK to acknowledge that the script was parsed successfully, and then click OK.

12 Click OK again and then click the Queries tab.

You can provide up to four separate query types: insert, update, delete, and select. Since the ActiveX transformation calls an insert query and an update query, you will define these two queries in this procedure.

▶ **Important**   The queries that you define for each query type can be any that you deem appropriate. They do not have to match the query types. These names are just placeholders. For example, you could have four different types of update queries.

13 Verify that Insert is selected in the Query Type list, open C:\Microsoft Press\SQL DTS SBS\Ch4\ChapterFiles\Insert.txt in Microsoft Notepad, copy the script from this file to the clipboard, and then paste the script in the query window.

This query contains a Transact-SQL *INSERT INTO* statement that inserts data into columns in the *ProductDim* table. The data values for this statement are represented by parameters that you will map to the columns in the binding table.

Data Driven Query Task Properties

Source | Bindings | Transformations | Queries | Lookups | Options

For each query type used, provide a SQL statement, choosing a destination column to fill each parameter.

Query type: Insert   Build...

```
INSERT INTO dbo.ProductDim
(ProductCode, ProductName, ReorderLevel, ObsoleteFlag,
CategoryName, CategoryDescription, UnitPrice, QuantityPerUnit)
Values (?, ?, ?, ?, ?, ?, ?, ?)
```

Destination to parameter mapping: Parse/Show Parameters

Destination	Parameters

OK   Cancel   Help

14 Click Parse/Show Parameters and then click OK to acknowledge that the query was parsed successfully.

The binding columns are now mapped to parameters in the query. In this procedure, the binding columns are in the proper order, so you do not need to rearrange them to match the parameters in the query.

Data Driven Query Task Properties

Source | Bindings | Transformations | Queries | Lookups | Options

For each query type used, provide a SQL statement, choosing a destination column to fill each parameter.

Query type: Insert   Build...

```
INSERT INTO dbo.ProductDim
(ProductCode, ProductName, ReorderLevel, ObsoleteFlag,
CategoryName, CategoryDescription, UnitPrice, QuantityPerUnit)
Values (?, ?, ?, ?, ?, ?, ?, ?)
```

Destination to parameter mapping: Parse/Show Parameters

Destination	Parameters
ProductCode	Parameter 1
ProductName	Parameter 2
ReorderLevel	Parameter 3
ObsoleteFlag	Parameter 4

OK   Cancel   Help

> ▶ **Tip** You must always ensure that the order of the parameters being passed from the binding table are in the proper order for the question marks in the queries you create. If the binding columns are not in the necessary order, you must resequence them appropriately.

15 Select Update in the Query Type list, open C:\Microsoft Press\SQL DTS SBS\Ch4\ChapterFiles\Update.txt in Notepad, copy the script in this file, and then paste the script in the query window.

This query contains a Transact-SQL *UPDATE* statement that updates existing data in the *ProductDim* table. The data values for this statement are represented by parameters that you will map to the columns in the binding table.

16 Click Parse/Show Parameters and then click OK to acknowledge that the query was parsed successfully.

In this case, the parameters are not mapped to the correct destination columns. *ProductCode* in the destination column is mapped to parameter 1 in the update query. However, *ProductCode* should be mapped to parameter 8. *ProductName* should be mapped to parameter 1, *ReorderLevel* should be mapped to parameter 2, and so on.

17 In the Destination To ParameterMapping box, map the following parameters:

Parameter 1	ProductName
Parameter 2	ReorderLevel
Parameter 3	ObsoleteFlag
Parameter 4	CategoryName
Parameter 5	CategoryDescription
Parameter 6	UnitPrice
Parameter 7	QuantityPerUnit
Parameter 8	ProductCode

18 Click OK to save the configuration of the DDQ task.

19 Click the ProductStage connection on the design sheet, hold the Ctrl key down, and click the Insert Or Update ProductDim Table step.

20 Right-click the Insert Or Update ProductDim Table step, point to Workflow, and then click On Completion.

You are using an On Completion constraint to enable the *Insert or Update ProductDim Table* step to execute even if the *Load Product-Stage Table* step fails. For example, if no new data is available for loading, you might still want to update the *ProductDim* table for data previously loaded into the *ProductStage* table. Chapter 10 will demonstrate this concept more fully.

21 On the Package menu, click Save As.

22 Type **mypassword** in the Owner Password box, type **C:\Microsoft Press\SQL DTS SBS\DataMovementApplication\ UpdateProductDim.dts** in the File Name box, and then click OK to save the UpdateProductDim package with the DDQ task into the data movement application folder.

23 Type **mypassword** in the Password box, click OK, and then click OK again to acknowledge that you cannot execute the package without the owner password.

Now that you have saved this package, you are ready to test its execution.

Test the DDQ task in the *UpdateProductDim* package

1 Switch to SQL Query Analyzer and then click Clear Window on the toolbar.

2 In the query pane, type the following statements:

SELECT * FROM SBS_OLAP.dbo.ProductStage
SELECT * FROM SBS_OLAP.dbo.ProductDim WHERE
ProductCode IN (6,78,79)

3 Click Execute on the toolbar. Do not close this query.

The *ProductStage* table is currently empty and the name of the product in the *ProductDim* table with a product code of 6 is Grandma's Boysenberry Spread.

4 Switch to the UpdateProductDim package in DTS Designer.

5 On the toolbar, click Execute.

6 Click OK to acknowledge that the package executed successfully, and then click Done.

Three rows of data were added from the NewProducts.txt file into the *ProductStage* table and three rows were either inserted or updated in the *ProductDim* table.

7 Switch to SQL Query Analyzer and then click Execute on the toolbar to execute the previous query.

The three records added to the *ProductStage* table from the text file appear in the first result set. The second result set shows the changes to the *ProductDim* table. The product name for product code 6 was changed from Grandma's Boysenberry Spread to Grandma's Blueberry Spread, and the products with the product codes of 78 and 79 were added to the *ProductDim* table.

You have successfully created and tested a DDQ task that will retrieve a row from the *ProductStage* table, read the value of the *InsertOrUpdate* column to determine whether to perform the insert or the update query, execute the insert or update query using the values from the row of data, and repeat the process until all rows of data have been processed. Now you are ready to learn how to improve the performance of this task by using a stored procedure rather than a table as the data source for the DDQ task.

▶ **Important** When you use a stored procedure or a query as the data source, you can take advantage of the performance benefits of set-oriented processing to populate an entire rowset in memory from the source table or tables; in contrast, when you use a table as the data source, the DDQ task retrieves one row at a time from the table. Although the DDQ task retrieves only one row at a time from the rowset in memory, this is much faster than retrieving one row at a time from the underlying table. Using a stored procedure or query as the data source also enables you to perform a multi-table join to generate the rowset.

Add the *ProductStageRowsetSP*

1   On the SQL Query Analyzer toolbar, click Load SQL Script. When prompted to save the query, click No.

2   In the Look In list, navigate to C:\Microsoft Press\SQL DTS SBS\ Ch4\ChapterFiles and then double-click CreateProduct-StageRowsetSP.sql.

This script creates a stored procedure that generates the rowset required by the DDQ task to populate the *ProductDim* table with new and updated values.

> ▶ **Tip**   You can generate the source rowset using complex stored procedures that pull data from multiple tables across multiple servers, perform a variety of aggregations, and include parameters passed to it by the DDQ task upon execution. When you do so, you must create a table matching the schema generated by the stored procedure that the DDQ task can use for the binding table if the generated rowset does not exactly match the schema of the destination table. If it does match the schema of the destination table, you can use the destination table as the binding table.

3   Execute the CreateProductStageRowsetSP.sql script to create this stored procedure and then close SQL Query Analyzer.

Now that you have created this stored procedure, you are ready to modify the DDQ task in the *UpdateProductDim* package to use this stored procedure.

Modify the DDQ task in the *UpdateProductDim* package

1 Switch to DTS Designer in SQL Server Enterprise Manager.

2 In the UpdateProductDim package, double-click the Insert Or Update ProductDim Table step.

3 On the Source tab, click SQL Query.

4 In the query window, type **EXEC dbo.ProductStageRowsetSP**.

5 Click the Bindings tab and verify that ProductStage is still selected as the binding table.

6 Click the Transformations tab and verify that the previously configured transformations are still valid.

Since the substitution of the stored procedure for the table as the data source generates the same rowset, you are not prompted to update the previously configured transformations.

> ▶ **Tip** If you change the data source or the binding table in a DDQ task in a manner that invalidates the previously configured transformations, a dialog box will appear and inform you that some of the previous transformations are invalid. If you made a change that you expected would invalidate previously configured transformations, you can continue and choose to remove the invalid transformations or all the transformations. If you made a change that you did not expect would invalidate previously configured transformations, you can click Cancel and close the task to retain all previous settings in the task and then fix the previously made change.

7   Click OK to save the changes to the DDQ task.

8   On the toolbar, click Save.

9   On the toolbar, click Execute.

10 Click OK, and then click Done.

Three products were added to the *ProductStage* table and six products were either inserted or updated in the *ProductDim* table. Six products were inserted or updated this time rather than three because the original three entries in the *ProductStage* table were not deleted before the identical three entries were added again from the New-Products.txt file. In Chapter 7, you will create a delete phase for this package to solve this double-entry problem.

11 Close the UpdateProductDim package in DTS Designer.

You have modified the DDQ task to enable the row-by-row processing to retrieve one row of data at a time from memory rather than one row of data at a time from a table. This technique can substantially increase the performance of the DDQ task.

Accessing the Multiphase Data Pump

The multiphase data pump is the engine that handles the movement and transformation of data for the Transform Data and Data Driven Query tasks. When you modified the default transformation in the Transform Data task in the *UpdateCustomerDim* package to call the *CountryCodes* lookup query and when you modified the default transformation in the DDQ task in the *UpdateProductDim* package to call either the insert or update query, you were actually accessing the row transform phase of the multiphase data pump. The row transform phase is the only phase exposed by default in DTS Designer. In this chapter you will learn how to expose the additional phases and learn a little bit about each phase. In later chapters, you will extend the data movement application by using ActiveX transformation scripts to access the data pump at different phases.

The multiphase data pump actually has six phases that are entry points for customization of a data movement application. The data pump has three phases that allow you to interact with the data, one of which is the row transform phase. You can also access the data after each batch completes and again after all batches have completed. In addition to these phases that allow you to manipulate the data, there is one phase that allows you to access the data pump before any source rows are fetched and two phases that allow you to access the data pump after the data has been processed (but before the next task starts).

These phases can be accessed by ActiveX scripts and custom COM objects. The following list describes each of these phases.

- **Pre-Source phase**   This phase occurs before the first row of data is fetched from the data source and is executed only once unless you use an ActiveX script to create a loop. You can write a pre-source data pump function for a transformation that writes header rows containing meta data to a table or a file; truncates tables; drops indexes; or initializes objects, connections, and memory for use in later phases of the data pump. This phase does not allow access to the source data but does allow access to the data destination. You actually accessed this phase in Chapter 3 when you submitted global variable values to the *PopulateTimeDimension* package using the *DTSRun* command. You will continue to explore accessing this phase in Chapter 6 and Chapter 7.

- **Row Transform phase**   This phase is the default data pump phase and occurs once for each row being transformed. All transformations use this phase to move data between the source and destination. This phase is available through the Transformations mapping tab of the Transform Data task or the Data Driven Query task. This phase is also available through an ActiveX Scripting task or a custom task. In an ActiveX scripting task, the *Main* function placeholder in the transformation script is the default entry point for writing a transformation script for this phase. You accessed this phase using an ActiveX transformation script when you modified the default transformation script to call the lookup query in the Transform Data task and the insert or update query in the DDQ task. This phase allows read access to the source data and meta data and write access to the destination data.

- **Post Row Transform phase**   This phase occurs once for each row being transformed, regardless of the success or failure of the row transformation. This phase has three subphases:
  - **Transform Failure subphase**   This subphase occurs whenever an error is detected in the Row Transform phase for a particular row, indicated by the return of *DTSTransformStat_Error* or *DTSTransformStat_ExceptionRow*. These errors are typically caused by data conversion errors. You can write a function that handles transformation errors (such as type mismatches). You can override the value that generated the error and continue with the execution, or you can abort the execution and report a failure. You can also call this subphase and insert code that tests for failure conditions that DTS does not automatically detect at

this phase. Failure conditions include null conditions in the source data that will violate a null constraint at the data destination. If you do not write a function to handle a transform failure, execution will continue and DTS will attempt to insert the row containing the transformation error.

- **Insert Success subphase**   This subphase occurs when the current row is successfully inserted into the destination rowset. The data is not actually inserted into the data destination at this point. You can write a function to keep count of all rows that were successfully transformed and added to the destination rowset.

- **Insert Failure subphase**   This subphase occurs when the current row cannot be inserted into the destination rowset. You can write a function to keep a count of all rows that were not successfully transformed.

- **On Batch Complete phase**   This phase occurs once for each batch. By default, all rows are processed in one batch. You can define a batch size for the Transform Data task on the Options tab. You must set a batch size for the DDQ and other tasks programmatically. When this phase occurs, all rows in the destination rowset buffer are written to the destination table. You can write a function programmatically to audit the state of large, multi-batch load jobs. If an error occurs during the writing of this rowset, the number of rows written to the destination table depends upon whether the package is configured to use transactions. Transactions are discussed in Chapter 5.

- **Post Source Data phase**   This phase occurs after all batches have been processed (but before the final batch is committed). During this phase, you have full access to the data. For example, you could write a function that adds a footer row to the data destination.

- **On Pump Complete phase**   This phase occurs after all other phases are complete. During this phase, you do not have access to the destination data. During this phase, you can free up resources (such as closing a global ADO connection) and commit data held in global variables throughout the lifetime of the data pump (such as a value for total rows processed).

Figure 4-1 shows the data pump phases and how they map to the data flow.

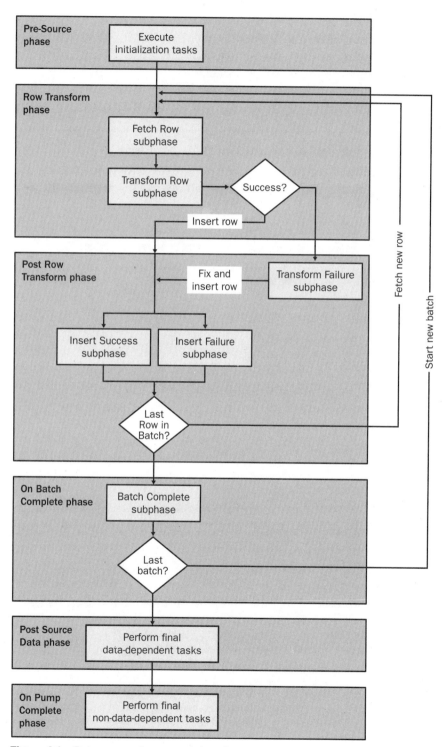

Figure 4-1   Data pump phases and data flow

By exposing these entry points to the multiphase data pump, DTS enables you to add great flexibility to the data movement application. You will learn to access these functions throughout the remainder of this book. However, because these entry points are not exposed by default, you must activate the data pump feature in SQL Server Enterprise Manager before you can access them directly in DTS Designer.

Access the data pump phases in DTS Designer

In this procedure, you will activate the multiphase data pump feature in DTS Designer and then review the data pump phases as they appear in DTS Designer.

1   In the SQL Server Enterprise Manager console tree, right-click Data Transformation Services and then click Properties.

2   Select the Show Multi-Phase Pump In DTS Designer check box. You could also select the Turn On Cache check box and clear the Enable Save To Meta Data Services check box at this point if you so desire.

> ► **Important**   In the Package Properties dialog box, you can also turn on caching, which can reduce the time required to load large packages in DTS Designer. When caching is not turned on, DTS Designer queries the Windows registry each time a package is opened to determine what scripting languages, custom transformations, OLE-DB Providers, and custom tasks are registered on the computer. If you turn on caching, you must click Refresh to update the cache after changing one of these objects.

3 Click OK.

4 In the SQL Server Enterprise Manager console tree, right-click Data Transformation Services and then click Open Package.

5 Navigate to C:\Microsoft Press\SQL DTS SBS\Ch1\WorkingFolder in the Look In list, and then double-click SQL_DTS_SBS_1.1.dts.

6 Double-click SQL_DTS_SBS_1.1 in the Select Package dialog box, type **mypassword** in the Password box, and then click OK.

7 Double-click the Transform Data step and then click the Transformations tab.

The phases filter list allows you to view, edit, or create transformations at different phases. The only transformation in this package is the DirectCopyXform transformation in the row transform phase.

8 Click Delete All, click Select All, and then click New.

9 Click ActiveX Script, click OK, and then click Properties.

10 Click the Phases tab.

Notice that only the Row Transform phase is selected by default. In this procedure, you will select all the phases. Then you will generate default code to demonstrate where to add custom code to access each phase with an ActiveX transformation script.

11 Select all the check boxes on the Phases tab, and then click Auto Gen.
to add a function placeholder, and the *DTSTransformstat_OK* constant as an exit value, for each phase.

DTSTransformstat_OK indicates to the DTS task that it can continue with the next task. You can add ActiveX script within the function blocks of any phase of the multiphase data pump to enhance the
functionality of your data movement application.

12 Click Cancel, click No, click Cancel again, click Cancel once more,
and then close the SQL_DTS_SBS_1.1 package in DTS Designer.

You have now activated the multiphase data pump feature in DTS Designer. You will use the functionality exposed in this exercise throughout the remainder of this book.

Calling Subpackages

The final task that you will learn to use in this chapter is the Execute Package task. The Execute Package task enables you to call another package (called a subpackage) from within a package, pass parameters to the subpackage, and wait until the subpackage completes before continuing with additional tasks in the calling package.

Use the Execute Package task to modularize your data movement application. You can execute packages as a group, in a defined order, or using a common set of global variables. You can use specialized packages for particular functionality (such as error control). You can use a single package to begin the execution of the entire data movement application (called a master package) and initialize all variables used for a particular execution of the entire application.

The Execute Package task executes in the same process space as the calling task (which enables it to use the same global variables values as the master package). If you call multiple Execute Packages simultaneously, they execute in parallel. The number of tasks that execute in parallel is one of the package properties of the calling package. By default, the number of tasks in a package that can execute in parallel is limited to four. If you parallelize the data movement application, and the computer on which the application is executing has sufficient processing power to handle the execution of additional tasks in parallel, you should increase the number of tasks that can execute in parallel in the master package. In Chapter 5, you will learn how to set the number of tasks that a package will execute in parallel.

To allow your packages to scale this way, you must design this type of parallelism into the data movement application. Remember also that you must use separate connection objects for each task that you want to run in parallel. Using multiple packages, each with their own connection objects, helps you parallelize a data movement application.

In the following procedure, you will create a package that containing two Execute Package tasks. These execution tasks will call the *UpdateProductDim* and the *UpdateCustomerDim* packages. These packages will become the primary packages in the data movement application you are building that will periodically update each of the dimension tables used by the *Sales* cube and then update the fact table used by the *Sales* cube. Although these two packages do not yet accomplish all the tasks necessary for the data movement application, this master package will provide a starting place for configuring the entire application.

Create a master package containing Execute Package tasks

1   In the SQL Server Enterprise Manager console tree for your default instance, right-click Data Transformation Services, and then click New Package.

2   On the Task menu, click Execute Package Task, which prompts you to provide the package name, location, and connection information.

3   Type **Call UpdateProductDim Subpackage** in the Description box, click Structured Storage File in the Location list, and then type **C:\Microsoft Press\SQL DTS SBS\DataMovementApplication\ UpdateProductDim.dts** in the File Name box.

4   Click the ellipsis to the right of the Package Name box, double-click UpdateProductDim, and then type **mypassword** in the Password box.

The package ID for this subpackage is retrieved and will be saved as part of this Execute Package task. Because the package ID is used, this Execute Package task will always execute the most recent version of the *UpdateProductDim* package. However, if you change the package ID of this package, this Execute Package task will fail.

The Execute Package Task Properties dialog box includes two additional tabs: the Inner Package Global Variables tab and the Outer Package Global Variables tab. You can use these tabs to pass global variable values to the subpackage. You will incorporate this functionality into the data movement application in Chapter 6 and Chapter 7.

▶ **Important**   A package called by an Execute Package task can process global variable data passed to it in any ActiveX script in its executable workflow. Inner package global variables enable you to set values for global variables that are defined in the package being called. Outer package global variables enable you to define which of the global variable values defined in the calling package will be passed to the package being called.

5   Click OK to save this Execute Package task and then click Execute Package Task on the Task menu.

6   Type **Call UpdateCustomerDim Subpackage** in the Description box, click Structured Storage File in the Location list, type **C:\Microsoft Press\SQL DTS SBS\DataMovementApplication\ UpdateCustomerDim.dts** in the File Name box, type **UpdateCustomerDim** in the Package Name box, type **mypassword** in the Password box, and then click OK.

You have successfully created a simple master package that calls two subpackages. Notice that because this package does not contain precedence constraints, both tasks will execute simultaneously as soon as the package is executed.

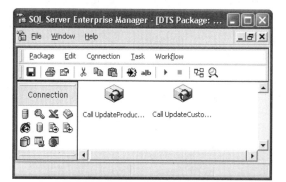

7   On the toolbar, click Save.

8   Type **MasterUpdate** in the Package Name box, type **mypassword** in the Owner Password box, click Structured Storage File in the Location list, type **C:\Microsoft Press\SQL DTS SBS\DataMovementApplication\ MasterUpdate.dts** in the File Name box, and then click OK.

9   Type **mypassword**, click OK, and then click OK again.

10   Close the MasterUpdate package in DTS Designer and then close SQL Server Enterprise Manager.

You have successfully created the master package for this prototype of a data movement application. In subsequent chapters, you will add functionality to this package. For example, in Chapter 6 you will configure global variables in the *MasterUpdate* package that will be passed to each subpackage, and in Chapter 7 you will add some initialization steps that will populate global variable values from a table in the SBS_OLAP database before these Execute Package tasks execute. In addition, in Chapter 9 you will add a task that updates the *SalesFact* table in the SBS_OLAP database after the *UpdateProductDim* and *UpdateCustomerDim* packages update the appropriate dimension tables.

Chapter Summary

In this chapter, you learned about the range of DTS tasks that you can add to a package. You learned how to add additional functionality to the Transform Data task with the lookup query and learned how to use a Data Driven Query to add even more flexibility to your packages. It both cases, you were introduced to the use of ActiveX transformation scripts to enable this additional functionality at the Row Transform phase of the multiphase data pump. You were also introduced to the additional phases of the data pump that you can access in a package. Finally, you learned how to use the Execute Package task to begin creating a modularized data movement application.

5

Working with Advanced DTS Options

In this chapter, you will learn how to:

■ Configure package and task execution properties

■ Enable transactions and join packages and tasks into existing transactions

■ Enable and configure exception files

DTS provides a number of advanced options that enable you to control the execution of tasks and packages and enhance their functionality. These options include the ability to configure execution priorities, the number of tasks that execute in parallel, definitions of packages, properties of transactions, and exception files. For example, you can design a modularized data movement application with many packages that can execute in parallel. You can then adjust the number of packages that actually execute in parallel based on the capabilities of the production computer on which the data movement application is deployed. You might also want to increase the execution priority of the entire data movement application when it is being executed on a multi-processor computer, or increase the execution priority of a particular task or package within the data movement application.

To design your data movement application to take advantage of the advanced options, and to ensure the proper functionality of tasks and packages, you must understand the consequences of using the options and know where their use is required.

Configuring Execution Properties

Execution properties modify and control how entire packages as well as individual tasks execute. In this section, you will learn to configure the number of tasks that will be executed in parallel, the execution priority of packages and tasks, and the point at which a task failure constitutes a package failure. You will also learn how to work with tasks that are not free-threaded.

Configuring Parallel Execution of Tasks

In Chapter 2, you learned about the use of precedence constraints to control the order in which tasks execute within a package. You also learned that tasks that are not limited by precedence constraints execute in parallel unless the tasks share the same connection object. By definition, tasks that share a connection object execute serially because only one task can use a connection object at any point in time.

After you determine which tasks you want to execute in parallel and you ensure that each task needing to execute simultaneously has a separate connection object, you must decide how many tasks you actually want DTS to execute in parallel. By default, the maximum number of tasks that DTS can execute in parallel is four. You can increase the performance of a well-designed data movement application on a multiprocessor computer by increasing the number of steps that execute concurrently in each package. If, however, you set the number of concurrently executing steps too high, the overall performance of the data movement application can suffer because the processors will be switching between tasks rather than finishing each task sequentially.

You can use DTS Designer to configure the maximum number of tasks that execute concurrently in a package in the Properties dialog box for the package. Figure 5-1 displays the properties of the *MasterUpdate* package that you created in Chapter 4.

Notice that the *MasterUpdate* package is configured to execute up to four tasks in parallel. You can increase or decrease the number of tasks that will execute in parallel at run time by dynamically changing the *MaxConcurrentSteps* property of the package. (For more information about changing package and task properties at run time, see Chapter 6.)

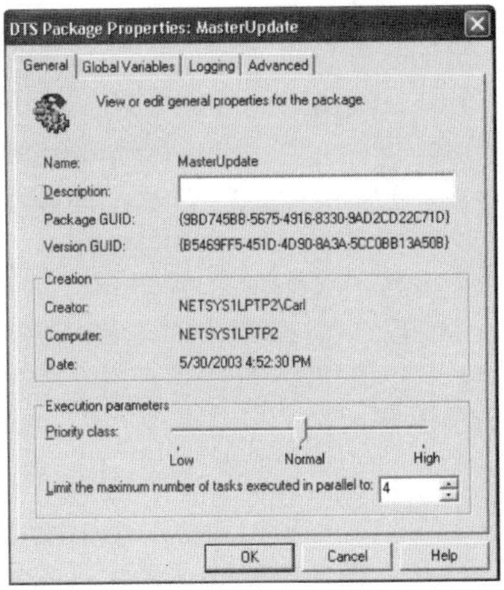

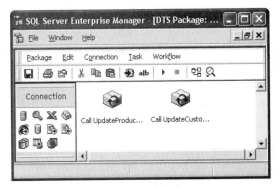

Figure 5-1   Properties of the *MasterUpdate* package

In a modularized data movement application, you can control the number of subpackages that are executed simultaneously from a master package by configuring the number of tasks that execute concurrently. Figure 5-2 displays the *MasterUpdate* package that you created in Chapter 4. This package contains two Execute Package tasks that update dimensions in the *Sales* cube. In a complex Analysis Services cube, you might have 15 to 20 dimensions, each of which is updated using a separate subpackage.

Figure 5-2   *MasterUpdate* package

The two subpackages called by this master package will execute concurrently because the package does not contain precedence constraints, the number of packages in the package does not exceed the number of tasks that can execute in parallel, and the tasks in the subpackages have their own connection objects.

Advanced DTS Options

5

As you add Execute Package tasks to a master package, you will quickly exceed the number of packages that executes concurrently unless you increase the setting for parallelism. However, the number of tasks that you actually want to execute in parallel on any particular computer depends upon the number of processors on that computer and the other tasks on that computer that are competing for processor resources. You can increase or decrease the number of subpackages that executes concurrently in your modular data movement application by using only the parallelism setting. This design enables you to develop and test the data movement application on one computer and then tune its performance in the production environment without having to edit each individual subpackage.

Configuring Execution Priority

Another execution property that you can configure is the execution priority of the operating system thread on which a package and its subpackages run. By default, packages execute at normal priority relative to other applications running on the same server. Increasing the execution priority for the package might improve its performance, but potentially at the expense of the responsiveness of other applications. However, if the data movement application executes a multiprocessor computer, you can configure the computer to execute SQL Server tasks only on particular processors. In this environment, you can increase the execution priority of the packages in the data movement application relative to other SQL Server tasks. On the other hand, if the data movement application is using too many resources relative to other tasks on either a single or a multiple processor computer, you can decrease the execution priority of the data movement application, albeit at the price of poorer performance.

You can use DTS Designer to increase or decrease the priority of a package relative to other applications in the package's Properties dialog box, which was shown in Figure 5-1. You can also set this value at run time by changing the *PackagePriorityClass* property of the package.

By default, all package tasks inherit the thread priority of the package, and tasks that execute in parallel execute with equal priority. You can use DTS Designer to increase or decrease the priority of a task within a package relative to other tasks on the Options tab of the task's Workflow Properties dialog box. Figure 5-3 displays this dialog box for the *DTSStep_DTSExecutePackageTask_1* step in the *MasterUpdate* package. This is the step that executes the Execute Package task and calls the *UpdateProductDim* subpackage. Execution priority is determined by a property of the step; it is not a function of the task itself.

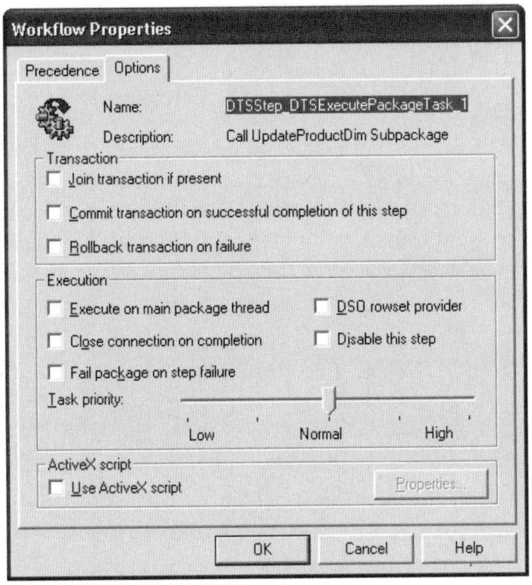

Figure 5-3   Options tab of the Workflow Properties dialog box for the *DTSStep_DTSExecutePackageTask_1* step

▶ **Important**   Tasks and steps are related but different. Whereas a *task* defines a unit of work within a package, a *step* actually executes the task. In the first half of this book, you are learning about tasks. In the second half of this book, you will learn about manipulating the execution of these tasks by using the step object associated with the task.

You can also set this task priority value at run time by changing the *RelativePriority* property of the step. In the data movement application you are building, all packages and tasks will execute at normal priority.

Configuring the Definition of Package Failure

Another execution property that you can set is the definition of package failure. If a package completes all the tasks within it (regardless of their success or failure), the package completes successfully unless you define the failure of a particular task as a package failure. You can use DTS Designer to configure a task so that its failure will cause the entire package to fail. You set this definition on the Options tab of the task's Workflow Properties dialog box. (See Figure 5-3.) If you call a subpackage from a master package by using the Execute Package task and configure the failure of one of its steps to cause it to fail, the failure of the step in the subpackage will cause the failure of the master package and all its subpackages. In the data movement application you are building, you will not configure the failure of any particular task to cause the failure of the entire data movement application. Rather, you will use error handling routines to capture error information to enable you to recover from errors. For more information, see Chapter 8.

> ▶ **Tip**   Configuring a package to fail when one of its steps fails does not undo any steps performed by the package and its subpackages before the step failure occurs. To automatically roll back package changes when a package failure occurs, you must create one or more transactions in the data movement application and have tasks enlist in an ongoing transaction. (For more information, see the section "Working with Transactions" later in this chapter.)

Working with Tasks That Are Not Free-Threaded

The other execution property of a step that you might need to configure is the execution thread on which the task will execute. DTS executes each task on a separate thread unless you configure a step to execute a task on the main package thread. Spawning new threads for each task enables DTS to take advantage of the operating system's ability to distribute execution threads among available processors. Executing tasks on separate threads increases the performance of DTS packages, particularly when the tasks execute on computers with multiple processors. However, tasks that use an OLE DB provider that is not free-threaded, or that were developed using a language not supporting the Free-Threaded model (or the Apartment Threading model), must execute on the main thread. (You can use DTS Designer to specify whether a task executes on the main thread or on its own thread by modifying the properties of the step that executes the task in the task's Workflow Properties dialog box.) Microsoft Visual Basic tasks, such as the Analysis Services Processing task or custom Visual Basic tasks, are not free-threaded. The following providers are not free-threaded:

- Microsoft OLE DB Provider for Jet
- Microsoft Excel provider
- dBase provider
- Paradox provider
- HTML source files provider

> ▶ **Important**   Attempting parallel execution on a provider that does not support it can result in serious errors.

Rather than run tasks that are not free-threaded on the main thread, you can choose to run these tasks in a separate process by using the Execute Process task to execute them. For example, to process multiple Analysis Services cubes in parallel, you must run each execution of the Analysis Services Processing task in a separate process.

Working with Transactions

A DTS transaction ensures that all its tasks complete successfully and all task changes are committed; or, if the transaction fails, it rolls back the changes made by any task in the transaction. DTS transactions enable you to keep data consistent across multiple servers, incorporate all tasks in a package into a single transaction, utilize multiple transactions in a single package, and control errors in an asynchronous environment. To automatically roll back changes made by a DTS package whenever a package failure occurs, you must enable and configure transactions at the package level, and then configure tasks to join ongoing transactions when they execute. However, some tasks and some connection objects do not support transactions. Furthermore, you must limit the execution parallelism of your data movement application if you want to incorporate transactions into your application.

Enabling and Configuring Transactions

Packages do not use transactions unless you enable transactions at the package level. You can use DTS Designer to enable a package to use transactions on the Advanced tab of the package's DTS Package Properties dialog box. Figure 5-4 displays this dialog box for the *MasterUpdate* package.

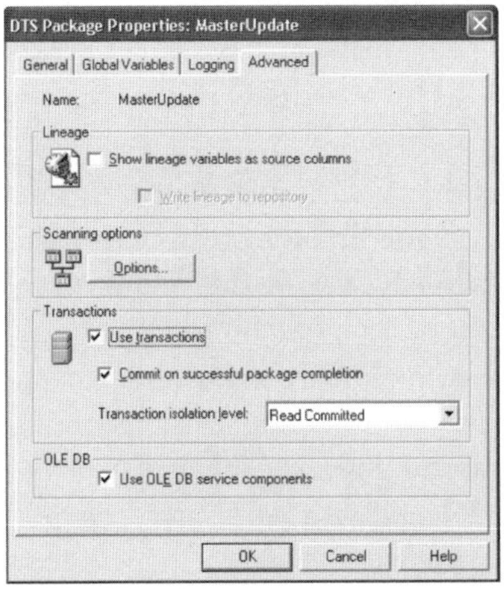

Figure 5-4   The Advanced tab of DTS Package Properties dialog box for the *MasterUpdate* package

After you enable a package to use transactions, you have access to two transaction configuration options. Your first option allows you to choose whether to commit an open transaction when the package completes successfully. At the task level, you can also choose to have a transaction commit whenever a particular step succeeds. If a package completes successfully with an uncommitted transaction, you must select the Commit On Successful Package Completion check box on the Option tab in the Workflow Properties dialog box, or else the uncommitted transaction will be rolled back with all pending changes lost.

A list box option on the Advanced tab for the package lets you configure the transaction isolation level used for every task that joins the package transaction. The isolation level controls the extent to which data in other transactions that have not been committed is visible to the transaction (including other transactions in the package as well as transactions started by other users of the data source). Transaction isolation levels include the following:

- **Read Committed**   A package operating at this isolation level cannot see uncommitted changes to data made by other transactions but can incur nonrepeatable or phantom reads. A *nonrepeatable read* is a read of one or more rows of data within a transaction that, when repeated, yields different values for the same rows. A *phantom read* is a read of data on one or more rows within a transaction that, when repeated, yields a different number of rows. Read Uncommitted is the default isolation mode for all SQL Server operations, including DTS.

- **Repeatable Read**   A package operating at this isolation level cannot see uncommitted changes to data made by other transactions and does not permit changes to the rows previously read within the transaction until the transaction completes. However, new phantom rows can still be inserted.

- **Serializable**   A package operating at this isolation level cannot see data in uncommitted changes to data made by other transactions, does not permit changes to rows previously read within the transaction, and does not permit the insertion of new rows into the data set.

- **Read Uncommitted**   A package operating at this isolation level can see uncommitted changes to data made by other transactions and might also incur nonrepeatable or phantom reads. This isolation mode is similar to the Chaos isolation level but is supported by SQL Server.

- **Chaos**   A package operating at this isolation level can see uncommitted changes to data made by other transactions. Changes made to data by a package operating at this isolation level cannot be rolled back. This isolation mode is not allowed by SQL Server but is permitted by non–SQL Server data sources. No locks are held by transactions running at this isolation level.

For more information on isolation levels other than Chaos, see SQL Server Books Online.

▶ **Important**   The Microsoft Distributed Transaction Coordinator (MS DTC) service must be running on the computer on which a package is executing in order for DTS packages to use transactions. For some data sources such as Oracle, additional services or configuration might be necessary for the package to enlist the data source in a transaction.

Enlisting Tasks in Transactions

A package transaction begins when a task in a package attempts to join a transaction (provided the package is configured to use transactions). If an ongoing transaction exists, the task joins the open transaction. If no ongoing transaction exists, a new package transaction is started. Only one transaction can be active in a package at any one time. In DTS Designer, on the Options tab of a task's Workflow Properties dialog box, you can enable a task to join a transaction if one is present. On this same tab, you configure whether an ongoing transaction is committed when the task completes successfully or is rolled back when the task fails.

Transactions cannot be used unless the destination connection supports them. The following connection types do support joining transactions:

- Microsoft OLE DB Provider for SQL Server
- ODBC data source, provided the ODBC driver supports the *SQL_ATT_ENLIST_IN_DTC* connection attribute and this attribute is set
- Microsoft Data Link, provided the OLE DB provider implements the *ITransactionJoin* interface

▶ **Note**   A connection to a Microsoft Access connection cannot join a transaction.

In addition, only certain tasks can join transactions. The following tasks can participate in transactions if the destination connection they are using supports joining transactions:

- Transform Data task
- Data Driven Query task
- Execute SQL task
- Bulk Insert task
- Execute Package task
- Message Queue task

Note that neither the Execute Process task nor the ActiveX Script task can join an ongoing transaction. A transaction can be used within both of these tasks, but the tasks themselves cannot join an ongoing transaction within the package. However, a task that is not part of an ongoing transaction, including a task that cannot join transactions, can be configured to cause an ongoing transaction to commit upon the success of the step or to roll back upon the failure of the step.

▶ **Note**   When a step joins a transaction, each connection used by the step joins the transaction. This means that updates for other tasks in the package that use the connection become part of the transaction, even though those tasks did not enlist in the ongoing transaction. Use separate connections to a database to enable both transactional and non-transactional updates to the same database.

Inheriting Transactions

When a subpackage is called from a master package by the Execute Package task, the subpackage will inherit the parent package transaction if the Execute Package task that fired the subpackage joined the parent transaction. When a subpackage runs within an inherited transaction, no commit takes place within the subpackage (although a step failure can still cause a transaction rollback). This means that you cannot cause a transaction to commit when a step in the subpackage, or the subpackage itself, completes successfully. You can, however, cause the transaction to commit when the step that called the subpackage completes successfully.

▶ **Note**   A transaction rollback in a subpackage does not cause the subpackage to fail unless you configure the failure of the step to cause package failure. This means that even though a step in a subpackage can fail and roll back the entire open transaction, the subpackage can complete successfully and report this success back to the calling package.

Considerations When Working with Transactions

The next few sections provide guidelines for working with transactions in packages.

Organize the Package Steps Sequentially

Sequentially executing packages simplify your work with transactions. You can use precedence constraints to make all tasks execute sequentially after successful completion of the previous task, cause the failure of any task to roll back the transaction, and ensure the final step in the package commits the transaction when the step completes successfully.

Plan Carefully When Executing Package Steps in Parallel

When executing tasks in parallel, you must take steps to avoid anomalous results. First, use DTS package failure to roll back the transaction in the event that a step fails. Not following this rule can result in steps continuing even though a transaction rolled back when one task in the transaction failed. For example, suppose Task C is configured to execute after the successful completion of Task A, and Task A and Task B execute in parallel within a single transaction. If Task B fails, all changes made by Task A and Task B are rolled back after Task A completes. However, since Task A completed successfully, Task C will commence, starting a new transaction because there is no existing transaction. If the failure of a single task causes the failure of the entire package, no additional steps will start.

When using separate connections to a SQL Server instance, multiple steps cannot execute in parallel within the same transaction. To avoid this problem, you can either use a single connection for each step to serialize the steps or execute each of the separate steps on the main package thread. This problem will not appear with Execute SQL tasks that SQL Server can execute very quickly because they will actually execute serially rather than in parallel.

Branch upon the Success or Failure of a Transaction

As you learned in Chapter 2, you can use precedence constraints to cause a task to execute based on the success, failure, or completion of a previous task. For example, you can configure one or more tasks in a package to execute only after the failure of a previous package step. When the step fails, you can roll back the transaction and use a failure precedence constraint to execute error-handling tasks, such as Send Mail, Execute SQL, and ActiveX Script tasks, to report and record error information.

Use Transaction Checkpointing for Multiple Transactions

If the logic of your package enables you to use multiple transactions in a single package, use an ActiveX Script task as a placeholder, and use precedence constraints to have the tasks in the first transaction trigger the execution of the ActiveX Script task. You can then configure the ActiveX Script task to commit this first transaction upon the successful completion of the ActiveX Script task. The ActiveX Script task itself does not actually execute any script; rather it merely marks the transition between one set of tasks in one transaction and another set of tasks in another transaction.

▶ **Note**   Because of the limitations on using transactions with parallel task execution, you will not utilize transactions in your data movement application. Rather, the application will incorporate into its design the ability to partially or completely roll back batches that fail based on a batch ID value.

Test the *TransactionDemo* package

In this procedure, you will test the *TransactionDemo* package without transaction control.

1   Open SQL Server Enterprise Manager, expand your local instance, right-click Data Transformation Services, and then click Open Package.

2   In the Look In list, navigate to C:\Microsoft Press\SQL DTS SBS\Ch5\ChapterFiles and then double-click TransactionDemo.dts.

3   Double-click TransactionDemo in the Select Package dialog box.

This package includes four Execute SQL tasks that execute in sequence. The first task deletes one row from each of three tables (to clean up from a previous execution of this package), and each of the other three tasks adds one row to one of these three tables.

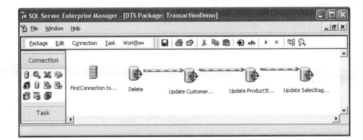

4   On the toolbar, click Execute.

5   Click OK, verify that all four tasks executed successfully, and then click Done.

6   Open SQL Query Analyzer and connect to your local instance as a system administrator.

7   On the toolbar, click Load SQL Script, navigate to C:\Microsoft Press\SQL DTS SBS\Ch5\ChapterFiles, and then double-click TransactionTestScript.sql.

This script queries the *ProductStage*, *CustomerStage*, and *SalesStage* tables to determine whether a particular row has been added to each table.

8 On the toolbar, click Execute.

One row was successfully added to each table by the *Transaction-Demo* package.

9 Switch to the TransactionDemo package in DTS Designer and then double-click the Update SalesStage Table step on the design sheet.

10 Delete the closing parenthesis in the VALUES list in the INSERT statement, and then click OK to save the modified Execute SQL task.

11 On the toolbar, click Execute.

12 Click OK to acknowledge that one task failed, verify that the Update SalesStage Table step failed, verify that the other three steps succeeded, and then click Done.

13 Switch to SQL Query Analyzer and re-execute the TransactionTest-Script query.

The *Delete* step successfully deleted the rows previously entered into these tables, but only the *ProductStage* and *CustomerStage* tables were repopulated because the Execute SQL task called by the *Update SalesStage Table* step failed to execute properly.

Now that you see how this simple package works in the absence of transaction control, you are ready to add transaction control to the *TransactionDemo* package.

Enlist tasks that execute sequentially in a single transaction

In this procedure, you will configure four tasks to execute as part of a single transaction.

1   Switch to the TransactionDemo package in DTS Designer.

2   Right-click an open area of the design sheet and click Package Properties.

3   On the Advanced tab, verify that the Use Transactions and Commit On Successful Package Completion check boxes are selected, and then click OK.

4   On the design sheet, right-click the Delete step, point to Workflow, and then click Workflow properties.

5   On the Options tab, select the Join Transaction If Present check box, select the Rollback Transaction On Failure check box, and then click OK.

Workflow Properties

Precedence | Options

Name: DTSStep_DTSExecuteSQLTask_4
Description: Delete

Transaction
☑ Join transaction if present
☐ Commit transaction on successful completion of this step
☑ Rollback transaction on failure

Execution
☐ Execute on main package thread   ☐ DSO rowset provider
☐ Close connection on completion   ☐ Disable this step
☐ Fail package on step failure
Task priority:

        Low   Normal   High

ActiveX script
☐ Use ActiveX script   Properties...

OK   Cancel   Help

6 On the design sheet, right-click the Update CustomerSales Table step on the design sheet, point to Workflow, and then click Workflow properties.

7 On the Options tab, select the Join Transaction If Present check box, select the Rollback Transaction On Failure check box, and then click OK.

8 Right-click Update ProductStage Table on the design sheet, point to Workflow, and then click Workflow properties.

9 On the Options tab, select the Join Transaction If Present check box, select the Rollback Transaction On Failure check box, and then click OK.

10 Right-click Update SalesStage Table on the design sheet, point to Workflow, and then click Workflow properties.

11 On the Options tab, select the Join Transaction If Present check box, select the Rollback Transaction On Failure check box, and then click OK.

Now that you have enlisted these tasks to execute in a single transaction, you need to start the Distributed Transaction Coordinator (if it is not already started).

Start Distributed Transaction Coordinator

1 Click Start, point to All Programs, point to Microsoft SQL Server, and then click Service Manager.

2 Verify that your local server appears in the Server list and then select Distributed Transaction Coordinator in the Services list.

3 If the Distributed Transaction Coordinator service is not started, click Start.

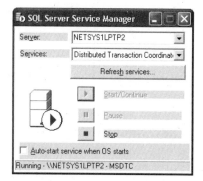

4 Verify the Distributed Transaction Coordinator started and then close SQL Server Service Manager.

Now that you have started the Distributed Transaction Coordinator, you are ready to test the execution of the *TransactionDemo* package with transaction control.

Test the *TransactionDemo* package

In this procedure, you will modify the *Update CustomerStage Table* step to cause it to fail and observe the consequences now that you have enabled transaction control for the *TransactionDemo* package.

1 Switch to the TransactionDemo package in DTS Designer and then double-click the Update CustomerStage Table step.

2 Delete the closing parenthesis in the VALUES list in the INSERT statement, and then click OK to save the modified Execute SQL task.

3 On the toolbar, click Execute.

4 Click OK, verify that only the Delete step executed successfully, and then click Done.

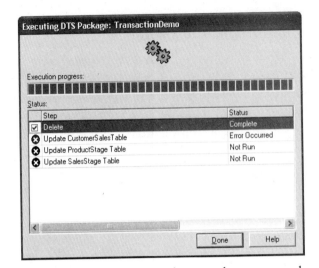

5   Switch to SQL Query Analyzer and re-execute the query.

Although the *Delete* step executed successfully, its actions were rolled back because the package was executed under transaction control. Because all the transactions were part of a single transaction and one of the steps failed, the entire transaction failed. As a result, no rows were deleted.

Now that you understand how transaction control works within a package when a single transaction is involved, you are ready to add a second transaction to this package.

Enlist tasks into multiple transactions using checkpointing

In this procedure, you will configure the *Delete* step to commit the initial transaction when it completes successfully. This means that the subsequent tasks in the package will be part of a second transaction.

1   Switch to the TransactionDemo package in DTS Designer.

2   On the design sheet, right-click the Delete step, point to Workflow, and then click Workflow Properties.

3   On the Options tab, select the Commit Transaction On Successful Completion Of This Step check box, and then click OK.

> ▶ **Tip**   Although you have now incorporated two transactions within a single package, this fact is not obvious to someone new to the package. To make it more obvious, you could add an ActiveX Script task between the *Delete* step and the *Update CustomerStage Table* step as a placeholder and label it as the transaction checkpoint task.

Now that you have enabled the *TransactionDemo* package to use two transactions, you are ready to test its execution.

Test the *TransactionDemo* package with two transactions

In this procedure, you will test the execution of the *TransactionDemo* package to demonstrate how DTS can use two separate transactions within a single package.

1 On the DTS Designer toolbar, click Execute.

2 Click OK to acknowledge that one task failed, verify that only the Delete step succeeded, and then click Done.

3 Switch to SQL Query Analyzer and then re-execute the query.

   The *Delete* step was not rolled back because the ongoing transaction committed after this step finished and the *Update CustomerSales Table* step began a new transaction when it started.

4 Switch to the TransactionDemo package in DTS Designer and then double-click the Update CustomerStage Table step.

5 Add the closing parenthesis to the VALUES list in the INSERT statement that you removed in a previous procedure, and then click OK.

6 On the toolbar, click Execute.

7 Click OK to acknowledge that one task failed, notice that only the Update SalesStage Table step failed, and then click Done.

8 Switch to SQL Query Analyzer and re-execute the query.

Although the *Update CustomerStage Table* and *Update ProductStage Table* steps executed successfully, the actions of those steps were rolled back because the *Update SalesStage Table* step failed.

9 Switch to the TransactionDemo package in DTS Designer and then double-click the Update SalesStage Table step on the design sheet.

10 Add the closing parenthesis to the VALUES clause of the INSERT statement that you removed in a previous procedure and then click OK.

11 Click Execute on the toolbar.

12 Click OK, verify that all four steps completed successfully, and then click Done.

Now that you understand how to incorporate multiple transactions into a single package, you are ready to add connection objects to enable tasks to execute in parallel.

Add separate connections to the *TransactionDemo* package

In this procedure, you will add three new connection objects to the *Transaction-Demo* package and configure each step in the package to use a different connection. You will then test the package's execution.

1 On the design sheet, right-click the FirstConnection to SBS_OLAP connection object, and then click Copy.

2 In a open area of the design sheet, click Paste.

3 Repeat the previous step two more times.

This package now contains four connection objects.

4 Right-click an open area of the design sheet and click Disconnnected Edit.

5 In the console tree, expand Connections and click FirstConnection To SBS_OLAP Copy.

6 Double-click Name in the details pane, change the value to **Second-Connection to SBS_OLAP**, and then click OK.

7 In the console tree, click FirstConnection To SBS_OLAP Copy 2.

8 Double-click Name in the details pane, change the value to **Third-Connection to SBS_OLAP**, and then click OK.

9 In the console tree, click FirstConnection To SBS_OLAP Copy 3.

10 Double-click Name in the details pane, change the value to **Fourth-Connection to SBS_OLAP**, and then click OK.

11 Click Close.

12 On the design sheet, double-click the Update CustomerStage Table step.

13 In the Existing Connection list, select SecondConnection To SBS_OLAP, and then click OK.

14 On the design sheet, double-click the Update ProductStage Table step.

15 In the Existing Connection list, select ThirdConnection to SBS_OLAP, and then click OK.

16 On the design sheet, double-click the Update SalesStage Table step.

17 In the Existing Connection list, select FourthConnection to SBS_OLAP, and then click OK.

> ▶ **Tip** The renamed connection objects will not be displayed properly on the design sheet until you open and then close each of them to refresh their presentation on the design sheet.

18 On the toolbar, click Execute.

19 Click OK, verify that all four steps executed successfully, and then click Done.

Now that you have added separate connections to the *TransactionDemo* package, you are ready to change the task flow to parallel execution rather than sequential.

Change the task flow to parallel

In this procedure, you will configure the three update steps to execute in parallel within the second transaction. The *Delete* step will continue to execute in its own transaction.

1 On the design sheet, delete the On Success precedence constraint between the Update CustomerStage Table step and the Update ProductStage Table step.

2 On the design sheet, delete the On Success precedence constraint between the Update ProductStage Table step and the Update SalesStage Table step.

3 On the design sheet, click the Delete step, and then hold down the Ctrl key while you click the Update ProductStage Table step.

4 Right-click the Update ProductStage Table step, point to Workflow, and then click On Success.

5 On the design sheet, click the Delete step, and then hold down the Ctrl key while you click the Update SalesStage Table step.

6 Right-click the Update SalesStage Table step, point to Workflow, and then click On Success.

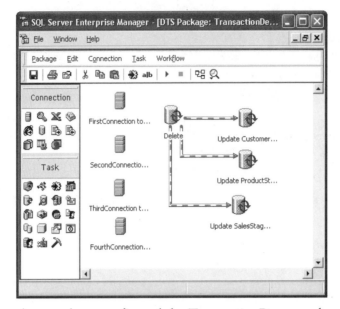

Now that you have configured the *TransactionDemo* package to execute tasks in parallel within the second transaction, you are ready to test its execution.

Test the execution of the *TransactionDemo* package with parallel steps

1   On the toolbar, click Execute.

    If more than one of these three Execute SQL tasks executes simultaneously, you will receive an error message. However, with these simple tasks, it is unlikely that you will receive an error message because they execute so quickly.

2   Click OK and then click Done.

3   On the design sheet, double-click the Update CustomerStage Table step.

4   Copy the INSERT statement, paste it into the SQL Statement box 100 times, and then click OK.

5   On the design sheet, double-click the Update ProductStage Table step.

6   Copy the INSERT statement, paste it into the SQL Statement box 100 times, and then click OK.

7   On the design sheet, double-click the Update SalesStage Table step.

8 Copy the INSERT statement, paste it into the SQL Statement box 100 times, and then click OK.

9 On the toolbar, click Execute.

10 Click OK to acknowledge that two tasks failed during execution. (On a very fast computer, only a single task might fail. You might also need to execute that task a second or third time to see the failure.)

11 Double-click one of the steps that failed to display the error.

Each step failed because the ongoing transaction that the step attempted to join was being used by another step. A package cannot have more than one task within a transaction simultaneously making a connection to a SQL Server database.

12 Click OK, and then click Done.

Now that you have demonstrated the problem with multiple tasks connecting to SQL Server over separate connections within the same transaction, you are ready to solve this problem by having each simultaneously executing task execute on the main execution thread.

Advanced DTS Options

5

Enable the tasks executing in parallel to execute on the main thread

In this procedure, you will configure the *Update CustomerStage Table*, the *Update ProductStage Table*, and *Update SalesStage Table* steps to execute on the same thread.

1   On the design sheet, right-click the Update CustomerStage Table step, point to Workflow, and then click Workflow Properties.

2   On the Options tab, select the Execute On Main Package Thread check box and then click OK.

3   On the design sheet, right-click the Update ProductStage Table step, point to Workflow, and then click Workflow Properties.

4   On the Options tab, select the Execute On Main Package Thread check box and then click OK.

5   On the design sheet, right-click the Update SalesStage Table step, point to Workflow, and then click Workflow Properties.

6   On the Options tab, select the Execute On Main Package Thread check box and then click OK.

7   On the toolbar, click Execute.

8   Click OK, verify that all four steps executed successfully, and then click OK.

All four tasks executed successfully because they executed on the same thread. This setting effectively serialized these tasks, negating the benefits of parallel execution.

9 On the Package menu, click Save As.

10 In the File Name box, change the save location to **C:\Microsoft Press\SQL DTS SBS\Ch5\WorkingFolder\TransactionDemo**, and then click OK.

11 Close the TransactionDemo package in DTS Designer.

Working with Exception Files

In Chapter 3, you learned how to enable package execution and error logging to assist you in package debugging and auditing. However, these logs contain information only about the success or failure of individual packages. If you want to record package and step execution information, error information (such as the error number and its description), and the actual source and destination rows that generate errors, you must configure exception files for each transformation task (any task that uses the data pump). These files record these additional details with only a small performance penalty.

In DTS Designer, on the Options tab for the transformation task, you can define and configure three different exception files. Figure 5-5 displays the Options tab for the *Load CustomerStage Table* step in the *UpdateCustomerDim* package.

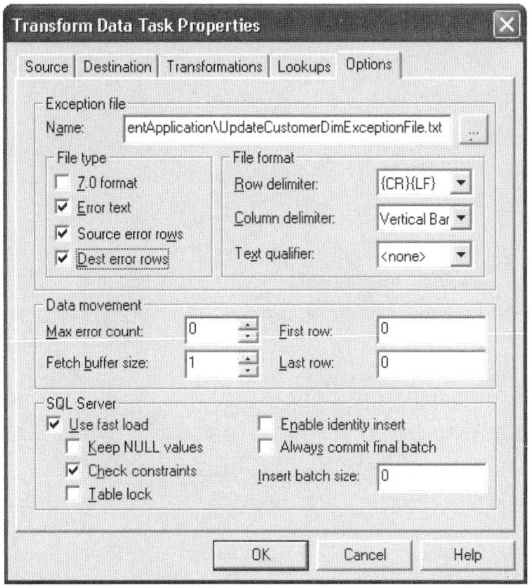

Figure 5-5 Options tab for the *Load CustomerStage Table* step in the *UpdateCustomerDim* package

The first file that you define is a general error information text file that records step execution and error information, including any SQL exception errors that are raised during the package execution. If you choose to use the Microsoft SQL Server 2000 format rather than the Microsoft SQL Server 7 format, you have three additional options. The first option lets you choose whether to record the text of any error messages in the main exception file. The error description and number would be identical to what you would receive if you executed the SQL statement directly via a Transact-SQL script in SQL Query Analyzer. The second and third options let you choose to have the actual source and destination error rows recorded in separate text files. These text files are created only if errors are detected in source or destination rows. Figure 5-6 displays the exception file generated when the *UpdateCustomerDim* package executes and then encounters an error during the transformation of one of the 30 rows being inserted into the destination table.

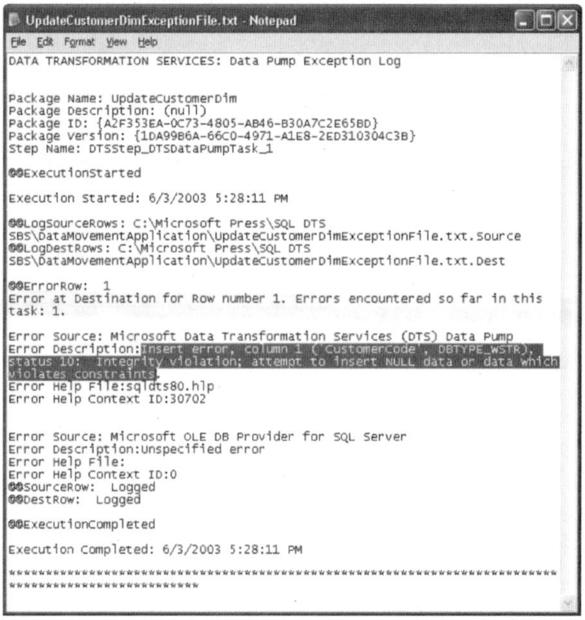
```
UpdateCustomerDimExceptionFile.txt - Notepad
File Edit Format View Help
DATA TRANSFORMATION SERVICES: Data Pump Exception Log


Package Name: UpdateCustomerDim
Package Description: (null)
Package ID: {A2F353EA-0C73-4805-AB46-B30A7C2E65BD}
Package Version: {1DA99B6A-66C0-4971-A1E8-2ED310304C3B}
Step Name: DTSStep_DTSDataPumpTask_1

@@ExecutionStarted

Execution Started: 6/3/2003 5:28:11 PM

@@LogSourceRows: C:\Microsoft Press\SQL DTS
SBS\DataMovementApplication\UpdateCustomerDimExceptionFile.txt.Source
@@LogDestRows: C:\Microsoft Press\SQL DTS
SBS\DataMovementApplication\UpdateCustomerDimExceptionFile.txt.Dest

@@ErrorRow:  1
Error at Destination for Row number 1. Errors encountered so far in this
task: 1.

Error Source: Microsoft Data Transformation Services (DTS) Data Pump
Error Description:Insert error, column 1 ('CustomerCode', DBTYPE_WSTR),
status 10:  Integrity violation; attempt to insert NULL data or data which
violates constraints.
Error Help File:sqldts80.hlp
Error Help Context ID:30702


Error Source: Microsoft OLE DB Provider for SQL Server
Error Description:Unspecified error
Error Help File:
Error Help Context ID:0
@@SourceRow:  Logged
@@DestRow:  Logged

@@ExecutionCompleted

Execution Completed: 6/3/2003 5:28:11 PM

*************************************************************************************
*****************************
```

Figure 5-6 Exception file generated when the *UpdateCustomerDim* package encounters an error

Notice that the exception file in Figure 5-6 indicates that a null constraint violation occurred when DTS attempted to insert a row into the *CustomerCode* column. This exception file also indicates that both the source row and the destination row were logged. The source row was logged to the UpdateCus-tomerDimExceptionFile.txt.Source file, and the destination row was logged to the UpdateCustomerDimExceptionFile.txt.Dest file.

▶ **Important** Destination rows that are rejected by the data destination are recorded in the destination exception file. A row is not logged when DTS detects the error before the row is submitted to the data destination. For example, if an input row contains missing or incorrectly formatted data, the transformation task will fail the row, and it won't pass it to the data destination. The row containing the failure is counted toward the maximum number of errors permitted by the task. However, data integrity violations, such as duplicate keys or foreign key constraint violations, cannot be detected by DTS and are detected only after the destination rows are passed to the data destination. These types of errors are noted in the main exception file and recorded in the destination exception files.

You will incorporate this ability to capture rows of data that cannot be inserted or updated properly into the data movement application prototype. This will enable you to fix errors in these rows and resubmit them.

▶ **Note** If you skipped Chapter 4, execute the IfYouSkippedChapter4.cmd batch file. This batch file restores the SBS_OLTP and SBS_OLAP databases and copies the DTS packages that would have been created in Chapters 1 through 4 into the appropriate folders. If you do not want this batch file to overwrite any packages that you created in Chapters 1 through 4, you must move them or rename them before you execute this batch file.

Define exception files

In this procedure, you will define exception files for the transformation tasks in the *UpdateCustomerDim* and *UpdateProductDim* packages.

1 Switch to SQL Server Enterprise Manager.

2 In your local SQL Server instance, right-click Data Transformation Services, and then click Open Package.

3 Navigate to C:\Microsoft Press\SQL DTS SBS\DataMovementApplication in the Look In list, and then double-click UpdateProduct-Dim.dts.

4 Double-click UpdateProductDim in the Select Package dialog box, type **mypassword** in the Password text box, and then click OK.

5 On the design sheet, double-click the Load ProductStage Table step, and then click the Options tab.

6 Type **C:\Microsoft Press\SQL DTS SBS\DataMovementApplication\ LoadProductStageTableExceptionFile.txt** in the Name box.

7 Clear the 7.0 Format check box, select the Error Text check box, select the Source Error Rows check box, select the Dest Error Rows check box, and then click OK.

8 On the design sheet, double-click the Insert Or Update ProductDim Table step, and then click the Options tab.

▶ **Tip** You can configure exception files for any task that uses the data pump, namely the Transform Data and the Data Driven Query tasks. You cannot configure an exception file for Execute SQL and Bulk Insert tasks.

9 Type **C:\Microsoft Press\SQL DTS SBS\DataMovementApplication\ LoadProductDimTableExceptionFile.txt** in the Name box.

10 Clear the 7.0 Format check box, select the Error Text check box, select the Source Error Rows check box, select the Dest Error Rows check box, and then click OK.

11 On the toolbar, click Save and then close the UpdateProductDim package in DTS Designer.

12 In the SQL Server Enterprise Manager console tree, right-click Data Transformation Services, and then click Open Package.

13 Navigate to C:\Microsoft Press\SQL DTS SBS\DataMovementApplication in the Look In list, and then double-click UpdateCustomerDim.dts.

14 Double-click UpdateCustomerDim in the Select Package dialog box, type **mypassword** in the Password text box, and then click OK.

15 On the design sheet, double-click the Load CustomerStage Table step, and then click the Options tab.

16 Type **C:\Microsoft Press\SQL DTS SBS\DataMovementApplication\ LoadCustomerStageTableExceptionFile.txt** in the Name box.

Notice that the default number of permitted errors is zero in the Max Error Count box.

17 Clear the 7.0 Format check box, select the Error Text check box, select the Source Error Rows check box, select the Dest Error Rows check box, and then click OK.

18 On the toolbar, click Save.

Now that you have configured exception files, you are ready to modify the NewCustomers.txt file to demonstrate the use of exception files.

Modify the NewCustomers.txt file

In this procedure, you will introduce errors into the NewCustomers.txt file to generate errors when this data is loaded into the *CustomerStage* table.

1   Open the C:\Microsoft Press\SQL DTS SBS\Ch4\ChapterFiles\New-Customers.txt file in Microsoft Notepad.

This file contains 29 rows of new customer data, with each column separated by a vertical bar.

2   Delete the first column of data from the sixth and fourteenth rows, and then save and close this changed file.

The deletion of the data in the first column for these two rows of data will cause null constraint violations in the data destination when these rows are submitted to the data destination.

Now that you have modified the NewCustomers.txt file, you are ready to test the execution of the *UpdateCustomerDim* package with this source file.

Test the execution of the *UpdateCustomerDim* package with the modified source file

1   Switch to SQL Query Analyzer, and then click Clear Window on the toolbar.

2   Type **DELETE FROM SBS_OLAP.dbo.CustomerStage** in the query pane, and then click Execute on the toolbar.

This deletes all existing data in the *CustomerStage* table, so you can easily see the effect of importing data containing errors.

3   Switch to the UpdateCustomerDim package in DTS Designer.

4   On the toolbar, click Execute to attempt to import new customers from the newly modified NewCustomers.txt file into the Customer-Stage table.

5   Click OK to acknowledge that one task failed during execution.

6   Double-click the Load CustomerStage Table step in the Status window to view the error message.

The task failed because the first column in the destination table contains a NOT NULL constraint and the first column in two of the data rows being inserted contains a null value. Notice the error message states that the number of failing rows exceeds the maximum specified.

7   Click OK and then click Done.

8   Switch to SQL Query Analyzer, and then click New Query on the toolbar.

9   Type **SELECT * FROM SBS_OLAP.dbo.CustomerStage** in the query
pane, and then click Execute on the toolbar.

No rows were added to the *CustomerStage* table because the maximum errors permitted by the *Load CustomerStage Table* step is zero,
and the step uses the default batch size, which processes all rows in
one batch.

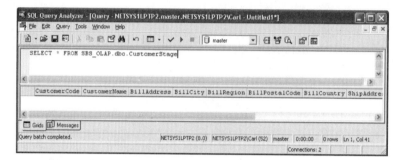

10   Use Notepad to open LoadCustomerStageTableExceptionFile.txt in
the C:\Microsoft Press\SQL DTS SBS\DataMovementApplication
folder.

This main error file recorded the error information. Notice that no
rows were copied from the data source to the data destination
because the error occurred in the sixth row and the task was set to
permit a maximum of zero errors.

11 In Notepad, open LoadCustomerStageTableExceptionFile.txt.Source in the C:\Microsoft Press\SQL DTS SBS\DataMovementApplication folder.

The row from the source table that caused the error is displayed. Vertical bars separate each column in this file, and the value for the first column in this error row is a null value, which is not permitted in the destination table.

12 In Notepad, open LoadCustomerStageTableExceptionFile.txt.Dest in the C:\Microsoft Press\SQL DTS SBS\DataMovementApplication folder.

The row that DTS attempted to insert into the destination table is displayed. Depending on the transformations performed in the DTS package, the destination row might be significantly different from the source row. This row could not be inserted into the destination table because a null value was provided for the *CustomerCode* column, and that column does not permit nulls.

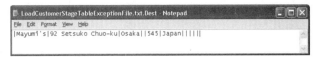

13 Close Notepad.

Now that you understand how the exception files work, you are ready to increase the maximum error count permitted (the *MaximumErrorCount* property) for the *Load CustomerStage Table* step and execute the *UpdateCustomerDim* package.

Execute the *UpdateCustomerDim* package with a modified *MaximumErrorCount* property for the *Load CustomerStage Table* step

1 Switch to the UpdateCustomerDim package in DTS Designer, and then double-click the Load CustomerStage Table step on the design sheet.

2 On the Options tab, change the value in the Max Error Count box to 5, and then click OK to save this change.

3   On the toolbar, click Execute.

4   Click OK to acknowledge that one task failed.

Notice that all 29 rows in the NewCustomers.txt text file were processed by this task, although this dialog box does not indicate how many rows were successfully inserted. Because the maximum error count value is more than the number of errors encountered, the task did not terminate when the first error was detected. Instead, the task completed, reporting that a failure had occurred. Remember that by default, the failure of a task does not cause a package to fail. In this case, you could choose to have this package continue executing other tasks and have the data movement application continue executing other packages despite this error. Because the error rows are captured in the exception files, you can fix the error and reinsert the corrected error rows as a separate execution of the data movement application. In Chapter 8, you will add more complete error handling routines, and in Chapter 10, you will learn how to insert error rows that originally failed.

5 Click Done, switch to SQL Query Analyzer, and then re-execute the SELECT * FROM SBS_OLAP.dbo.CustomerStage query.

All rows in the NewCustomers.txt file other than rows 6 and 14 were added to the *CustomerStage* table.

6 Using the Window menu in SQL Query Analyzer, switch to the first query.

The DELETE FROM SBS_OLAP.dbo.CustomerStage query appears.

7 On the toolbar, click Execute to delete all 27 rows from the CustomerStage table, and then close the current query window without saving the query.

8 Switch to the UpdateCustomerDim package in DTS Designer, and then double-click the Load CustomerStage Table step.

9 On the Options tab, change the value in the Max Error Count box to 1, change the value in the Insert Batch Size box to 5, and then click OK.

The Insert Batch Size box sets the InsertCommitSize property for the *Load CustomerStage Table* step. DTS will commit rows in batches of five until the maximum error count is reached. When the maximum error value is reached, the task will discard any processed rows in the current batch and terminate.

▶ **Important**   Committed batches will not be rolled back if the maximum error count is reached before all source rows have been processed unless the task is participating in a transaction.

10 Click Execute on the toolbar.

11 Click OK to acknowledge that one task failed during execution, and then click Done.

Notice that although all 29 rows were not processed, you are unable to determine whether some of these rows were processed.

12 Switch to SQL Query Analyzer and click Execute on the toolbar to execute the SELECT * FROM SBS_OLAP.dbo.CustomerStage script.

Because the batch size was set to 5 and the maximum error count was set to 1, the first two batches committed before the maximum error count was reached. Rows 12 and 13 in the third batch before the error in row 14 were not committed.

13 Close SQL Query Analyzer without saving any queries, and then switch to the UpdateCustomerDim package in DTS Designer.

14 On the toolbar, click Save and then close SQL Server Enterprise Manager.

You have now configured data transformation steps in two DTS packages to capture error rows in exception files, and you've learned how to use the *Insert-CommitSize* and *MaximumErrorCount* properties.

Chapter Summary

In this chapter, you learned about a number of advanced DTS package and task options that you can use to develop a data movement application. You also learned that, due to both performance limitations and task restrictions, transactional control will not be utilized in the prototype of the data movement application you are building throughout the course of this book. Finally, you learned how to capture error rows, which enables you to configure the packages in the data movement application to continue inserting good data rather than fail the entire package. The *InsertCommitSize* and *MaximumErrorCount* properties of the Transform Data and Data Driven Query tasks enable you to determine how many errors your application will tolerate before the package fails. In the next two chapters, you will learn how to configure the data movement application so that you can dynamically set task properties at run time.

Chapter 6

Dynamically Configuring DTS Package Objects

In this chapter, you will learn how to:

- Use a data link connection

- Use the Dynamic Properties task

- Dynamically change global variable values in another package

In this chapter, you will learn to use data link connection objects, INI files, global variables, and Dynamic Properties tasks to enable the dynamic reconfiguration of packages in the data movement application at run time. A data movement application that supports dynamic configuration can be flexibly executed without multiple packages being edited each time a change is required for new circumstances. Dynamic configuration enables you to easily migrate an application from a development computer to quality assurance (QA) and production servers, changing data sources and destinations as needed, without editing packages. Dynamic configuration also allows you to use global variables to change the batch size or number of errors permitted when loading data, control the type of cube or dimension processing based on the data being added, or bypass certain packages in the data movement application during a particular execution.

In addition, you will learn how to change the values of global variables in subpackages from the context of the master package. This capability is particularly important as you begin adding packages and complexity to the data movement application. For example, you can specify the number of errors permitted during the execution of each step in each package in the data movement application using a single global variable value in the master package.

Using Data Link Connection Objects

In the packages you created in previous chapters, each connection object was defined within each package in the data movement application. Embedding connection information in each package, however, makes it difficult to migrate the data movement application—a process that involves changing data sources and destinations—without opening and editing each connection object in each package. Opening and manually editing packages is time consuming and error prone.

In Microsoft SQL Server 2000, you can solve this migration problem by configuring each connection object to read a Universal Data Link (UDL) file at run time and retrieve connection information. This retrieval process is called a *data link connection*. A UDL file is an external file that you can configure to access an OLE DB data source using any of the system-installed OLE DB providers. A UDL file, which is configured to connect to an OLE DB data source, is similar to a file Data Source Name (DSN), which is configured to connect to an ODBC data source. The connection information in the UDL file is not resolved until run time, and each UDL file can be edited independently of the DTS packages that refer to it. A single UDL file can be used by multiple packages within the data movement application without affecting parallelism.

Implementing a data link connection involves creating a UDL file in Microsoft Windows Explorer, storing connection information in the UDL file, and then configuring a connection object to use the UDL file. In the following procedures, you will create two UDL files in Windows Explorer, store information about how to connect to the SBS_OLTP and SBS_OLAP databases in these UDL files, and then configure the connections in the *UpdateCustomerDim*, *UpdateProductDim*, *PopulateTimeDimension*, and *LoadHistoricalData* packages to use these UDL files.

▶ **Note**   If you skipped Chapter 5, execute the IfYouSkippedChapter5.cmd batch file in the C:\Microsoft Press\SQL DTS SBS\Ch6\SkippedChapterFiles folder. This batch file restores the SBS_OLTP and SBS_OLAP databases and copies the DTS packages that would have been created in Chapters 1 through 5 into the appropriate folders. If you do not want this batch file to overwrite any packages that you created in Chapters 1 through 5, you must move them or rename them before you execute this batch file.

Create UDL files

1 Click Start and then click Run.

2 In the Open box, type **C:\Microsoft Press\SQL DTS SBS\ DataMovementApplication,** and then click OK.

3 On the Tools menu, click Folder Options.

4 Click View, clear the Hide Extensions For Known File Types check box, and then click OK.

5 Right-click an open area in the Windows Explorer window, point to New, and then click Text Document.

6 Type **SBS_OLTP.udl,** click Enter, and then click Yes.

Until you configure a UDL file, the file is simply a blank text file with the .udl extension.

7 Right-click an open area in the Windows Explorer window, point to New, and then click Text Document.

8 Type **SBS_OLAP.udl,** click Enter, and then click Yes.

You have successfully created two UDL files. Next you need to configure these files.

Configure UDL files

1 In Windows Explorer, double-click SBS_OLTP.udl.

Windows recognizes the .udl extension and opens a Data Link Properties dialog box to enable you to configure the properties of this UDL file.

Click the Provider tab, which lists the different providers from which you can choose, and select the Microsoft OLE DB Provider For SQL Server.

2   Click Next, type (**local**), click Use Windows NT Integrated Security, and then select SBS_OLTP in the Select The Database On The Server list.

▶   **Tip**   This UDL file will always try to connect to the default instance on the local server. If you later want to configure this UDL file to connect to a named instance on the local server or to an instance on a remote server, you can change this UDL file to point to a specific SQL Server instance without directly editing the packages that use the file.

3 Click Test Connection, click OK, and then click OK again to save your changes. This completes the configuration of the SBS_OLTP.udl file.

4 Double-click SBS_OLAP.udl.

5 Click the Provider tab, and then click Microsoft OLE DB Provider For SQL Server.

6 Click Next, type (**local**), click Use Windows NT Integrated Security, and then select SBS_OLAP in the Select The Database On The Server list.

7 Click Test Connection, click OK, and then click OK again to save your changes.

You have successfully configured two UDL files. Now you are ready to use these files in your existing packages.

Configure the connections in the *UpdateProductDim* package to use a UDL file

1 Open Microsoft SQL Server Enterprise Manager.

2 In the SQL Server Enterprise Manager console tree, expand your local SQL Server instance, right-click Data Transformation Services, and then click Open Package.

3 Navigate to C:\Microsoft Press\SQL DTS SBS\DataMovementApplication in the Look In list, and then double-click UpdateProduct-Dim.dts.

4 Double-click UpdateProductDim in the Select Package dialog box, type **mypassword** in the Password text box, and then click OK.

5 Double-click the ProductStage connection object to change the data source for the ProductStage connection object to the SBS_OLAP.udl file that you previously configured.

6 Select Microsoft Data Link in the Data Source list, and then type **C:\Microsoft Press\SQL DTS SBS\DataMovementApplication\ SBS_OLAP.udl** in the UDL File Name box.

> ▶ **Tip**   If you click Properties in this dialog box after entering a valid UDL file and path, you can edit the properties of the UDL file from within DTS.

7 Select the Always Read Properties From UDL File check box.

> ▶ **Important**   If you do not select the Always Read Properties From UDL File check box, DTS will copy the connection string into the package and will not update it in the package when you make changes to the UDL file.

8   Click OK to save the modified connection object, and then click OK to keep all existing transformations that reference this connection object.

You have successfully modified the *ProductStage* connection object to use the SBS_OLAP.udl file. Notice that the icon representing the connection object on the design sheet has changed.

9   Double-click the SBS_OLAPAdditionalConnection connection object to change the data source for the SBS_OLAPAdditionalConnection connection object to the SBS_OLAP.udl file that you previously configured.

10   Select Microsoft Data Link in the Data Source list, type **C:\Microsoft Press\SQL DTS SBS\DataMovementApplication\SBS_OLAP.udl** in the UDL File Name box, select the Always Read Properties From UDL File check box, and then click OK to save the modified connection object.

11   Click OK to keep all existing transformations that reference this connection object. Since you are not actually changing the data source, you do not need to modify any transformation in the package.

12   On the toolbar, click Execute to verify the connection objects in the package function properly.

13   Click OK and then click Done.

> ▶ **Tip**   If you save your package each time you make a few changes, the size of the structured storage file can get very large by the time you finish modifying your packages because each version of the package is saved in the structured storage file. However, if you delete underlying structured storage file while a package is open and then save the open package, only the most recent version is saved and the package GUID is not changed.

You have successfully modified all connections in the *UpdateProductDim* package to allow them to be dynamically configured.

Configure the connections in the *UpdateCustomerDim* package to use a UDL file

1   Switch to the SQL Server Enterprise Manager console tree, right-click Data Transformation Services in your local instance, and then click Open Package.

2   Navigate to C:\Microsoft Press\SQL DTS SBS\DataMovementApplication in the Look In list, and then double-click UpdateCustomerDim.dts.

3   Double-click UpdateCustomerDim in the Select Package dialog box, type **mypassword** in the Password text box, and then click OK.

4   Double-click the CustomerStage connection object to change the data source for the CustomerStage connection object to the SBS_OLAP.udl file that you previously configured.

> ▶ **Note**   When multiple connection objects use the same UDL file, parallelism is not affected. The UDL file contains only the connection information; it does not make the actual connection.

5   Select Microsoft Data Link in the Data Source list, type **C:\Microsoft Press\SQL DTS SBS\DataMovementApplication\SBS_OLAP.udl** in the UDL File Name box, select the Always Read Properties From UDL File check box, and then click OK to save the modified connection object.

6   Click OK to keep all existing transformations that reference this connection object.

7   Double-click the SBS_OLAPAdditionalConnection connection object to change the data source for the SBS_OLAPAdditionalConnection connection object to the SBS_OLAP.udl file that you previously configured.

8   Select Microsoft Data Link in the Data Source list, type **C:\Microsoft Press\SQL DTS SBS\DataMovementApplication\SBS_OLAP.udl** in the UDL File Name box, select the Always Read Properties From UDL File check box, and then click OK to save the modified connection object.

9   On the toolbar, click Execute to verify that the connection objects in the package function properly.

Even though the connection object functions properly, the *Load CustomerStage Table* step still fails because the number of errors in the source file exceeds the number of errors permitted by the *Load CustomerStage Table* step.

10   Click OK and then click Done.

You have successfully modified each of the connections in the *UpdateCustomerDim* package to allow them to be dynamically configured.

Configure the connection in the *PopulateTimeDimension* package to use a UDL file

1   Switch to the SQL Server Enterprise Manager console tree, right-click Data Transformation Services in your local instance, and then click Open Package.

2   Navigate to C:\Microsoft Press\SQL DTS SBS\DataMovementApplication in the Look In list, and then double-click PopulateTimeDimension.dts.

3   Double-click PopulateTimeDimension in the Select Package dialog box, type **mypassword** in the Password text box, and then click OK.

4   Double-click the SBS_OLAPDestination connection object to change the data source for the SBS_OLAPDestination connection object to the SBS_OLAP.udl file that you previously configured.

5   Select Microsoft Data Link in the Data Source list, type **C:\Microsoft Press\SQL DTS SBS\DataMovementApplication\SBS_OLAP.udl** in the UDL File Name box, select the Always Read Properties From UDL File check box, and then click OK to save the modified connection object.

6   On the toolbar, click Save and then close the PopulateTimeDimension package in DTS Designer.

Dynamic Configuration

6

You have successfully modified the connection in the *PopulateTimeDimension* package to allow it to be dynamically configured.

Configure the *LoadHistoricalData* package to use the UDL files

1 Switch to the SQL Server Enterprise Manager console tree, right-click Data Transformation Services in your local instance, and then click Open Package.

2 Navigate to C:\Microsoft Press\SQL DTS SBS\DataMovementApplication in the Look In list, and then double-click LoadHistorical-Data.dts.

3 Double-click LoadHistoricalData in the Select Package dialog box, type **mypassword** in the Password text box, and then click OK.

4 Double-click the ProductsSource connection object to change its data source to the SBS_OLTP.udl file that you previously configured.

5 Select Microsoft Data Link in the Data Source list, type **C:\Microsoft Press\SQL DTS SBS\DataMovementApplication\SBS_OLTP.udl** in the UDL File Name box, select the Always Read Properties From UDL File check box, and then click OK to save the modified connection object.

6 Click OK to keep all existing transformations that reference this connection object.

7 Double-click the CustomersSource connection object to change its data source to the SBS_OLTP.udl file that you previously configured.

8 Select Microsoft Data Link in the Data Source list, type **C:\Microsoft Press\SQL DTS SBS\DataMovementApplication\SBS_OLTP.udl** in the UDL File Name box, select the Always Read Properties From UDL File check box, and then click OK to save the modified connection object.

9 Click OK to keep all existing transformations that reference this connection object.

10 Double-click the ProductsDestination connection object to change its data source to the SBS_OLAP.udl file that you previously configured.

11 Select Microsoft Data Link in the Data Source list, type **C:\Microsoft Press\SQL DTS SBS\DataMovementApplication\SBS_OLAP.udl** in the UDL File Name box, select the Always Read Properties From UDL File check box, and then click OK to save the modified connection object.

12 Click OK to keep all existing transformations that reference this connection object.

13 Double-click the CustomersDestination connection object to change its data source to the SBS_OLAP.udl file that you previously configured.

14 Select Microsoft Data Link in the Data Source list, type **C:\Microsoft Press\SQL DTS SBS\DataMovementApplication\SBS_OLAP.udl** in the UDL File Name box, select the Always Read Properties From UDL File check box, and then click OK to save the modified connection object.

15 Click OK to keep all existing transformations that reference this connection object.

16 Double-click the 1996DataDestination connection object to change its data source to the SBS_OLAP.udl file that you previously configured.

17 Select Microsoft Data Link in the Data Source list, type **C:\Microsoft Press\SQL DTS SBS\DataMovementApplication\SBS_OLAP.udl** in the UDL File Name box, select the Always Read Properties From UDL File check box, and then click OK to save the modified connection object.

Notice that you are not prompted to update transformations because this connection is used by a Bulk Insert task rather than a Transform Data task. There are no transformations to be updated.

18 Double-click the 1997DataDestination connection object to change its data source to the SBS_OLAP.udl file that you previously configured.

19 Select Microsoft Data Link in the Data Source list, type **C:\Microsoft Press\SQL DTS SBS\DataMovementApplication\SBS_OLAP.udl** in the UDL File Name box, select the Always Read Properties From UDL File check box, and then click OK to save the modified connection object.

20 Double-click the SBS_OLAPAdditionalConnection connection object to change its data source to the SBS_OLAP.udl file that you previously configured.

21 Select Microsoft Data Link in the Data Source list, type **C:\Microsoft Press\SQL DTS SBS\DataMovementApplication\SBS_OLAP.udl** in the UDL File Name box, select the Always Read Properties From UDL File check box, and then click OK to save the modified connection object.

22 Click OK to keep all existing transformations that reference this connection object.

23 Double-click the SalesFactDataDestination connection object to change its data source to the SBS_OLAP.udl file that you previously configured.

24 Select Microsoft Data Link in the Data Source list, type **C:\Microsoft Press\SQL DTS SBS\DataMovementApplication\SBS_OLAP.udl** in the UDL File Name box, select the Always Read Properties From UDL File check box, and then click OK to save the modified connection object.

25 Click OK to keep all existing transformations that reference this connection object.

26 On the toolbar, click Execute to verify that the connection objects in the package function properly.

> ▶ **Tip**   It is a good idea to open each connection object to verify that the
> Always Read Properties From UDL File check box is selected. Verifying
> that the option is selected is easy to forget, but you will not see an error
> until you change the connection information in the UDL file and execute
> the package. Unless this check box is selected, the package will not use
> the updated information in the UDL file.

27 Click OK and then click Done.

You have successfully configured each connection object in each of these packages to use UDL files. As you can see, even when only four packages are involved in a data movement application, opening and modifying each connection object in each package every time connection information changes is a tedious process. Now that your connection objects are using UDL files, merely editing these two UDL files enables the tasks in each package to access different data sources and destinations.

However, your data movement application is still dependent on hard-coded paths in the packages that specify the names and locations of these UDL files. Furthermore, these packages still contain hard-coded paths to identify the names and locations of the delimited text files used in the Bulk Insert tasks. In the next section, you will learn how to use the Dynamic Properties task and an initialization file to enable these paths to be set dynamically at run time.

Using the Dynamic Properties Task

The Dynamic Properties task enables you to modify the properties of virtually any item within a DTS package at run time. The Dynamic Properties task works by retrieving values from sources outside the DTS package at run time and assigning the values retrieved to selected package and task properties. Values can be retrieved from one or more of the following sources:

- **INI file field** A single .ini file can contain multiple fields for many different properties within a package, and the fields are grouped into one or more sections. Each field in an .ini file is limited to a single line.

- **Data file contents** A data file supports multiple lines for a property value but can contain only the value for a single package property.

- **Query column** Values can be retrieved from the first column of the first row returned from a query.

- **Global variable value** Global variable values can be changed at run time by using the *DTSRun* command, an ActiveX Script task, or an Execute Package task.

- **Environmental variable value** Values can be retrieved from a System or User variable, such as *COMPUTERNAME* or *PATH*.

- **Constant value** You can set a package or task property to a constant so that you can return the property to a known value or a default value in between tasks.

Storing values outside the packages in a data movement application enables these values to be modified at run time; you do not have to open and edit multiple packages to modify the values. As already discussed, dynamic configuration is very useful when migrating the data movement application. Dynamic configuration also enables you to execute the packages in the data movement application under circumstances that change, such as when the batch size or the maximum error count settings need to be updated.

In the following procedures, you will create an initialization file that provides the paths to the UDL files you created in the previous procedure, as well as the paths to the delimited text files used in the data movement application. You will then create Dynamic Properties tasks in each package that uses this initialization file. You will also create a global variable that one of these Dynamic Properties tasks will use to dynamically configure the number of permitted errors before a task terminates.

Create an initialization file

1   Open Microsoft Notepad and then open the Config.txt file in C:\Microsoft Press\SQL DTS SBS\Ch6\ChapterFiles folder.

    This text file contains four sections: UDL, Products, Customers, and HistoricalData. Each section contains path and file name information that the data movement application can use to dynamically configure tasks and connection objects.

2   On the File menu, click Save As.

3   In the Save In list, navigate to C:\Microsoft Press\SQL DTS SBS\DataMovementApplication.

4   Type **Config.ini** in the File Name box, select All Files in the Save As Type list, select Unicode in the Encoding list, and then click Save. Do not close Notepad.

You have successfully created an initialization file. You can add or modify sections and keys in this initialization file based on the requirements of your data movement application.

Configure a Dynamic Properties task in the *UpdateProductDim* package

1   Switch to the UpdateProductDim package in DTS Designer.

2   On the Task menu, click Dynamic Properties task and then type **Properties From INI File** in the Description box.

    In this procedure, you will configure this task to dynamically set the properties of the connection objects in this package.

3   Click Add to select a property to be dynamically set.

The Dynamic Properties Task: Package Properties dialog box displays the connection, task, step, and global variable objects in the *UpdateProductDim* package in the left pane, and the properties and values for the selected object in the right pane.

4   Expand each node in the console tree to see each object in the UpdateProductDim package.

Notice that each task has a step associated with it and that the names for the tasks and steps are generated by DTS when the task is created. The name you enter when you create a task is its description, not its name.

Dynamic Configuration

5   Select the Leave This Dialog Box Open After Adding A Setting check box.

▶ **Tip**   The Package Properties dialog box will close after each property is modified if you do not select the Leave This Dialog Box Open After Adding A Setting check box. Leaving the dialog box open after each modification will save you time if you are making more than one modification.

6   In the left pane, click ProductStage in the Connections node.

The properties and values for this connection object are displayed in the right pane. The value for the *UDLPath* property is C:\Microsoft Press\SQL DTS SBS\DataMovementApplication\SBS_OLAP.udl.

▶ **Tip**   To see the full path, expand the size of the Default Value column so that a scroll bar appears at the bottom of the right pane. Continue expanding the size of the default value column until you can use the scroll bar to view the full file path.

7   In the right pane, double-click UDLPath.

In this procedure, you will specify the Config.ini file as the source from which the *UDLPath* property will be retrieved at run time.

8   In the Source list, select INI File, type **C:\Microsoft Press\SQL DTS SBS\DataMovementApplication\Config.ini** in the File box, select UDL in the Section list, and then select SBS_OLAPUDLFilePath in the Key list.

The Preview box displays the value stored in the Config.ini file for this key, and the Refresh button enables you to see its updated value if you change its value while configuring this assignment in the Dynamic Properties task.

9   Click OK to save this assignment.

You have successfully configured the Dynamic Properties task to dynamically configure the location of the UDL file used by the *ProductStage* connection object.

10   Click SBS_OLAPAdditionalConnection in the left pane, and then double-click UDLPath in the right pane.

11   Select INI File in the Source list, type **C:\Microsoft Press\SQL DTS SBS\DataMovementApplication\Config.ini** in the File box, select UDL in the Section list, select SBS_OLAPUDLFilePath in the Key list, and then click OK.

You have successfully configured the Dynamic Properties task to dynamically configure the location of the UDL file used by the *SBS_OLAPAdditionalConnection* connection object.

12   Click NewProductsSource in the left pane, and then double-click DataSource in the right pane.

13   Select INI File in the Source list, type **C:\Microsoft Press\SQL DTS SBS\DataMovementApplication\Config.ini** in the File box, select Products in the Section list, and select NewProductData in the Key list.

Notice that the path specified for NewProducts.txt file is C:\Microsoft Press\SQL DTS SBS\DataMovementApplication. However, the NewProducts.txt file you have been using for testing is located in the C:\Microsoft Press\SQL DTS SBS\Ch4\ChapterFiles folder. This will introduce an intentional error to demonstrate the functionality of the initialization file.

14   Click OK and then click Close.

You have successfully configured the Dynamic Properties task to dynamically configure the location of the delimited text file used by the *NewProductsSource* connection object.

15 Click OK to save the Dynamic Properties task.

Next you need to configure the *UpdateProductDim* package to execute the *Set-PropertiesFromInitializationFile* step before it executes any other steps in the package.

Configure the *SetPropertiesFromInitializationFile* step to execute first

1 On the design sheet, select the SetPropertiesFromInitializationFile step, and then hold down the Ctrl key while you click the NewProductsSource connection object.

> ▶ **Tip** You might want to rearrange the objects on the design sheet before you configure this precedence constraint.

2 On the Workflow menu, click On Success.

You can now change the data sources and destinations used in the *UpdateProductDim* package without having to edit the package directly. At run time, the *UpdateProductDim* package retrieves information from the Config.ini file and uses this information during execution. You are now ready to perform similar steps in the *UpdateCustomerDim* package.

Configure a Dynamic Properties task in the *UpdateCustomerDim* package

1   Switch to the UpdateCustomerDim package in DTS Designer.

2   On the Task menu, click Dynamic Properties task and then type **Properties From INI File** in the Description box.

3   Click Add to select a property to be dynamically set.

4   Select the Leave This Dialog Box Open After Adding A Setting check box.

5   In the left pane, expand Connections and then click CustomerStage.

6   In the right pane, double-click UDLPath.

7   In the Source list, select INI File, type **C:\Microsoft Press\SQL DTS SBS\DataMovementApplication\Config.ini** in the File box, select UDL in the Section list, select SBS_OLAPUDLFilePath in the Key list, and then click OK.

8   Click SBS_OLAPAdditionalConnection in the left pane, and then double-click UDLPath in the right pane.

9   Select INI File in the Source list, type **C:\Microsoft Press\SQL DTS SBS\DataMovementApplication\Config.ini** in the File box, select UDL in the Section list, select SBS_OLAPUDLFilePath in the Key list, and then click OK.

10 Click NewCustomersSource in the left pane, and then double-click DataSource in the right pane.

11 Select INI File in the Source list, type **C:\Microsoft Press\SQL DTS SBS\DataMovementApplication\Config.ini** in the File box, click Customers in the Section list, and then click NewCustomerData in the Key list.

Notice that the path specified for NewCustomers.txt file is C:\Microsoft Press\SQL DTS SBS\DataMovementApplication. However, the NewCustomers.txt file you have been using for testing is located in the C:\Microsoft Press\SQL DTS SBS\Ch4\ChapterFiles folder. This will introduce an intentional error to demonstrate the functionality of the initialization file.

12 Click OK, click Close, and then click OK again to save the Dynamic Properties task.

Next you need to configure the *UpdateCustomerDim* package to execute the *Properties From INI File* step before it executes any other steps in the package.

Configure the *Properties From INI File* step to execute first

1 On the design sheet, select the Properties From INI File step, and then hold down the Ctrl key while you click the NewCustomers-Source connection object.

2 On the Workflow menu, click On Success.

You can now change the data sources and destinations used in the *UpdateCustomerDim* package without having to edit the package directly. You are now ready to perform similar steps in the *LoadHistoricalData* package.

Configure a Dynamic Properties task in the *LoadHistoricalData* package

1 Switch to the LoadHistoricalData package in DTS Designer.

2 On the Task menu, click Dynamic Properties task, type **Properties From INI File** in the Description box, and then click Add.

3 Select the Leave This Dialog Box Open After Adding A Setting check box.

4 In the left pane, expand Connections and then click ProductsSource.

5 In the right pane, double-click UDLPath.

6 In the Source list, select INI File, type **C:\Microsoft Press\SQL DTS SBS\DataMovementApplication\Config.ini** in the File box, select UDL in the Section list, select SBS_OLTPUDLFilePath in the Key list, and then click OK.

> ▶ **Tip**   Take the extra time to make sure you select the correct Key value in the Config.ini file. Debugging errors later will consume much more time.

7 Click CustomersSource in the left pane, and then double-click UDL-Path in the right pane.

 8 Select INI File in the Source list, type **C:\Microsoft Press\SQL DTS SBS\DataMovementApplication\Config.ini** in the File box, select UDL in the Section list, select SBS_OLTPUDLFilePath in the Key list, and then click OK.

 9 Click ProductsDestination in the left pane, and then double-click UDLPath in the right pane.

 10 Select INI File in the Source list, type **C:\Microsoft Press\SQL DTS SBS\DataMovementApplication\Config.ini** in the File box, select UDL in the Section list, select SBS_OLAPUDLFilePath in the Key list, and then click OK.

 11 Click CustomersDestination in the left pane, and then double-click UDLPath in the right pane.

 12 Select INI File in the Source list, type **C:\Microsoft Press\SQL DTS SBS\DataMovementApplication\Config.ini** in the File box, select UDL in the Section list, select SBS_OLAPUDLFilePath in the Key list, and then click OK.

 13 Click 1996DataDestination in the left pane, and then double-click UDLPath in the right pane.

 14 Select INI File in the Source list, type **C:\Microsoft Press\SQL DTS SBS\DataMovementApplication\Config.ini** in the File box, select UDL in the Section list, select SBS_OLAPUDLFilePath in the Key list, and then click OK.

 15 Click 1997DataDestination in the left pane, and then double-click UDLPath in the right pane.

 16 Click INI File in the Source list, type **C:\Microsoft Press\SQL DTS SBS\DataMovementApplication\Config.ini** in the File box, select UDL in the Section list, select SBS_OLAPUDLFilePath in the Key list, and then click OK.

 17 Click SBS_OLAPAdditionalConnection in the left pane, and then double-click UDLPath in the right pane.

 18 Click INI File in the Source list, type **C:\Microsoft Press\SQL DTS SBS\DataMovementApplication\Config.ini** in the File box, select UDL in the Section list, select SBS_OLAPUDLFilePath in the Key list, and then click OK.

 19 Click SalesFactDataDestination in the left pane, and then double-click UDLPath in the right pane.

20 Click INI File in the Source list, type **C:\Microsoft Press\SQL DTS SBS\DataMovementApplication\Config.ini** in the File box, select UDL in the Section list, select SBS_OLAPUDLFilePath in the Key list, and then click OK.

21 Expand Task, click DTSTask_DTSBulkInsertTask_1 in the left pane, and then double-click DataFile in the right pane.

The data source for the Bulk Insert task is configured within the task itself; it does not have a separate connection object. As a result, to enable a Bulk Insert task to be configured dynamically, you must configure the task to read its data source from the initialization file.

22 Click INI File in the Source list, type **C:\Microsoft Press\SQL DTS SBS\DataMovementApplication\Config.ini** in the File box, select HistoricalData in the Section list, select 1996Data in the Key list, and then click OK.

23 Double-click FormatFile in the right pane.

24 Click INI File in the Source list, type **C:\Microsoft Press\SQL DTS SBS\DataMovementApplication\Config.ini** in the File box, select HistoricalData in the Section list, select FormatFile in the Key list, and then click OK.

25 Click DTSTask_DTSBulkInsertTask_2 in the left pane, and then double-click DataFile in the right pane.

26 Click INI File in the Source list, type **C:\Microsoft Press\SQL DTS SBS\DataMovementApplication\Config.ini** in the File box, select HistoricalData in the Section list, select 1997Data in the Key list, and then click OK.

27 Double-click FormatFile in the right pane.

28 Click INI File in the Source list, type **C:\Microsoft Press\SQL DTS SBS\DataMovementApplication\Config.ini** in the File box, select HistoricalData in the Section list, select FormatFile in the Key list, and then click OK.

29 Click Close and then click OK to save the Dynamic Properties task.

Now you need to configure the *LoadHistoricalData* package to execute the *Properties From INI File* step before it executes any other steps in the package.

Configure the *Properties From INI File* step to execute first

1 On the design sheet, select the Properties From INI File step, and then hold down the Ctrl key while you click the TruncateData step.

2 On the Workflow menu, click On Success.

3 On the toolbar, click Save.

You can now change the data sources and destinations used in the *LoadHistoricalData* package without having to edit the package.

Test the *LoadHistoricalData*, *UpdateCustomerDim*, and *UpdateProductDim* packages

1 On the DTS Designer toolbar for the LoadHistoricalData package, click Execute.

The *LoadHistoricalData* package executes successfully.

2 Click OK and then click Done.

3 On the toolbar, click Save and then close the LoadHistoricalData package in DTS Designer.

4 On the DTS Designer toolbar for the UpdateCustomerDim package, click Execute. One task failed during execution.

5   Click OK.

Notice that the *Properties From INI File* step succeeded, but the *Load CustomerStage Table* step failed.

6   Double-click Load CustomerStage Table in the Status window.

The *Load CustomerStage Table* step failed because it could not find the file specified in the initialization file.

Load CustomerStage Table

Error opening datafile: The system cannot find the file specified.

OK

7   Click OK and then click Done.

8   Switch to Windows Explorer and then navigate to C:\Microsoft Press\SQL DTS SBS\Ch4\ChapterFiles.

9   Select and then copy the NewCustomers.txt and NewProducts.txt files.

10   Navigate to C:\Microsoft Press\SQL DTS SBS\DataMovementApplication and paste these two files into this folder.

11   Switch to the UpdateCustomerDim package in DTS Designer and then click Execute on the toolbar.

A task in the package still fails.

12 Click OK and then double-click Load CustomerStage Table in the Status window.

The *Load CustomerStage Table* step failed due to the errors you introduced in the NewCustomers.txt file in the previous chapter, which means that the initialization file is pointing the *Load CustomerStage Table* step to the file that you just moved into the C:\Microsoft Press\SQL DTS SBS\DataMovementApplication folder.

13 Click OK and then click Done.

14 Switch to the UpdateProductDim package in DTS Designer, and then click Execute on the toolbar.

The *UpdateProductDim* package executes successfully because you moved the NewProducts.txt file to the C:\Microsoft Press\SQL DTS SBS\DataMovementApplication, which is where the initialization file configured the *Load ProductStage Table* step to look for the file.

15 Click OK and then click Done.

You have now verified that the initialization file works properly and that you can use it to change the data sources used by the data movement application to load data. Obviously, the schema for the data sources cannot change or the packages will fail. Now that you have learned to configure a Dynamic Properties task to read information from a configuration file, you will learn how to configure the Dynamic Properties task to read values from global variables.

Configure a Dynamic Properties task to use global variable values

1 In the UpdateProductDim package, double-click the Properties From INI File step on the design sheet and then click Add.

2 Select the Leave This Dialog Box Open After Adding A Setting check box.

3 Expand Tasks in the left pane, and then click DTSTask_DTSDataPumpTask_1.

The *DTSTask_DTSDataPumpTask_1* task is the task described on the design sheet as the *Load ProductStage Table* task.

4   In the right pane, double-click MaximumErrorCount.

5   In the Source list, click Global Variable to configure the Maximum-ErrorCount property to be set at run time based on the value of a global variable.

6   Click Create Global Variables.

Because you have not previously created a global variable to hold this value, you will create a global variable and then specify its default value.

7 Type **giMaxErrorCount** in the Name box, select Integer (1 byte) in the Type list, type 5 in the Value box, and then click OK.

> ▶ **Important**   Global variable names are case-sensitive, so when you create them, pay attention to case. Establishing a naming convention that you follow for all global variables can be helpful.

Now that you have added this global variable to the *UpdateProduct-Dim* package, you need to map this variable to the *MaximumError-Count* property.

> ▶ **Tip**   The prefix used in naming this global variable will be used in an ActiveX script in Chapter 7 to identify the type of data stored in this variable: *g* stands for global variable, and *i* stands for integer data type.

8 In the Variable list, select giMaxErrorCount.

9   Click OK to save this assignment.

10 In the right pane, double-click InsertCommitSize.

11 In the Source list, click Global Variable, and then click Create Global Variables.

12 Type **giBatchSize** in the Name column, select Integer (small) in the Type list, type 500 in the Value column, and then click OK.

13 In the Variable list, select giBatchSize, and then click OK to save this assignment.

14 Click Close and then click OK to save these changes to the Dynamic Properties task.

15 On the toolbar, click Save and then close the UpdateProductDim package in DTS Designer.

You have successfully configured the Dynamic Properties task to read configuration values at run time from two different data sources.

16 In the UpdateCustomerDim package in DTS Designer, double-click the Properties From INI File step on the design sheet and then click Add.

17 Select the Leave This Dialog Box Open After Adding A Setting check box.

18 Expand Tasks in the left pane and then click DTSTask_DTSDataPumpTask_1.

19 In the right pane, double-click MaximumErrorCount.

20 In the Source list, click Global Variable, and then click Create Global Variables.

21 Type **giMaxErrorCount** in the Name box, select Integer(1 byte) in the Type list, type 5 in the Value box, and then click OK.

22 In the Variable list, select giMaxErrorCount, and then click OK.

23 In the right pane, double-click InsertCommitSize.

24 In the Source list, click Global Variable, and then click Create Global Variables.

25 Type **giBatchSize** in the Name box, select Integer(small) in the Type list, type 500 in the Value box, and then click OK.

26 In the Variable list, select giBatchSize, and then click OK.

27 Click Close and then click OK again to save this change to the Dynamic Properties task.

28 On the toolbar, click Execute.

The *Load CustomerStage Table* step processed all 29 rows because there were only two errors in the NewCustomers.txt file and the maximum error count was set to 5.

29 Click OK and then click Done.

30 On the toolbar, click Save, and then close the UpdateCustomerDim package in DTS Designer.

You have now configured the *UpdateProductDim* and *UpdateCustomerDim* packages to support the dynamic configuration of the maximum number of errors permitted before a Transfer Data task terminates, and also the number of rows that will be committed in a single batch.

Dynamically Changing Global Variable Values in Another Package

Global variable values can be updated at run time using a number of different mechanisms, for example, by using the DTSRun utility (see Chapter 3) or the Execute Package task. Using the Execute Package task enables a master package to communicate with subpackages and modify global variable values in them at run time.

The Execute Package task supports inner package and outer package global variables. *Inner package global variables* specify values for subpackage global variables. *Outer package global variables* specify the master package global variables that are passed to the subpackage. For a given execution, identically named global variables in the subpackage use the values of the global variables passed from the master package.

In the following procedures, you will learn how to use inner package and outer package global variables. First, you will modify the *MasterUpdate* package to use an inner package variable when executing the *UpdateCustomerDim* package. You will then modify the *MasterUpdate* package to use outer package global variables when executing both the *UpdateCustomerDim* and *UpdateProductDim* packages.

Configure an inner package global variable

1   In the SQL Server Enterprise Manager console tree, right-click Data Transformation Services in your local instance and then click Open.

2   Navigate to C:\Microsoft Press\SQL DTS SBS\DataMovementApplication and then double-click MasterUpdate.dts.

3   Double-click MasterUpdate in the Select Package dialog box, type **mypassword** in the Password text box, and then click OK.

4   On the design sheet, double-click the Call UpdateCustomerDim Subpackage step, and then click the Inner Package Global Variables tab.

5   In the Variables window, select giMaxErrorCount in the Name list.

    The global variable type and current value are retrieved from the *UpdateCustomerDim* package.

6   Type 0 in the Value box and then click OK.

7   On the toolbar, click Execute.

8   Click OK to acknowledge that one task failed during execution, and then double-click Call UpdateCustomerDim Subpackage in the Status window.

    The *UpdateCustomerDim* package did not transform any rows because the *MaximumErrorCount* property in this package was changed to 0 at run time by the *MasterUpdate* package, and the NewCustomers.txt source file contains two errors. As a result, the number of failing rows exceeded the maximum number permitted by the Transform Data task.

9   Click OK and then click Done.

You have successfully configured a master package to change the global variable value in a subpackage. However, when you use this approach, you must edit the master package each time you want to change this value. As you will learn in the following procedure, using outer package global variables solves this problem by enabling you to configure the global variable value passed to the subpackage at run time from outside the package.

Configure an outer package global variable

1   Verify that no tasks are selected on the design sheet, and then right-click an open area of the design sheet and click Package Properties.

In this procedure, you will create the *giMaxErrorCount* and *giBatch-Size* global variables in the *MasterUpdate* package that will be passed to each of the subpackages.

2   Click the Global Variables tab and then click New.

3   Type **giMaxErrorCount** in the Name box, select Integer (1 byte) in the Type list, and type **5** in the Value box.

4   In the next line in the Variables window, type **giBatchSize** in the Name box, select Integer (small) in the Type list, type **500** in the Value box, and then click OK.

You have successfully created the global variables in the master package that match the global variables you want to manipulate in the *UpdateCustomerDim* and *UpdateProductDim* subpackages.

> ▶ **Important**   Since global variable names are case-sensitive, you must ensure that the name of the global variable in the master package and the name in each subpackage are identical, including case. If not, the global variable in the subpackage will not be updated.

5   On the design sheet, double-click the Call UpdateCustomerDim Subpackage step, and then click the Inner Package Global Variables tab.

6   Click giMaxErrorCount and click Delete.

7   Click the Outer Package Global Variables tab.

8   In the first row in the Variables window, select giMaxErrorCount in the Name list. In the second row, select giBatchSize in the Name list.

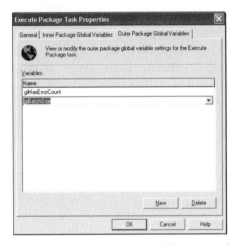

9   Click OK to save the modification of the Execute Package task.

You have successfully configured the *Call UpdateCustomerDim Subpackage* step to pass global variable values to the *UpdateCustomerDim* package when it executes the subpackage. Next you will configure the *Call UpdateProductDim Subpackage* step to pass the same global variable values to the *UpdateProductDim* subpackage.

10   On the design sheet, double-click the Call UpdateProductDim Subpackage step, and then click the Outer Package Global Variables tab.

11   In the first row in the Variables window, select giMaxErrorCount in the Name list. In the second row, select giBatchSize in the Name list.

12   Click OK to save the modification of the Execute Package task.

13 On the toolbar, click Execute.

Both packages complete successfully, although one task failed in the *UpdateCustomerDim* subpackage. All 29 rows were processed in the *UpdateCustomerDim* subpackage, and 27 of the 29 rows were inserted successfully because the *MaximumErrorCount* property in the *UpdateCustomerDim* subpackage was set to 5.

14 Click OK and then click Done.

15 On the toolbar, click Save.

16 Close the MasterUpdate package in DTS Designer, and then close SQL Server Enterprise Manager.

You have successfully configured the *MasterUpdate* package to dynamically update global variable values in each of the subpackages that it calls based on the values of identically named global variables in the master package. Changes to these global variable values in the *MasterUpdate* package modify the operation of each subpackage. However, if you want to have different values for the the global variables in each subpackage and have them set dynamically at run time, you can use separate global variables for each subpackage (which can become confusing), or you can use ActiveX Script tasks, Execute SQL tasks, and SQL Server tables to solve this problem. You will learn how to accomplish this in the next chapter.

Chapter Summary

In this chapter, you learned how to enable properties in your packages to be dynamically configured at run time without opening and editing each package. You learned how to use data link connection objects, an initialization file, global variables, and Dynamic Properties tasks to dynamically control the execution of tasks and the configuration of connection objects at run time. Furthermore, you learned two methods for setting global variable values in a subpackage from a master package. In the next chapter you will learn how to use an ActiveX Script task to set global variable values in the packages in the data movement application.

Chapter

7

Using ActiveX Script Tasks

In this chapter, you will learn how to:

■ Set global variable values

■ Read registry values

■ Enable package branching

In previous chapters, you learned how to use Microsoft ActiveX scripts in conjunction with the Data Driven Query task to add functionality to your data movement application. In this chapter, you will learn to use the ActiveX Script task to expand your application's functionality beyond what is available in the built-in tasks. Specifically, you will learn to set global variable values, read registry values, and enable package branching. These are examples of some of the functionality that you can add to packages by using ActiveX Script tasks.

Using the ActiveX Script task, you can access a variety of COM objects, such as the DTS object model, the WSH (Windows Scripting Host) object model, and the *FileSystemObject* object model, to dynamically configure DTS tasks and packages and control package workflow. Figure 7-1 shows Part 1 and Figure 7-2 shows Part 2 of the DTS object model.

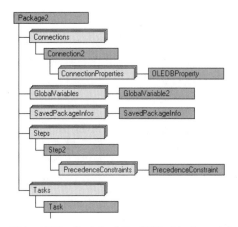

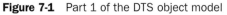

Figure 7-1 Part 1 of the DTS object model

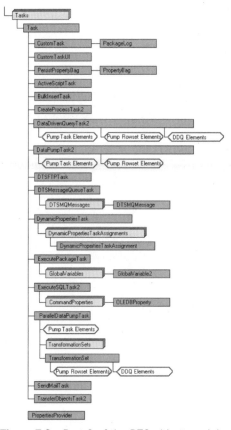

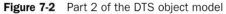

Figure 7-2 Part 2 of the DTS object model

The root-level object of the DTS object model is the *Package2* object. (The Microsoft SQL Server 7 version of DTS uses the *Package* object.) In an ActiveX task, you can access any of the connection objects, tasks, steps, or global variables in a package through the *Package2* object. Similarly, you can access any file in the Microsoft Windows file system through the *FileSystemObject* object, and any key or value in the Windows registry through the *WScript* object. In this chapter, you will learn how to access the DTS object model and the WSH object model to add additional dynamic configuration capabilities to your data movement application. (For more information on DTS programming, see *http://msdn.microsoft.com/library/default.asp?url=/library/en-us/dtsprog /dtsptasks_4yp1.asp?frame=true*. For information about the WSH object model, see *http://www.microsoft.com/technet/treeview/default.asp?url=/technet /scriptcenter/scrguide/sas_wsh_rjma.asp*.)

You can use one of many interpreted scripting languages within an ActiveX Script task. Interpreted languages are not compiled until run time, which means that you can change the code without having to recompile it after each change. However, this flexibility comes at the price of performance—each ActiveX Script task is compiled before it is executed. As a result, you should use ActiveX Script tasks only for tasks that you cannot perform using one of the built-in tasks. DTS compiles Microsoft Visual Basic Script (VBScript) more efficiently than JavaScript, and it compiles JavaScript more efficiently than PerlScript. Furthermore, Microsoft has fully tested only VBScript and JavaScript with the ActiveX Script task. Although the examples in this book use VBScript, you could write them using any interpreted language. This book assumes that you are familiar with VBScript and does not attempt to explain the details of the VBScript used in the ActiveX Script tasks, although the overall concept of each script is explained. For information about VBScript, see *http://msdn.microsoft.com/library/default.asp?url=/library/en-us/script56 /html/vtoriVBScript.asp* or *Microsoft® Windows® 2000 Scripting Guide,* published by Microsoft Press (*http://www.microsoft.com/MSPress/books /6417.asp*).

When you incorporate ActiveX scripts to change package properties during execution, the changed objects in the package can be left without a context after the package is executed. When you execute such a package within DTS Designer, make further edits to the package, and then save it, package corruption can result. To avoid this potential problem, you should always save your package before you test its execution and then use the saved package for further edits. Do not use the executed package for further edits. Close and then re-open the package.

Setting Global Variable Values at Run Time

In previous chapters, you learned how to define global variables in DTS packages, use these global variable values in tasks, pass these global variables between packages by using the Execute Package task, and modify these global variable values at run time using the *DTSRun* command. In this chapter, you will learn how to use the ActiveX Script task to set global variable values at run time based on the value of each variable that is stored in a SQL table. You will take this concept one step further by creating a configuration ID column in the SQL table to permit you to store different possible values for the same global variable. When you retrieve global variable values at run time, you will retrieve the appropriate values based on the value of the configuration ID passed into the package by the *DTSRun* command. As the number of global variables and the number of packages in the data movement application increase, the ability to set variations of these values for multiple packages in one place and control which set of values are used at run time can save you a significant amount of time and confusion.

▶ **Note**   If you skipped Chapter 6, execute the IfYouSkippedChapter6.cmd batch file in the C:\Microsoft Press\SQL DTS SBS\Ch7\SkippedChapterFiles folder. This batch file restores the SBS_OLTP and SBS_OLAP databases and copies the DTS packages that would have been created in Chapters 1 through 6 into the appropriate folders. If you do not want this batch file to overwrite any packages that you created in Chapters 1 through 6, you must move them or rename them before you execute this batch file.

Creating a Configuration Table in SQL Server

In the following procedure, you will create and populate a global variable configuration table in the SBS_OLAP database. In subsequent procedures, you will create tasks that read global variable values from this table to modify task properties at run time.

Create a global variable configuration table

1   Open SQL Query Analyzer and connect to your local SQL Server instance as a system administrator.

2   On the File menu, click Open.

3 In the Look In list, navigate to C:\Microsoft Press\SQL DTS SBS\Ch7\ChapterFiles and then open the PackageGVs.sql script.

This script creates a five-column table to hold global variable names and values for each package in the data movement application. The *ConfigID* column enables you to store different values for the same package global variable, and the *Description* column enables you to describe each configuration. This script also loads six records into this new table. The first two records define a default configuration of the data movement application (the Default configuration). The next four records define an alternate configuration of global variable values (the No Errors Unless Override configuration). In the Default configuration, a value is set for each global variable in the *MasterUpdate* package, and this value carries to each subpackage. In the No Errors Unless Override configuration, a value is set for each global variable in the *MasterUpdate* package, and then a different value for the *giMaxErrorCount* global variable is specified for the *UpdateCustomerDim* and the *UpdateProductDim* subpackages.

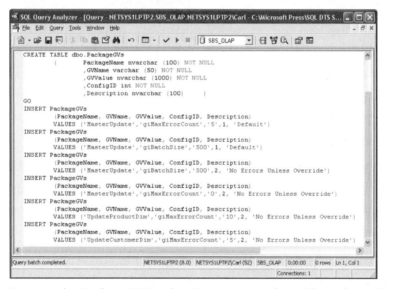

4 Execute the PackageGVs.sql script to create this table and populate its values.

Now that you have created and populated this table, you are ready to modify the *MasterUpdate* package to connect to and read this table.

Updating Global Variable Values in the *MasterUpdate* Package from the Configuration Table

In the following procedures, you will add a dynamically configured connection object to the SBS_OLAP database and then create an Execute SQL task in the *MasterUpdate* package that will use this connection object to read the global variable configuration table at run time and store the rowset in a global variable. You will then create an ActiveX Script task in this package to read the stored rowset and update the package global variable values before executing the remaining tasks in the package.

Create a dynamically configured data link connection in the *MasterUpdate* package to the SBS_OLAP database

1   Open SQL Server Enterprise Manager and then right-click Data Transformation Services in your local instance.

2   Click Open Package and then open the most recent version of the MasterUpdate package in the C:\Microsoft Press\SQL DTS SBS\ DataMovementApplication folder using a password of **mypassword**.

3   On the Connection menu, click Microsoft Data Link.

Before you can create an Execute SQL task, you must define a connection object for the Execute SQL task to use.

4   Type **SBS_OLAP** in the New Connection box, type **C:\Microsoft Press\SQL DTS SBS\DataMovementApplication\SBS_OLAP.udl** in the UDL File Name box, select Always Read Properties From UDL File, and then click OK to save the connection object.

5   On the Task menu, click Dynamic Properties Task, type **Properties From INI File** in the Description box, and then click Add.

> ▶   **Tip**   As you add objects to your data movement application, remember to set them up for dynamic configuration.

6   In the left pane, expand Connections and then click SBS_OLAP.

7   In the right pane, double-click UDLPath.

8   In the Add/Edit Assignment dialog box, verify that INI File is selected in the Source list, type **C:\Microsoft Press\SQL DTS SBS\ DataMovementApplication\Config.ini** in the File box, select UDL in the Section list, select SBS_OLAPUDLFilePath in the Key list, and then click OK.

9   Click OK to save this Dynamic Properties task.

Now that you have configured a dynamic connection object in the *Master-Update* package to the SBS_OLAP database, you are ready to add an Execute SQL task to retrieve global variable values from the *PackageGVs* table.

Read the *PackageGVs* configuration table into a global variable in the *MasterUpdate* package

1   On the Task menu, click Execute SQL Task.

2   Type **PickupGVs** in the Description box and then click Browse.

3   In the Look In list, navigate to C:\Microsoft Press\SQL DTS SBS\Ch7\ChapterFiles and double-click PickupGVsMaster.sql.

Based on a configuration ID, this script retrieves each *MasterUpdate* package global variable and its value from the *PackageGVs* table. As you learned in Chapter 2, the question mark in this script represents a parameter that is populated from a global variable in the package.

4   Click Parameters to create a global variable that will store the value for the configuration ID parameter and then map this global variable to the parameter in this query.

5   Click Create Global Variables on the Input Parameters tab, type **giConfigID** in the Name column, select Integer (1 byte) in the Type list, type **1** in the Value column, and then click OK.

Using a default value of 1 for this global variable specifies that only the global variable values in the *PackageGVs* table with a configuration ID of 1 will be retrieved, unless a different value for the *giConfigID* global variable is passed to the package at execution time.

> ▶ **Tip**   The prefix of *gi* used in the global variable naming will indicate to the ActiveX script you will use that the data type for this variable is an integer. Additional prefixes that you will use include *gs* for string data types, *gb* for Boolean data types, and *go* for other. Also, remember that global variable names are case sensitive, so make sure you type them exactly as they appear in this text to prevent the saved scripts that you use from failing.

6   Select giConfigID from the Input Global Variables list.

Click the Output Parameters tab, where you can map the output from the SQL query to none, one, or many global variables.

By default, no data is stored when you run an Execute SQL task and any output generated by the SQL statement is not preserved within the package. You can choose to either store each value returned in a separate global variable or store the entire rowset returned in a single global variable as a disconnected Microsoft ActiveX Data Objects (ADO) recordset. For the *PickupGVs* task, you will store the data returned in a single global variable that will be read by the ActiveX Script task that you will configure in the next procedure.

7   Click Create Global Variables, type **goGVsPickedUp** in the Name column, select String in the Type column, and then click OK. No default value applies in this context, and the prefix *go* signifies that this global variable is used to hold the output from a SQL query.

8 Click Rowset and then click goGVsPickedUp in the global variables list.

9 Click OK to save the parameter mapping for the query and then click OK to save the Execute SQL task.

Now that you have configured an Execute SQL task to retrieve global variable values from the *PackageGVs* table, you are ready to create an ActiveX Script task to read each of the records in the recordset stored in the global variable and update the applicable global variables in the *MasterUpdate* package.

Update global variable values in the *MasterUpdate* package by creating an ActiveX Script task

1 On the Task menu, click ActiveX Script Task and then type **SetGVs** in the Description box.

The default code in the ActiveX Script task executes in the Main phase, and since no code has been added to perform any action, the Main phase simply reports that the phase completed successfully and then exits.

2   Click Browse, navigate to C:\Microsoft Press\SQL DTS
SBS\Ch7\ChapterFiles, and then double-click SetGVs.bas.

This script begins by declaring a variable and placing a reference to the
package into the variable. This script then declares a second variable
to contain the disconnected recordset from the Execute SQL task
(which is passed through the *goGVsPickedUp* global variable). This
script then declares three additional variables for the retrieved information: the global variable name, the value, and the type. This script
parses each row in the recordset and sets the value of the appropriate
global variable in the package to the value retrieved from the *Package-
GVs* table. This script uses the *Case* statement and VBScript type
conversion functions (*CStr*, *CInt*, or *CBool*) to convert the global
variable values retrieved from the recordset to the correct data type
(*string*, *integer*, or *Boolean*) for the global variable. This script uses
the first two characters of the global variable name to determine the
appropriate data type to which to convert the retrieved value. This
script also uses the *CStr* function to convert the variable name
retrieved from the recordset to a string value.

▶   **Note**   Conversion functions are required in ActiveX scripts when working
with the DTS object model because all variables within a VBScript data
type are defined as variant. The conversion function ensures that the
variable value is set to the appropriate data type.

3   Click OK to save the ActiveX Script task.

You have just configured tasks to read new global variable values from a SQL table and then update global variable values in the *MasterUpdate* package. Now you need to pass the *giConfigID* global variable as an outer package global variable to each subpackage. This enables you to set a configuration ID value for the *MasterUpdate* package and allow this value to be used by all subpackages to retrieve and update global variable values unique to each subpackage. You will also add another dynamic configuration step to the *MasterUpdate* package using information you will store in the initialization file.

Passing the *giConfigID* Value to Subpackages and Dynamically Configuring the Execute Package Tasks in the *MasterUpdate* Package

In the following procedures, you will configure each of the Execute Package tasks in the *MasterUpdate* package to pass the *ConfigID* global variable value from the *MasterUpdate* package to each subpackage. You will also add a Dynamic Properties task to the *MasterUpdate* package to read the location of each subpackage from the Config.ini initialization file.

Pass the *giConfigID* value from the *MasterUpdate* package to each subpackage by updating the Execute Package tasks

1   On the design sheet, double-click the Call UpdateProductDim Sub-package step and then click the Outer Package Global Variables tab.

To pass the value for the *giConfigID* global variable from the master package to the *UpdateProductDim* subpackage, you must specify this variable as an outer package global variable in the *Call UpdateProductDim Subpackage* step.

2   In the Name list, select giConfigID to add this global variable to the list of global variables passed to the *UpdateProductDim* subpackage.

3   Click OK and then double-click the Call UpdateCustomerDim Sub-package step.

4   On the Outer Package Global Variables tab, select giConfigID in the Name list to add this global variable to the list of global variables passed to the *UpdateCustomerDim* subpackage, and then click OK.

Before configuring precedence constraints between the newly added steps, you will modify the *Properties From INI File* step to read subpackage location information from the Config.ini initialization file. This will enable you to move the structured storage files for each subpackage to a new location without breaking the data movement application. To do this, you must first add an entry in the Config.ini file to point to each of these subpackages.

Add subpackage location information to the Config.ini initialization file

1   Using Microsoft Windows Explorer, navigate to C:\Microsoft Press\SQL DTS SBS\DataMovementApplication and then double-click Config.ini.

2   On a new line at the end of the file, type [**SubPackages**] and then press Enter.

3   Type **UpdateProductDim=C:\Microsoft Press\SQL DTS SBS\ DataMovementApplication\UpdateProductDim.dts** and then press Enter.

4   Type **UpdateCustomerDim=C:\Microsoft Press\SQL DTS SBS\ DataMovementApplication\UpdateCustomerDim.dts** and then click Save on the File menu. Do not close the Config.ini file.

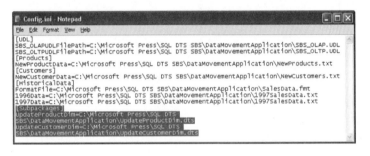

Now that you have entries for the file locations of each subpackage called from the *MasterUpdate* package, you are ready to dynamically configure the *File-Name* property in each Execute Package task in this package.

Read subpackage location information into the *MasterUpdate* package from the Config.ini initialization file

1   Switch to the MasterUpdate package in SQL Server Enterprise Manager.

2   On the design sheet, double-click the Properties From INI File step and then click Add.

3   Select the Leave This Dialog Box Open After Adding A Setting check box.

4   In the left pane, expand Tasks and then click DTSTask_DTSExecutePackageTask_1.

DTSTask_DTSExecutePackageTask_1 is the name for the Execute Package task called by the *Call UpdateProductDim Subpackage* step.

5   In the right pane, double-click FileName, verify INI is selected in
     the Source list, type **C:\Microsoft Press\SQL DTS SBS\
     DataMovementApplication\Config.ini** in the File list, select SubPack-
     ages in the Section list, select UpdateProductDim in the Key list, and
     then click OK.

6   In the left pane, click DTSTask_DTSExecutePackageTask_2 in the
     Tasks node.
     DTSTask_DTSExecutePackageTask_2 is the name for the Execute
     Package task called by the *Call UpdateCustomerDim Subpackage*
     step.

7   In the right pane, double-click FileName, verify INI is selected in
     the Source list, type **C:\Microsoft Press\SQL DTS SBS\
     DataMovementApplication\Config.ini** in the File list, select Sub-
     Packages in the Section list, select UpdateCustomerDim in the Key
     list, and then click OK.

8   Click Close and then click OK.

Now that you have added these new steps to the *MasterUpdate* package, you
need to configure the appropriate precedence constraints to ensure that they
execute in the proper order.

Specifying Step Execution Order in the *MasterUpdate* Package and Testing the Package

In the following procedures, you will configure the step that sets the path to the
SBS_OLAP database to execute first, followed by the step that reads updated
global variable values from the *PackageGVs* table, and then the step that
updates the global variable values from the rowset global variable. You will
configure the step that dynamically updates the Execute Package tasks to execute after these steps complete, followed by the steps that call the subpackages.
You will then test the execution of the *MasterUpdate* package as updated by the
previous procedures.

Ensure package steps execute in the proper order by configuring precedence constraints in the *MasterUpdate* package

1   On the design sheet, click the Properties From INI File step, and then
     hold down the Ctrl key and click the PickUpGVs step.

     ▶ **Tip** For easier viewing, as you are adding the precedence constraints,
     arrange the tasks on the design sheet in logical execution order.

2 On the Workflow menu, click On Success.

3 On the design sheet, click the PickupGVs step, and then hold down the Ctrl key and click the SetGVs step.

4 On the Workflow menu, click On Success.

5 On the design sheet, click the SetGVs step, and then hold down the Ctrl key and click the Call UpdateProductDim Subpackage step.

6 On the Workflow menu, click On Success.

7 On the design sheet, click the SetGVs step, and then hold down the Ctrl key and click the Call UpdateCustomerDim Subpackage step.

8 On the Workflow menu, click On Success.

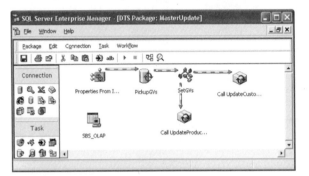

9 On the toolbar, click Save.

Now that you have successfully configured the *MasterUpdate* package to read global variable values from the *PackageGVs* table in SQL Server and update them in the package, you are ready to test the execution of the *MasterUpdate* package.

Test the execution of the *MasterUpdate* package

1 On the toolbar, click Execute to execute the package tasks.

All tasks in the *MasterUpdate* package complete successfully, but one task in the *UpdateCustomerDim* subpackage failed. The *Update-CustomerDim* package, which was called by the *Call Update-CustomerDim Subpackage* step, processed all 29 rows (inserting 27 of these rows) of data because the *giMaxErrorCount* global variable value is set to 5 and the *giBatchSize* global variable is set to 500 for the *MasterUpdate* package by the *SetGVs* step, and these values are passed to the *UpdateCustomerDim* package as outer package global variables.

2 Click OK and then click Done.

3   Switch to SQL Query Analyzer and then click Load SQL Script on the toolbar.

4   Navigate to C:\Microsoft Press\SQL DTS SBS\Ch7\ChapterFiles in the Look In list and then double-click ModifyDefaultConfig.sql.

This script modifies the default configuration by setting the value of the *giMaxErrorCount* global variable to 0 for the *MasterUpdate* package where the *ConfigID* value is 1.

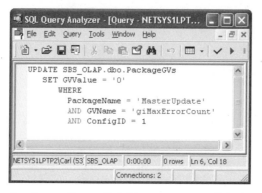

5   On the toolbar, click Execute to modify the default configuration and then switch to the MasterUpdate package in DTS Designer.

6   On the toolbar, click Execute to verify the execution of this package with this new configuration value for the giMaxErrorCount global variable.

One task fails.

7   Click OK and then double-click Call UpdateCustomerDim Subpackage in the Status window to verify the reason the task in the *Update-CustomerDim* subpackage failed.

The *UpdateCustomerDim* package that was called by the *Call UpdateCustomerDim Subpackage* step did not process all 29 rows; the number of failing rows exceeded the maximum number specified. This is because the *MasterUpdate* package was executed using the default configuration. This configuration specifies that the *giMax-ErrorCount* global variable value is 0 and that the *giBatchSize* global variable value is 500 for the *MasterUpdate* package. The *SetGVs* step in the *MasterUpdate* package sets these values at run time, and these values are passed to the *UpdateCustomerDim* and *Update-ProductDim* packages as outer package global variables.

8   Click OK and then click Done.

9   Close the MasterUpdate package in DTS Designer.

Now that you have verified that the *MasterUpdate* package can read global variable values from the *PackagesGVs* table in SQL Server and update them in the package, you are ready to configure the *UpdateProductDim* and *Update-CustomerDim* packages to also read global variable values from the *Package-GVs* table. This will enable you to use different global variable values in each package if circumstances require this capability.

Updating Global Variable Values in the *UpdateProductDim* Package from the Configuration Table

In the following procedures, you will create an Execute SQL task in the *UpdateProductDim* package that will read the global variable configuration table at run time and store the rowset in a global variable. You will then create an ActiveX Script task in this package to read the stored rowset and update the package global variable values before executing the remaining tasks in the package.

Read the *PackageGVs* configuration table into a global variable in the *UpdateProductDim* package by creating an Execute SQL task

1   In the SQL Server Enterprise Manager console tree, right-click Data Transformation Services in your local instance.

2   Click Open Package and then open the most recent version of the *UpdateProductDim* package in the C:\Microsoft Press\SQL DTS SBS\ DataMovementApplication folder using a password of **mypassword**.

3   On the Task menu, click Execute SQL Task.

4   Type **PickupGVs** in the Description box, click SBS_OLAPAdditionalConnection in the Existing Connection list, and then click Browse.

You could select either of the connection objects to the SBS_OLAP database because neither of them will be in use when this task executes. This is because the *PickupGVs* task will complete before any other task needs either of the connection objects.

5   In the Look In list, navigate to C:\Microsoft Press\SQL DTS SBS\Ch7\ChapterFiles, and double-click PickupGVsUpdateProduct-Dim.sql.

Based on a configuration ID, this script retrieves each *Update-ProductDim* package global variable and its value from the *Package-GVs* table.

6   Click Parameters to create a global variable that will store the value for the configuration ID parameter and then map this global variable to the parameter in this query.

7   Click Create Global Variables on the Input Parameters tab, type **giConfigID** in the Name column, select Integer (1 byte) in the Type list, type **1** in the Value column, and then click OK.

8   Select giConfigID in the Input Global Variables list.

9   Click the Output Parameters tab.

10   Click Create Global Variables, type **goGVsPickedUp** in the Name column, select String in the Type column, and then click OK.

11   Click Rowset, click goGVsPickedUp in the global variables list, click OK to save the parameter mapping for the query, and then click OK to save the Execute SQL task.

You have just configured an Execute SQL task to retrieve global variable values from the *PackageGVs* table. Now you are ready to create an ActiveX Script task to read each of the records in the rowset stored in the global variable, and update the applicable global variables in the *UpdateProductDim* package.

Set global variable values in the *UpdateProductDim* Package by creating an ActiveX Script task

1   On the Task menu, click ActiveX Script Task and then type **SetGVs** in the Description box.

2   Click Browse, navigate to C:\Microsoft Press\SQL DTS SBS\ Ch7\ChapterFiles, and then double-click SetGVs.bas.

This code is identical to the code used in the *MasterUpdate* package because it performs exactly the same function in this package and the global variable holding the rowset has the same name in both packages.

3   Click OK.

Before configuring precedence constraints between these newly added steps, you will modify the *Properties From INI File* step to specify dynamically configured exception file paths for use by the *Load ProductStage Table* step and the *Insert Or Update ProductDim Table* step. Configuring dynamic paths for these exception files will enable you to specify valid paths if you move the data movement application. To do this, you must first add entries in the Config.ini file to point to the locations for these exception files.

Updating Exception File Location Information Dynamically for *UpdateProductDim* Package Tasks

In the following procedures, you will add exception file location information for the *Load ProductStage Table* and *Insert Or Update ProductDim Table* steps to the Config.ini initialization file. You will then modify the *Properties From INI File* step to read this information and update the appropriate steps before they are executed.

Add exception file location information to the Config.ini initialization file

1   Switch to the Config.ini file in Notepad.

2   On a new line at the end of the file, type [**ExceptionFiles**] and then press Enter.

3   Type **Load ProductStage Table= C:\Microsoft Press\SQL DTS SBS\ DataMovementApplication\LoadProductStageTableExceptionFile.txt** and then press Enter.

4   Type **Insert or Update ProductDim Table=C:\Microsoft Press\ SQL DTS SBS\DataMovementApplication\LoadProductDimTable ExceptionFile.txt** and then click Save on the File menu. Do not close the Config.ini file in Notepad.

Now that you have added these location entries to the Config.ini initialization file, you are ready to update the *Properties From INI File* step to use these entries to dynamically configure the *ExceptionFileName* property in the *Load ProductStage Table* step and the *Insert Or Update ProductDim Table* step.

Read exception file locations into the *UpdateProductDim* package from the Config.ini initialization file

1   Switch to the UpdateProductDim package in SQL Server Enterprise Manager.

2   On the design sheet, double-click the Properties From INI File step and then click Add.

3   Select the Leave This Dialog Box Open After Adding A Setting check box.

4   In the left pane, expand Tasks and then click DTSTask_DTSDataPumpTask_1.

   DTSTask_DTSDataPumpTask_1 is the name for the Transform Data task called by the *Load ProductStage Table* step.

5   In the right pane, double-click ExceptionFileName, verify INI is selected in the Source list, type **C:\Microsoft Press\SQL DTS SBS\ DataMovementApplication\Config.ini** in the File list, select ExceptionFiles in the Section list, select Load ProductStage Table in the Key list, and then click OK.

6   Click Close and then click OK.

7   In the left pane, click DTSTask_DTSDataDrivenQueryTask_1.

   DTSTask_DTSDataDriveQueryTask_1 is the name for the Data Driven Query task called by the *Insert Or Update ProductDim Table* step.

8   In the right pane, double-click ExceptionFileName, verify INI is selected in the Source list, type **C:\Microsoft Press\SQL DTS SBS\ DataMovementApplication\Config.ini** in the File list, select ExceptionFiles in the Section list, select Insert Or Update ProductDim Table in the Key list, and then click OK.

9   Click Close and then click OK to save these modifications to the Dynamic Properties task.

Now that you have added these new tasks, you need to ensure that they execute in the proper order.

Specifying Step Execution Order in the *UpdateProductDim* Package

In the following procedure, you will configure the step that reads the properties from the initialization file to execute first, followed by the step that reads updated global variable values from the *PackageGVs* table, and then the step that updates the global variable values from the rowset global variable. You will configure the step that updates task properties from global variables to execute after these steps are complete, followed by the step that updates the *ProductStage* table. You will then configure the step that updates the *ProductDim* table. However, the *UpdateProductDim* package currently contains a step that calls a single Dynamic Properties task that reads the values from the Config.ini initialization file and updates task properties from global variable values. You must split these operations into two separate steps by placing them in two separate Dynamic Properties tasks that are called at different points in the package execution.

Ensure package steps execute in the proper order by configuring precedence constraints in the *UpdateProductDim* package

1   On the design sheet, delete the On Success constraint between the Properties From INI File step and the NewProductsSource connection object. (To delete it, highlight the constraint and then press Delete.)

2   On the design sheet, double-click the Properties From INI File step, click MaximumErrorCount in the Destination Property column, and then click Delete.

3   Click InsertCommitSize in the Destination Property column, click Delete, and then click OK to save the modified Dynamic Properties task.

   These two properties of the Transform Data task that load data into the *ProductStage* table must be dynamically configured in a separate Dynamic Properties task that is called later in the execution order.

4   On the Task menu, click Dynamic Properties Task, type **Properties From GVs** in the Description box, and then click Add.

5   In the left pane, expand Tasks and then click DTSTask_DTSDataPumpTask_1.

   This is the task called by the *Load ProductStage Table* step.

6   Select the Leave This Dialog Box Open After Adding A Setting check box.

7   In the right pane, double-click MaximumErrorCount, click Global Variable in the Source list, click giMaxErrorCount in the Variable list, and then click OK.

8   In the right pane, double-click InsertCommitSize, select Global Variable in the Source list, select giBatchSize in the Variable list, and then click OK.

9   Click Close and then click OK to save this Dynamic Properties task.

10 On the design sheet, click the Properties From INI File step, and then hold down the Ctrl key and click the PickupGVs step.

11 On the Workflow menu, click On Success.

12 On the design sheet, click the PickupGVs step, and then hold down the Ctrl key and click the SetGVs step.

13 On the Workflow menu, click On Success.

   ▶ **Tip**   At this point, you will probably want to rearrange the visual display of these tasks on the design sheet to represent the actual workflow.

14 On the design sheet, click the SetGVs step, and then hold down the Ctrl key and click the Properties From GVs step.

15 On the Workflow menu, click On Success.

16 On the design sheet, click the Properties From GVs step, and then hold down the Ctrl key and click the NewProductsSource connection object.

17 On the Workflow menu, click On Success.

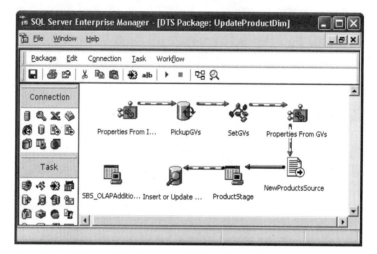

18 On the toolbar, click Save and then close the UpdateProductDim package in DTS Designer.

You have successfully configured the *UpdateProductDim* package to read global variable values from the *PackageGVs* table in SQL Server and update them in the package. Now you are ready to configure the *UpdateCustomerDim* package in the same manner.

Updating Global Variable Values in the *UpdateCustomerDim* Package from the Configuration Table

In the following procedures, you will create an Execute SQL task in the *Update-CustomerDim* package that will read the global variable configuration table at run time and store the rowset in a global variable. You will then create an ActiveX Script task in this package to read the stored rowset and update the package global variable values before executing the remaining tasks in the package.

Read the *PackageGVs* configuration table into a global variable in the *UpdateCustomerDim* package by creating an Execute SQL task

1   Switch to SQL Server Enterprise Manager, and then right-click Data Transformation Services in your local instance.

2   Click Open Package and then open the most recent version of the UpdateCustomerDim package in the C:\Microsoft Press\SQL DTS SBS\ DataMovementApplication folder using a password of **mypassword**.

3   On the Task menu, click Execute SQL Task.

4   Type **PickupGVs** in the Description box, select SBS_OLAPAdditionalConnection in the Existing Connection list, and then click Browse.

5   In the Look In list, navigate to C:\Microsoft Press\SQL DTS SBS\ Ch7\ ChapterFiles, and double-click PickupGVsUpdateCustomerDim.sql.

Based on a configuration ID, this script retrieves each *Update-CustomerDim* package global variable and its value from the *PackageGVs* table.

6   Click Parameters to create a global variable that will store the value for the configuration ID parameter and then map this global variable to the parameter in this query.

7   Click Create Global Variables on the Input Parameters tab, type **giConfigID** in the Name column, select Integer (1 byte) in the Type list, type **1** in the Value column, and then click OK.

8   Select giConfigID in the Input Global Variables list.

9   Click the Output Parameters tab.

10 Click Create Global Variables, type **goGVsPickedUp** in the Name column, select String in the Type column, and then click OK.

11 Click Rowset, select goGVsPickedUp in the global variables list, click OK to save the parameter mapping for the query, and then click OK to save the Execute SQL task.

You have just configured an Execute SQL task to retrieve global variable values from the *PackageGVs* table. Now you are ready to create an ActiveX Script task to read each of the records in the rowset stored in the global variable, and update the applicable global variables in the *UpdateCustomerDim* package.

Set global variable values in the *UpdateCustomerDim* package by creating an ActiveX Script task

1   On the Task menu, click ActiveX Script Task, and then type **SetGVs** in the Description box.

2   Click Browse, navigate to C:\Microsoft Press\SQL DTS SBS\ Ch7\ChapterFiles, and then double-click SetGVs.bas.

This code is identical to the code used in the *MasterUpdate* package because it performs exactly the same function in this package and the global variable holding the rowset has the same name in both packages.

3   Click OK.

Before configuring precedence constraints between these newly added steps, you will modify the *Properties From INI File* step to specify a dynamically configured exception file path for use by the *Load CustomerStage Table* step. Configuring a dynamic path for this exception file will enable you to specify a valid path if you move the data movement application. To do this, you must first add an entry in the Config.ini file to point to the location for this exception file.

Updating Exception File Location Information Dynamically for *UpdateCustomerDim* Package Tasks

In the following procedures, you will add exception file location information for the *Load CustomerStage Table* step to the Config.ini initialization file. You will then modify the *Properties From INI File* step to read this information and update the appropriate step before it is executed.

Add exception file location information to the Config.ini initialization file

1   Switch to the Config.ini file in Notepad.

2   On a new line at the end of the file, type **Load CustomerStage Table=C:\Microsoft Press\SQL DTS SBS\DataMovementApplication\ LoadCustomerStageTableExceptionFile.txt** and then click Save on the File menu.

Now that you have added this location entry to the Config.ini initialization file, you are ready to update the *Properties From INI File* step to use the entry to dynamically configure the *ExceptionFileName* property in the *Load Customer-Stage Table* step.

Read exception file locations from the Config.ini initialization file

1   Switch to the UpdateCustomerDim package in SQL Server Enterprise Manager.

2   On the design sheet, double-click the Properties From INI File step, and then click Add.

3   In the left pane, expand Tasks and then click DTSTask_DTSDataPumpTask_1.

   DTSTask_DTSDataPumpTask_1 is the name for the Transform Data task called by the *Load CustomerStage Table* step.

4   In the right pane, double-click ExceptionFileName, verify INI is selected in the Source list, type **C:\Microsoft Press\SQL DTS SBS\DataMovementApplication\Config.ini** in the File list, select ExceptionFiles in the Section list, select Load CustomerStage Table in the Key list, and then click OK.

5   Click OK to save these modifications to the Dynamic Properties task.

Now that you have added these new tasks, you need to ensure that they execute in the proper order.

Specifying Step Execution Order in the *UpdateCustomerDim* Package

In the following procedure, you will configure the step that reads the properties from the initialization file to execute first, followed by the step that reads updated global variable values from the *PackageGVs* table, and then the step that updates the global variable values from the rowset global variable. You will configure the step that updates task properties from global variables to execute after these steps complete, followed by the step that updates the *CustomerStage* table. In Chapter 8, you will add the steps that update and insert new data to the *CustomerDim* table. However, the *UpdateCustomerDim* package currently contains a step that calls a single Dynamic Properties task that reads the values from the Config.ini initialization file and updates task properties from global variable values. You must split these operations into two separate steps by placing them in two separate Dynamic Properties tasks that are called at different points in the package execution.

Ensure package steps execute in the proper order by configuring precedence constraints in the *UpdateCustomerDim* package

1   On the design sheet, delete the On Success constraint between the Properties From INI File step and the NewCustomersSource connection object.

2   On the design sheet, double-click the Properties From INI File step, click MaximumErrorCount in the Destination Property column, and then click Delete.

3   Click InsertCommitSize in the Destination Property column, click Delete, and then click OK to save the modified Dynamic Properties task.

These two properties of the Transform Data task that load data into the *CustomerStage* table must be dynamically configured in a separate Dynamic Properties task that is called later in the execution order.

4   On the Task menu, click Dynamic Properties Task, type **Properties From GVs** in the Description box, and then click Add.

5   Select the Leave This Dialog Box Open After Adding A Setting check box.

6   In the left pane, expand Tasks, and then click DTSTask_DTSDataPumpTask_1.

This is the task called by the *Load CustomertStage Table* step.

7   In the right pane, double-click MaximumErrorCount, click Global Variable in the Source list, click giMaxErrorCount in the Variable list, and then click OK.

8   In the right pane, double-click InsertCommitSize, select Global Variable in the Source list, select giBatchSize in the Variable list, and then click OK.

9   Click Close and then click OK to save this Dynamic Properties task.

10 On the design sheet, click the Properties From INI File step and then hold down the Ctrl key and click the PickUpGVs step.

11 On the Workflow menu, click On Success.

12 On the design sheet, click the PickupGVs step, and then hold down the Ctrl key and click the SetGVs step.

13 On the Workflow menu, click On Success.

▶ **Tip**   At this point, you will probably want to rearrange the visual display of these tasks on the design sheet to represent the actual workflow.

14 On the design sheet, click the SetGVs step, and then hold down the Ctrl key and click the Properties From GVs step.

15 On the Workflow menu, click On Success.

16 On the design sheet, click the Properties From GVs step, and then hold down the Ctrl key and click the NewCustomersSource connection object.

17 On the Workflow menu, click On Success.

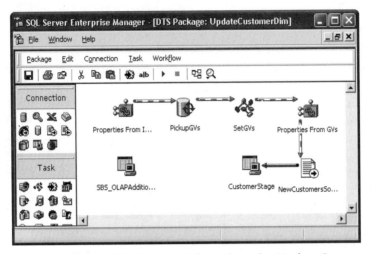

18 On the toolbar, click Save and then close the UpdateCustomerDim package in DTS Designer.

You have configured these three packages to enable them to dynamically retrieve and update task and package values at run time from a SQL table and from an initialization file. Now you are ready to test the execution of these packages with these new configuration steps.

Testing Configuration Table Configurations

In the following procedures, you will execute the *MasterUpdate* package and its subpackages from DTS Designer using the default *giConfigID* value. You will then create a DTSRun batch file that sets a different *giConfigID* value and then execute these packages using this batch file to verify that the new dynamic configuration steps work properly.

Execute the *MasterUpdate* package from DTS Designer

1   In SQL Server Enterprise Manager console tree, right-click Data Transformation Services in your local instance.

2   Click Open Package and then open the most recent version of the MasterUpdate package in the C:\Microsoft Press\SQL DTS SBS\ DataMovementApplication folder using a password of **mypassword**.

3   On the toolbar, click Execute.

One task fails.

4   Click OK and then double-click Call UpdateCustomerDim Subpackage in the Status window to verify the reason the task in the Update-CustomerDim subpackage failed.

The *UpdateCustomerDim* package that was called by the *Call UpdateCustomerDim Subpackage* step did not process all 29 rows; the number of failing rows exceeded the maximum number specified. This is because the *MasterUpdate* package was executed using the default configuration.

5   Click OK and then click Done.

6   Close the MasterUpdate package in DTS Designer.

Now that you have verified that the *MasterUpdate* package and its subpackages execute correctly while taking their settings from the Config.ini initialization file and the *PackageGVs* table, you are ready to create a DTSRun batch file to execute these packages using different configuration values.

Create and execute a DTSRun batch file

To execute the *MasterUpdate* package and its subpackages with different configuration values, you will create a batch file that will enable you to easily modify the value of the *giConfigID* global variable at run time, which in turn changes the values retrieved from the *PackageGVs* table by each package in the data movement application.

1   On the Windows Start menu, click Run, type **DTSRunUI** in the Open box, and then click OK.

2   In the Location list, select Structured Storage File, and then type **C:\Microsoft Press\SQL DTS SBS\DataMovementApplication\ MasterUpdate.dts** in the File Name box.

3   Click the ellipsis next to the Package Name text box, and then double-click MasterUpdate.

4 Click Advanced, type **mypassword** in the Password box, and then click OK.

5 Click the first row in the Name column, and then select giConfigID in the Name list.

6 Type **C:\Microsoft Press\SQL DTS SBS\DataMovementApplication\ MasterUpdateExecutionLog.txt** in the Log File text box.

7 Click Generate, and copy the generated DTSRun statement to the clipboard.

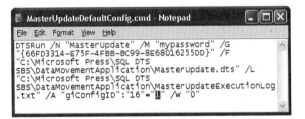

8 Click Cancel, and then click Cancel again.

9 Open Notepad, and then click Paste on the Edit menu. Notice that the value for the *giConfigID* variable is 1.

10 Click Save As on the File menu.

11 Navigate to C:\Microsoft Press\SQL DTS SBS\DataMovementApplication in the Save In list, type **MasterUpdateDefaultConfig.cmd** in the File Name box, select All Files in the Save As Type box, and then click Save. Do not close Notepad.

12 Using Windows Explorer, navigate to the C:\Microsoft Press\SQL
DTS SBS\DataMovementApplication folder and then double-click
MasterUpdateDefaultConfig.cmd.

The *MasterUpdate* package executes. To verify the tasks and packages that executed, you need to look at the log files for each package.

13 In the C:\Microsoft Press\SQL DTS SBS\DataMovementApplication
folder, double-click the MasterUpdateExecutionLog.txt file.

Notice that this log indicates that each task in the *MasterUpdate*
package succeeded. However, this log file does not tell you anything
about the success or failure of individual tasks in the subpackages.
Remember that by default the failure of a task in a package does not
cause the package to fail. To determine the success or failure of each
task in a subpackage, you must look at the log for each subpackage.

14 Close the MasterUpdateExecutionLog.txt file in Notepad and then
double-click the LoadCustomerStageTableExceptionFile.txt file in
the C:\Microsoft Press\SQL DTS SBS\DataMovementApplication
folder.

15 Scroll down in this file to the most recent execution of the Update-
CustomerDim package.

Notice that one error row was encountered in this task. However,
you cannot tell from this error log whether this error caused the task
to terminate or continue until a specific number of errors were
encountered (unless you happen to know that the source file also
contained an error in row 14, which was not processed). This log file
is the error log for the Transform Data task called by the *Load
CustomerStage Table* step, not an error log for the *UpdateCustomer-
Dim* package.

```
LoadCustomerStageTableExceptionFile.txt - Notepad
File  Edit  Format  View  Help
****************************************************************
****************************

Execution Started: 6/12/2003 10:13:39 AM

@@LogSourceRows: C:\Microsoft Press\SQL DTS
SBS\DataMovementApplication\LoadCustomerStageTableExceptionFile.txt.Source
@@LogDestRows: C:\Microsoft Press\SQL DTS
SBS\DataMovementApplication\LoadCustomerStageTableExceptionFile.txt.Dest

@@ErrorRow:  6
Error at Destination for Row number 6. Errors encountered so far in this
task: 1.

Error Source: Microsoft Data Transformation Services (DTS) Data Pump
Error Description:Insert error, column 1 ('CustomerCode', DBTYPE_WSTR),
status 10:  Integrity violation; attempt to insert NULL data or data which
violates constraints.
Error Help File:sqldts80.hlp
Error Help Context ID:30702

Error Source: Microsoft OLE DB Provider for SQL Server
Error Description:unspecified error
Error Help File:
Error Help Context ID:0
@@SourceRow:  Logged
@@DestRow:  Logged

@@ExecutionCompleted

Execution Completed: 6/12/2003 10:13:39 AM

****************************************************************
****************************
```

16 Close the LoadCustomerStageTableExceptionFile.txt file in Notepad.

You have successfully enabled the packages in the data movement application
to be updated at run time from a SQL Server configuration table.

Adding Package Logging and Error Handling Steps to Packages

To enable you to detect the success or failure of the individual tasks in each
subpackage when you execute the data movement application from a
DTSRun batch file, you need to configure logging and error handling in each
package in the data movement application. Only the *PopulateTimeDim* and

LoadHistoricalData packages have been enabled for package logging and error handling.

▶ **Note**   You cannot enable package logging for subpackages called from a master package by using the /L switch in the DTSRun command. You must enable logging in each subpackage. For more information, see Chapter 3.

In the following procedure, you will enable package logging and error handling in the *MasterUpdate* package. You will enable the locations of the error log files for each package in the data movement application to be configured dynamically by adding entries to the Config.ini initialization file and then configuring the *Properties From INI File* step in the *MasterUpdate*, *UpdateProductDim*, and *UpdateCustomerDim* packages to read the appropriate value from the initialization file and update the *LogFileName* property in each package. Finally, you will test the execution of these packages with different configuration values and review the generated error log files.

Enable package logging and error handling in the *MasterUpdate* package

1   Switch to SQL Server Enterprise Manager, and then right-click Data Transformation Services in your local instance.

2   Click Open Package and then open the most recent version of the MasterUpdate package in the C:\Microsoft Press\SQL DTS SBS\ DataMovementApplication folder using a password of **mypassword**.

3   On the Package menu, click Properties.

4   On the Logging tab, select the Log Package Execution To SQL Server check box, verify that (local) appears in the Server list box, and then verify that Use Windows Authentication is selected.

5   In the Error File text box, type **C:\Microsoft Press\SQL DTS SBS\ DataMovementApplication\MasterUpdatePackageErrorLog.txt**, and then click OK.

6   Switch to the Config.ini initialization file in Notepad.

7   On a new line at the end of the file, type **[ErrorHandlingFileNames]** and then press Enter.

8   Type **MasterUpdatePackage=C:\Microsoft Press\SQL DTS SBS\ DataMovementApplication\MasterUpdatePackageErrorLog.txt** and then press Enter.

9   On the new line, type **UpdateCustomerDimPackage= C:\Microsoft Press\SQL DTS SBS\DataMovementApplication\ UpdateCustomerDimPackageErrorLog.txt** and then press Enter.

10 On the new line, type **UpdateProductDimPackage=
C:\Microsoft Press\SQL DTS SBS\DataMovementApplication\
UpdateProductDimPackageErrorLog.txt** and then click Save on the
File menu.

11 Close the Config.ini file in Notepad and switch to the MasterUpdate
package in SQL Server Enterprise Manager.

Now that you have a location entry for the error handling file used
by the *MasterUpdate* package, you are ready to dynamically configure the *LogFileName* property in this package.

12 On the design sheet, double-click the Properties From INI File step
and then click Add.

13 Click MasterUpdate in the left pane, and then double-click LogFile-
Name in the right pane.

14 Verify INI is selected in the Source list, type **C:\Microsoft Press\SQL
DTS SBS\DataMovementApplication\Config.ini** in the File list,
select ErrorHandlingFileNames in the Section list, select MasterUpdatePackage in the Key list, click OK, and then click OK again to
save the modification to the Dynamic Properties task.

15 On the toolbar, click Save, and then close the MasterUpdate package.

Now that you have enabled package logging and error handling in the *Master-
Update* package, you need to do the same in the *UpdateCustomerDim* and
UpdateProductDim packages.

Enable package logging and error handling in the *UpdateCustomerDim* package

1 In the SQL Server Enterprise Manager console tree, right-click Data
Transformation Services in your local instance.

2 Click Open Package and then open the most recent version of the
UpdateCustomerDim package in the C:\Microsoft Press\SQL DTS
SBS\DataMovementApplication folder using a password of
mypassword.

3 On the Package menu, click Properties.

4 On the Logging tab, select the Log Package Execution To SQL Server
check box, verify that (local) appears in the Server list box, and then
verify that Use Windows Authentication is selected.

5   In the Error File text box, type **C:\Microsoft Press\SQL DTS SBS\ DataMovementApplication\UpdateCustomerDimPackageErrorLog.txt** box, and then click OK.

6   On the design sheet, double-click the Properties From INI File step and then click Add.

7   Click UpdateCustomerDim in the left pane, and then double-click LogFileName in the right pane.

8   Verify that INI is selected in the Source list, type **C:\Microsoft Press\SQL DTS SBS\DataMovementApplication\Config.ini** in the File list, select ErrorHandlingFileNames in the Section list, select UpdateCustomerDimPackage in the Key list, click OK, and then click OK again to save the modification to the Dynamic Properties task.

9   On the toolbar, click Save and then close the UpdateCustomerDim package.

Now that you have enabled package logging and error handling in the *Master-Update* and *UpdateCustomerDim* packages, you need to do the same in the *UpdateProductDim* package.

Enable package logging and error handling in the *UpdateProductDim* package

1   In the SQL Server Enterprise Manager console tree, right-click Data Transformation Services in your local instance.

2   Click Open Package and then open the most recent version of the UpdateProductDim package in the C:\Microsoft Press\SQL DTS SBS\ DataMovementApplication folder using a password of **mypassword**.

3   On the Package menu, click Properties.

4   On the Logging tab, select the Log Package Execution To SQL Server check box, verify that (local) appears in the Server list box, and then verify that Use Windows Authentication is selected.

5   In the Error File text box, type **C:\Microsoft Press\SQL DTS SBS\ DataMovementApplication\UpdateProductDimPackageErrorLog.txt,** and then click OK.

6   On the design sheet, double-click the Properties From INI File step and then click Add.

7 Click UpdateProductDim in the left pane, and then double-click Log-FileName in the right pane.

8 Verify that INI is selected in the Source list, type **C:\Microsoft Press\SQL DTS SBS\DataMovementApplication\Config.ini** in the File list, select ErrorHandlingFileNames in the Section list, select UpdateProductDimPackage in the Key list, click OK, and then click OK again to save the modification to the Dynamic Properties task.

9 On the toolbar, click Save and then close the UpdateProductDim package.

Now that you have enabled package logging and error handling in the *Master-Update*, *UpdateCustomerDim*, and *UpdateProductDim* packages, you are ready to test the DTSRun batch file with different configuration ID values.

Execute the DTSRun batch file with different configuration values

1 Using Windows Explorer, navigate to the C:\Microsoft Press\SQL DTS SBS\DataMovementApplication folder and then double-click MasterUpdateDefaultConfig.cmd.

After this batch file finishes executing, notice that the MasterUpdatePackageErrorLog.txt, UpdateProductDimPackageErrorLog.txt, and UpdateCustomerDimPackageErrorLog.txt files appear in the DataMovementApplication folder in Windows Explorer.

2 Double-click UpdateCustomerDimPackageErrorLog.txt in the C:\Microsoft Press\SQL DTS SBS\DataMovementApplication folder. Notice that the *DTSStep_DTSDataPumpTask_1* failed to copy any rows because the number of rows specified exceeded the maximum number specified. The *giConfigID* global variable has a value of 1, and no rows are added to the *CustomerDim* table because the *MaximumErrorCount* property is set to zero.

> ▶ **Tip** The step names that appear in these log files are the generated step names, not the user-friendly step names. Later in this chapter, you will learn how to change these generated step names to user-friendly step names to make it easier to interpret these log files.

```
UpdateCustomerDimPackageErrorLog.txt - Notepad
File  Edit  Format  View  Help
The execution of the following DTS Package succeeded:

Package Name: UpdateCustomerDim
Package Description: (null)
Package ID: {9B11616F-9037-4D60-9593-21AFACFDA123}
Package Version: {D4F77C80-64F5-4F89-ADDE-E1A249041206}
Package Execution Lineage: {4B0E7380-E322-452D-B6F3-AD365E3E006B}
Executed On: NETSYS1LPTP2
Executed By: Carl
Execution Started: 6/12/2003 11:15:14 AM
Execution Completed: 6/12/2003 11:15:15 AM
Total Execution Time: 0.931 seconds

Package Steps execution information:

Step 'DTSStep_DTSDataPumpTask_1' failed

Step Error Source: Microsoft Data Transformation Services (DTS) Data Pump
Step Error Description:The number of failing rows exceeds the maximum specified.
Step Error code: 8004206A
Step Error Help File:sqldts80.hlp
Step Error Help Context ID:0

Step Execution Started: 6/12/2003 11:15:14 AM
Step Execution Completed: 6/12/2003 11:15:14 AM
Total Step Execution Time: 0.391 seconds
Progress count in Step: 0

Step 'DTSStep_DTSDynamicPropertiesTask_1' succeeded
Step Execution Started: 6/12/2003 11:15:14 AM
Step Execution Completed: 6/12/2003 11:15:14 AM
Total Step Execution Time: 0.03 seconds
Progress count in Step: 0

Step 'DTSStep_DTSExecuteSQLTask_1' succeeded
Step Execution Started: 6/12/2003 11:15:14 AM
Step Execution Completed: 6/12/2003 11:15:14 AM
Total Step Execution Time: 0.16 seconds
Progress count in Step: 0

Step 'DTSStep_DTSActiveScriptTask_1' succeeded
Step Execution Started: 6/12/2003 11:15:14 AM
Step Execution Completed: 6/12/2003 11:15:14 AM
Total Step Execution Time: 0.02 seconds
Progress count in Step: 0

Step 'DTSStep_DTSDynamicPropertiesTask_2' succeeded
Step Execution Started: 6/12/2003 11:15:14 AM
Step Execution Completed: 6/12/2003 11:15:14 AM
Total Step Execution Time: 0.02 seconds
Progress count in Step: 0
************************************************************
```

3 Close the UpdateCustomerDimPackageErrorLog.txt file in Notepad.

4 Switch to the MasterUpdateDefaultConfig.cmd file in Notepad.

5 Change the value for the giConfigID global variable from 1 to **2** (the value of 16 immediately after giConfigID indicates the type of the parameter—integer (1 byte)), and then click Save As on the File menu.

6 In the File Name box, change the file name to **MasterUpdateConfig2.cmd**, select All Files in the Save As Type list, and then click Save.

7 Close the MasterUpdateConfig2.cmd file in Notepad.

8 In the DataMovementApplication folder, double-click MasterUpdateConfig2.cmd to execute the MasterUpdate package and its subpackages with the global variable values associated with configuration ID 2.

9 After the batch file completes, double-click the UpdateCustomer-DimPackageErrorLog.txt file in the DataMovementApplication folder. Scroll down to the end of the file to see the logging information for the most recent execution (package execution appends new logging data to the file).

The *MasterUpdate* package and its subpackages executed using the global variable values associated with the *ConfigID* value of 2 in the *PackageGVs* table. This resulted in the *MaximumErrorCount* property being set to 5 for the *UpdateCustomerDim* package and all 29 rows being processed because there were only two errors in the source file. Notice, however, that there is no way to tell from this error log that two rows were not inserted.

> ▶ **Tip**   To determine if any rows were not inserted by a Transform Data task or a Data Driven Query task if the number of rows failing did not exceed the value for the *MaximumErrorCount* property for the task, you must look at the exception file for each Transform Data and Data Driven Query task in the package. In Chapter 8, you will learn some additional error handling routines to simplify the task of tracking package and task errors in a single location.

10   Close the UpdateCustomerDimPackageErrorLog.txt file in Notepad and then open the LoadCustomerStageTableExceptionFile.txt file in the DataMovementAppplication folder.

The LoadCustomerStageTableExceptionFile.txt file contains the error information for each of the rows that failed. To determine the

actual error rows, you can look at the LoadCustomerStageTable-
ExceptionFile.txt.Source file, which contains the source row that
caused the error, and the LoadCustomerStageTableException-
File.txt.Dest file, which contains the transformed row that DTS
attempted to insert into the *CustomerStage* table.

> ▶ **Tip**   Since logging to SQL Server was enabled for the *MasterUpdate*
> package and its subpackages, you could also view the package log for
> each package using SQL Server Enterprise Manager (right-click Local
> Packages in the Data Transformation Services nodes and then click Pack-
> age Logs). However, the only way to capture the actual rows that failed is
> to configure exception files for each Transform Data and Data Driven
> Query task.

11 Close the LoadCustomerStageTableExceptionFile.txt file in Notepad.

You have successfully configured the packages in the data movement application and their tasks to be dynamically configured using values in an initialization file and a SQL table.

Reading Registry Values for Path Locations

The path to the initialization file is hard coded in each Dynamic Properties task in each package in the data movement application. If you want to move the data movement application files to any folder structure other than C:\Microsoft Press\SQL DTS SBS\DataMovementApplication, the packages in the data movement application will not be able to locate the initialization file and they will fail. A Windows application generally stores its installation path in the Windows registry and retrieves that information during execution from a known location in the registry.

Adding a Registry Entry

In the following procedure, you will add a subkey to the Windows registry that contains the location of the Config.ini initialization file. In subsequent procedures, you will configure the *MasterUpdate*, *UpdateProductDim*, and *UpdateCustomerDim* packages to read this subkey value before executing any other steps. This will enable you to move the location of the Config.ini initialization file to another folder, or rename that Config.ini file if necessary.

Add a subkey to the Windows registry that contains the location of the Config.ini initialization file

1 Using Windows Explorer, navigate to C:\Microsoft Press\SQL DTS SBS\Ch7\ChapterFiles.

2 Right-click DMA.reg, and then click Edit to view this text file.

   This text file creates the *ConfigFile* subkey containing the full path to the initialization file, as well as the *BuildNumber* and *BuildDate* subkeys.

3 Close Notepad, double-click DMA.reg, click Yes to confirm that you want to add the information in this reg file to the Windows registry, and then click OK.

Now that you have recorded the location for the Config.ini file in the Windows registry, you are ready to add a global variable to the *MasterUpdate* package to store this value and then create an ActiveX Script task that reads the *ConfigFile* subkey value into this global variable.

Updating the Dynamic Properties Task in the *MasterUpdate* Package with a Registry Key Value

In the following procedures, you will create an ActiveX Script task in the *MasterUpdate* package that reads the path to the Config.ini initialization file from the subkey you added to in the Windows registry into a global variable. You will then create another ActiveX Script task in this package that updates the Config.ini initialization file location information stored in *DTSTask_DTSDynamicPropertiesTask_1* task (the task called by the *Properties From INI File* step). You will then ensure that these new steps execute before any other steps in this package.

Read the *ConfigFile* registry key value into a global variable in the *MasterUpdate* package by creating an ActiveX Script task

1 Switch to SQL Server Enterprise Manager, and then right-click Data Transformation Services in your local instance.

2 Click Open Package and then open the most recent version of the MasterUpdate package in the C:\Microsoft Press\SQL DTS SBS\ DataMovementApplication folder using a password of **mypassword**.

3 Click Properties on the Package menu, and then click the Global Variables tab.

4 In the first empty line in the Name column, type **gsConfigINIPath**, select String in the Type column, and then click OK.

5 On the Task menu, click ActiveX Script Task, type **Set GV From Registry** in the Description box, click Browse, navigate to C:\Microsoft Press\SQL DTS SBS\Ch7\ChapterFiles, and then double-click ReadINIFromRegistry.bas.

This script begins by declaring a variable to hold the *WScript* object and then sets this variable to an instance of the *WScript* object. This script then declares an additional variable and retrieves the value of the *ConfigFile* subkey from the Windows registry into this variable. This script then sets the value of the *gsConfigINIPath* global variable in the package to the value retrieved from the Windows registry.

6 Click OK to save this ActiveX Script task.

Now that you have updated the value of the *gsConfigINIPath* global variable in the *MasterUpdate* package from the *ConfigFile* subkey, you will create an ActiveX Script task that updates the path the *Properties From INI File* step uses to locate the Config.ini file.

Set the INI file location from the global variable value in the *MasterUpdate* package by creating an ActiveX Script task

1 On the Task menu, click ActiveX Script Task, type **Set INI Location From GV**, click Browse, navigate to C:\Microsoft Press\SQL DTS SBS\Ch7\ChapterFiles, and then double-click SetINIFromGV.bas.

This script begins by declaring a variable and then populating the variable with the value of the *gsConfigINIPath* global variable stored in the package. This script then declares an additional variable and places a reference to the package into this variable. Next the script declares two additional variables, one to hold the task assignments collection from the package and one for each assignment in the package. This script uses a For Each loop to locate each reference to the Config.ini file in the *DTSTask_DTSDynamicPropertiesTask_1* task (the task called by the *Properties From INI File* step) and sets its value to the value of the *gsConfigINIPath* global variable retrieved from the package.

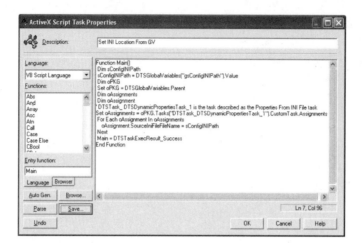

2   Click OK to save this ActiveX Script task.

You have configured a step in the *MasterUpdate* package that reads the Config.ini path from the registry into a global variable and a step that updates the *Properties From INI File* task with this value. Now you must configure the precedence constraints so that these two steps execute before any other steps in this package.

Ensure package steps execute in the proper order by configuring precedence constraints in the *MasterUpdate* package

1   On the design sheet, click the Set GV From Registry step, and then hold down the Ctrl key and click the Set INI Location From GV step.

2   On the Workflow menu, click On Success.

3   On the design sheet, click the Set INI Location From GV step, and then hold down the Ctrl key and click the Properties From INI File step.

4   On the Workflow menu, click On Success.

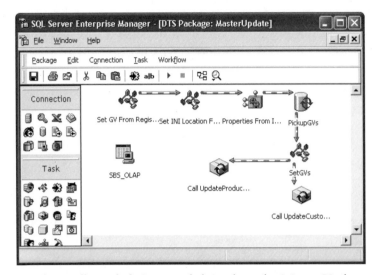

5   On the toolbar, click Save and then close the MasterUpdate package
    in DTS Designer.

You have now successfully modified each component of the *MasterUpdate*
package that relied on a hard-coded path within the package. Next you must
configure the subpackages called by the Execute Package tasks in the *Master-
Update* package to read the location of the Config.ini file from the registry as
well. If you do not, when you move the files in the data movement application,
these packages will fail when they attempt to read the Config.ini file from the
hard-coded location rather than the updated location in the initialization file
specified in the registry.

Updating the Dynamic Properties Task in the *UpdateCustomerDim* Package with a Registry Key Value

In the following procedures, you will create an ActiveX Script task in the
UpdateCustomerDim package that reads the path to the Config.ini initialization file from the subkey you added to in the Windows registry into a global
variable. You will then create another ActiveX Script task in this package that
updates the Config.ini initialization file location information stored in
DTSTask_DTSDynamicPropertiesTask_1 task (the task called by the *Properties
From INI File* step). You will then ensure that these new steps execute before
any other steps in this package.

Read the *ConfigFile* registry key value into a global variable in the *UpdateCustomerDim* package by creating an ActiveX Script task

1   In the SQL Server Enterprise Manager console tree, right-click Data Transformation Services in your local instance.

2   Click Open Package and then open the most recent version of the UpdateCustomerDim package in the C:\Microsoft Press\SQL DTS SBS\ DataMovementApplication folder using a password of **mypassword.**

3   Click Properties on the Package menu, and then click the Global Variables tab.

4   In the first empty line in the Name column, type **gsConfigINIPath,** select String in the Type column, and then click OK.

5   On the Task menu, click ActiveX Script Task, type **Set GV From Registry** in the Description box, click Browse, navigate to C:\Microsoft Press\SQL DTS SBS\Ch7\ChapterFiles, and then double-click ReadINIFromRegistry.bas.

    This code is identical to the code used in the *MasterUpdate* package because it performs exactly the same function in this package.

6   Click OK to save this ActiveX Script task.

Now that you have updated the value of the *gsConfigINIPath* global variable in the *UpdateCustomerDim* package from the *ConfigFile* subkey, you will create an ActiveX Script task that updates the path that the *Properties From INI File* step uses to locate the Config.ini file.

Set the INI File location from the global variable value in the *UpdateCustomerDim* package by creating an ActiveX Script task

1   On the Task menu, click ActiveX Script Task, type **Set INI Location From GV**, click Browse, navigate to C:\Microsoft Press\SQL DTS SBS\Ch7\ChapterFiles, and then double-click SetINIFromGV.bas.

    This code is identical to the code used in the *MasterUpdate* package because it performs exactly the same function in this package.

2   Click OK to save this ActiveX Script task.

You have configured a step in *UpdateCustomerDim* package that reads the Config.ini path from the registry into a global variable and a step that updates the *Properties From INI File* task with this value. Now you must configure the precedence constraints so that these two steps execute before any other steps in this package.

Ensure package steps execute in the proper order by configuring precedence constraints in the *UpdateCustomerDim* package

1   On the design sheet, click the Set GV From Registry step, and then hold down the Ctrl key and click the Set INI Location From GV step.

2   On the Workflow menu, click On Success.

3   On the design sheet, click the Set INI Location From GV step, and then hold down the Ctrl key and click the Properties From INI File step.

4   On the Workflow menu, click On Success.

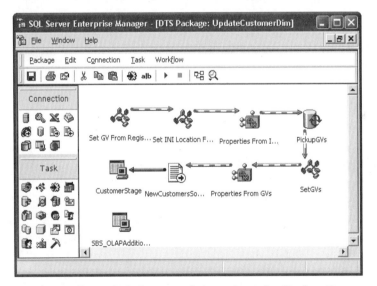

5   On the toolbar, click Save, and then close the UpdateCustomerDim package in DTS Designer.

Now that you have configured the *MasterUpdate* and *UpdateCustomerDim* packages to dynamically update the *Properties From INI File* step with the location of the Config.ini file from the registry, you need to update the *Properties From INI File* step in the *UpdateProductDim* package in the same fashion.

Updating the Dynamic Properties Task in the *UpdateProductDim* Package with a Registry Key Value

In the following procedures, you will create an ActiveX Script task in the *UpdateProductDim* package that reads the path to the Config.ini initialization file from the subkey you added to in the Windows registry into a global variable. You will then create another ActiveX Script task in this package that updates the Config.ini initialization file location information stored in *DTSTask_DTSDynamicPropertiesTask_1* task (the task called by the *Properties From INI File* step). You will then ensure that these new steps execute before any other steps in this package.

Read the *ConfigFile* registry key value into a global variable in the *UpdateProductDim* package by creating an ActiveX Script task

1   In the SQL Server Enterprise Manager console tree, right-click Data Transformation Services in your local instance.

2   Click Open Package and then open the most recent version of the UpdateProductDim package in the C:\Microsoft Press\SQL DTS SBS\ DataMovementApplication folder using a password of **mypassword**.

3   Click Properties on the Package menu, and then click the Global Variables tab.

4   In the first empty line in the Name column, type **gsConfigINIPath**, select String in the Type column, and then click OK.

5   On the Task menu, click ActiveX Script Task, type **Set GV From Registry** in the Description box, click Browse, navigate to C:\Microsoft Press\SQL DTS SBS\Ch7\ChapterFiles, and then double-click ReadINIFromRegistry.bas.

   This code is identical to the code used in the *MasterUpdate* and *UpdateCustomerDim* packages because it performs exactly the same function in this package.

6   Click OK to save this ActiveX Script task.

Now that you have updated the value of the *gsConfigINIPath* global variable in the *UpdateProductDim* package from the *ConfigFile* subkey, you will create an ActiveX Script task that updates the path the *Properties From INI File* step uses to locate the Config.ini file.

Set the INI file location from the global variable value in the *UpdateProductDim* package by creating an ActiveX Script task

1 On the Task menu, click ActiveX Script Task, type **Set INI Location From GV**, click Browse, navigate to C:\Microsoft Press\SQL DTS SBS\Ch7\ChapterFiles, and then double-click SetINIFromGV.bas.

This code is identical to the code used in the *MasterUpdate* and *UpdateCustomerDim* packages because it performs exactly the same function in this package.

2 Click OK to save this ActiveX Script task.

You have configured a step in the *UpdateProductDim* package that reads the Config.ini path from the registry into a global variable and a step that updates the *Properties From INI File* task with this value. Now you must configure the precedence constraints so that these two steps execute before any other steps in this package.

Ensure package steps execute in the proper order by configuring precedence constraints in the *UpdateProductDim* package

1 On the design sheet, click the Set GV From Registry step, and then hold down the Ctrl key and click the Set INI Location From GV step.

2 On the Workflow menu, click On Success.

3 On the design sheet, click the Set INI Location From GV step, and then hold down the Ctrl key and click the Properties From INI File step.

4 On the Workflow menu, click On Success.

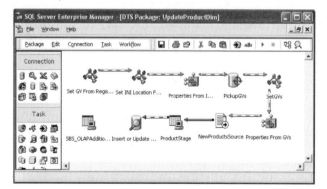

5 On the toolbar, click Save, and then close the UpdateProductDim package in DTS Designer.

Now that you have configured the *MasterUpdate*, *UpdateCustomerDim*, and *UpdateProductDim* packages to dynamically update package and task properties from the registry, an initialization file, and a SQL table, you are ready to test the execution of your packages from a different folder location.

Executing the Data Movement Application Packages from a New Folder Location

In the following procedure, you will copy all of the files required by the data movement application packages to a new folder structure to ensure that you have no hard-coded paths in any of the packages in the data movement application. To ensure the test is valid, you will rename the current data movement application folder in the file system and then execute the packages from the new folder structure.

Copy the data movement application to a new folder and then execute it

1   Using Windows Explorer, create the **DMA2** folder in the C:\Microsoft Press\SQL DTS SBS folder.

2   Using Windows Explorer, copy all the files in the C:\Microsoft Press\SQL DTS SBS\DataMovementApplication folder to the C:\Microsoft Press\SQL DTS SBS\DMA2 folder.

3   On the Windows Start menu, click Run, type **Regedt32** in the Open box, and then click OK.

4   In the Windows registry, navigate to HKEY_LOCAL_MACHINE\SOFTWARE\Microsoft\SQL DTS SBS in the left pane and then double-click ConfigFile in the right pane.

5   In the Value Data box, change the value to **C:\Microsoft Press\SQL DTS SBS\DMA2\Config.ini** and then click OK. Do not close the Registry Editor.

6   Using Windows Explorer, navigate to C:\Microsoft Press\SQL DTS SBS\DMA2 and then double-click Config.ini.

Notice that all references in the Config.ini initialization file refer to the C:\Microsoft Press\SQL DTS SBS\DataMovementApplication folder. To test your ability to move the data movement application, you need to change these references to the C:\Microsoft Press\SQL DTS SBS\DMA2 folder.

7   On the Edit menu, click Replace.

8 Type **DataMovementApplication** in the Find What box, type **DMA2** in the Replace With box, and then click Replace All.

9 Click Cancel, click Save on the File menu, and then close Notepad.

Now that you have changed these references in the initialization file, you will change the name of the original DataMovementApplication folder to ensure that the data movement application files in the DMA2 folder cannot access any of the files that were previously used.

10 Using Windows Explorer, rename the DataMovementApplication folder to **DataMovementApplication2**.

11 Switch to SQL Server Enterprise Manager, and then right-click Data Transformation Services in your local instance.

12 Click Open Package and then open the most recent version of the MasterUpdate package in the C:\Microsoft Press\SQL DTS SBS\DMA2 folder using a password of **mypassword**.

13 On the toolbar, click Execute.

One task in one of the subpackages fails.

14 Click OK.

Notice that the error occurred in the *UpdateCustomerDim* package.

15 Double-click Call UpdateCustomerDim Subpackage in the Status window to verify that a task in this subpackage failed because the number of failing rows exceeded the maximum specified. (If it fails for any other reason, you have made an error on one of the configuration steps.)

16 Click OK and then click Done.

17 Close the MasterUpdate package.

18 Switch to the Registry Editor and then change the value of the ConfigFile key to **C:\Microsoft Press\SQL DTS SBS\ DataMovementApplication\Config.ini** and then close the Registry Editor.

19 Using Windows Explorer, rename the DataMovementApplication2 folder to **DataMovementApplication**.

Your data movement application is now portable. Next you will learn how to create multiple branches in your application's packages using ActiveX Script tasks.

Enabling Package Branching

You can add different tasks for different situations in the same package and then use an ActiveX Script task to evaluate one or more global variable values at execution time to determine which of the tasks in a package should be called for a particular execution of the package. For example, sometimes you might want to have a package that normally adds new data to a staging table, delete data that has already been copied into the dimension tables before new data is added to the staging table. In a data warehouse environment, updates to the data in the dimension and fact tables are generally processed on a regular schedule (such as weekly) into the dimension and fact tables for the multidimensional cube. However, for a variety of reasons, you may want to add data to one or more staging tables incrementally during each week. In such a case, you will want to incrementally add data to the staging table until the weekly processing occurs. After you have updated the fact and dimension tables and processed their dimensions and partitions as appropriate (and ensured the data is processed successfully), you need to delete the data in the staging tables before you add any new data for the next week (to avoid adding duplicate data). Although you could create a new package associated with each staging table just for this delete task, you can also simply add a branch to each existing update package to perform the delete task. Reusing existing packages enables you to reuse the existing dynamic logic, use the same package names and GUIDs, and use the same DTSRun batch files. You can simply specify at run time whether the update branch or the delete branch of each package is executed by using a configuration ID. The package will use the configuration ID to retrieve appropriate global variable values from the global variable configuration SQL table to call the appropriate tasks for the delete branch of the package.

In addition, you might want to include an option in each package that enables you to bypass a package for a particular execution of the data movement application. For example, suppose you wanted to add data to only one particular dimension table. In the data movement application, a subpackage is created for each dimension table, and each time the data movement application is executed, the master package executes all of these subpackages. By adding a bypass branch to each subpackage, you can call the bypass branches of the appropriate subpackages. This enables you to control which subpackages actually add data and which ones simply log the fact that they were bypassed for a particular execution of the data movement application.

Adding a Branching Variable to the *MasterUpdate* Package

In the following procedure, you will create a global variable in the *Master-Update* package with a default value of 0 and pass this global variable to each subpackage. An ActiveX Script task in each subpackage will use this global variable to determine whether to execute the default workflow or a delete branch that you will add to each of these subpackages.

Add the *DeleteOrAdd* global variable to the *MasterUpdate* package and pass it to subpackages by editing the Execute Package tasks

1. Switch to SQL Server Enterprise Manager, and then right-click Data Transformation Services in your local instance.

2. Click Open Package and then open the most recent version of the MasterUpdate package in the C:\Microsoft Press\SQL DTS SBS\ DataMovementApplication folder using a password of **mypassword**.

3. Click Properties on the Package menu, and then click the Global Variables tab.

4. In the first empty line in the Name column, type **gbDeleteOrAdd**, select Boolean in the Type list, type 0 in the Value list, and then click OK.

   The value for this global variable will be passed to each subpackage and used to determine whether to execute the update or delete branch in each subpackage. You can change the value of this global variable at run time by placing a different value for it in the *Package-GVs* table and associating that value with the configuration ID that you pass when you execute the *MasterUpdate* package. The value for this variable will govern the execution flow in each subpackage unless a different value is specified in the *PackageGVs* table for a particular subpackage.

5. On the design sheet, double-click the Call UpdateProductDim Sub-package step, and then click the Outer Package Global Variables tab.

6. In the first empty line in the Names list, click gbDeleteOrAdd in the Variables list and then click OK.

7. On the design sheet, double-click the Call UpdateCustomerDim Sub-package step, and then click the Outer Package Global Variables tab.

8. In the first empty line in the Names list, click gbDeleteOrAdd in the Variables list and then click OK.

9. On the toolbar, click Save and then close the MasterUpdate package in DTS Designer.

Now that you have added this bypass package global variable to the *Master-Update* package and passed its value to each subpackage, you are ready to use this variable in each subpackage. You did not add a bypass package global variable to the *MasterUpdate* package because that package will always be executed.

Adding Branching Steps to the *UpdateCustomerDim* Package

In the following procedures, you will create the *gbDeleteOrAdd*, the *gbBypass-Package*, and the *gbBypassLoadDimensionTable* global variables in the *UpdateCustomerDim* package. You will then create a delete or add staging data step and a bypass package step in this package. (When you add a dimension table loading step to the *UpdateProductDim* package in Chapter 8, you will also add a bypass load dimension table step to that subpackage.) You will create ActiveX Script tasks in this package to read these variable values and determine the appropriate steps in the workflow based on the values of the these global variables. By default, the package bypass step will simply call the next step in the package unless the value of the bypass global variable is changed from 0 to 1. If it is changed to 1, the package bypass step will call a logging step that will log the fact that the remaining steps in the package were bypassed. By default, the delete or add staging data step will simply call the load staging table step unless the value of the delete or add global variable is changed from 0 to 1. If it is changed to 1, the delete or add staging data step will call a delete staging data step, which in turn will call a logging step that will log the fact that the delete staging data step executed.

Add branching global variables to the *UpdateCustomerDim* package

1 In the SQL Server Enterprise Manager console tree, right-click Data Transformation Services in your local instance.

2 Click Open Package and then open the most recent version of the UpdateCustomerDim package in the C:\Microsoft Press\SQL DTS SBS\DataMovementApplication folder using a password of **mypassword**.

3 Click Properties on the Package menu, and then click the Global Variables tab.

4 In the first empty line in the Name column, type **gbDeleteOrAdd**, select Boolean in the Type list, and then type 0 in the Value list.

   This global variable with a default value of 0 will indicate that new data will be added to the *CustomerStage* table from the data source. A value of 1 will indicate that all existing data in this table will be deleted. This value is passed from the *MasterUpdate* package, but it might be overwritten by a value retrieved from the *PackageGVs* table for this package.

5 In the next empty line in the Name column, type **gbBypassPackage**, select Boolean in the Type list, and then type 0 in the Value list.

This global variable with a default value of 0 will indicate that the tasks in this package after the branching step will be executed for a particular execution of the data movement application. A value of 1 will indicate that the tasks in this package after the branching step should not be executed for a particular execution of the data movement application. A value for this global variable in the *PackageGVs* table for this package will override the default value.

6 In the next empty line in the Name column, type **gbBypassLoad-DimensionTable**, select Boolean in the Type list, type 0 in the Value list, and then click OK.

You will use this global variable in Chapter 8 when you add a dimension table load step to this package.

Now that you have created these global variables in the *UpdateCustomerDim* package, you will create branching steps that will use these global variables.

Add a delete or add staging data branching step to the *UpdateCustomerDim* package by creating an ActiveX Script task

1 On the Task menu, click ActiveX Script Task, and then type **Delete Or Add Staging Data** in the Description box.

2 Click Browse, navigate to C:\Microsoft Press\SQL DTS SBS\Ch7\ChapterFiles, and then double-click DeleteOrAddStagingData.bas.

This script begins by declaring a variable and then placing a reference to the package into the variable. This script then enables the *DeleteStagingData* and the *PropertiesFromGVs* steps in the *UpdateCustomerDim* package using the *DisableStep* property of the *Step* object. (This ensures a known state for these objects.) Next the script reads the value of the *gbDeleteOrAdd* global variable from the *DTSGlobalVariables* object and then enables the appropriate step based on this variable's value. Notice that the *CInt* conversion function is used to convert the value to an integer so that it can be compared to the value of 0. Notice also that this script uses friendly names to refer to steps in the package rather than the DTS-generated names. In the procedures that follow, you will rename each step in the package to a user-friendly name.

> ▶ **Tip**   When writing the code for an ActiveX Script task that will perform branching, creating user-friendly names for each step in the package will make your coding and the reuse of existing code between packages easier. As you have seen, the default names for tasks and steps are not user-friendly. Renaming steps to user-friendly names will also make it easier to read the log files.

3   Click OK to save this ActiveX Script task.

Now that you have created the *Delete Or Add Staging Data* branching step, you will add a delete staging data step to this package. This step will call an Execute SQL task to delete all data in the *CustomerStage* table when the value of the *gbDeleteOrAdd* global variable is set to 1.

Add a delete staging data step to the *UpdateCustomerDim* package by creating an Execute SQL task

1   On the Task menu, click Execute SQL Task, and then type **Delete Staging Data** in the Description box.

2   In the Existing Connection list, select SBS_OLAPAdditionalConnection.

3   Type **TRUNCATE TABLE CustomerStage** in the SQL Statement box, and then click OK to save this Execute SQL task.

Now that you have created the *Delete Staging Data* step, you will add a bypass package step to this package.

Add a bypass package step to the *UpdateCustomerDim* package by creating an ActiveX Script task

1   On the Task menu, click ActiveX Script Task, and then type **Bypass Package** in the Description box.

2   Click Browse, navigate to C:\Microsoft Press\SQL DTS SBS\Ch7\ChapterFiles, and then double-click BypassPackage.bas.

   This script is very similar to the *DeleteOrAddStagingData* script you used earlier. You will notice, however, that this script calls a *Log-BypassPackage* step. This step will log the fact that the package was bypassed each time the data movement application executes and bypasses this package. You will fully configure this task and learn about creating a customized logging solution in Chapter 8. For now, you will simply configure a SQL statement that generates a null result set.

3   Click OK to save this ActiveX Script task.

Now that you have created the *Bypass Package* step, you will add a log package bypass step to this package.

Add a log package bypass step to the *UpdateCustomerDim* package by creating an Execute SQL task

1   On the Task menu, click Execute SQL Task, and then type **Log Package Bypass** in the Description box.

2   Select SBS_OLAPAdditionalConnection in the Existing Connection list, and then type the following Transact-SQL statement in the SQL Statement box:

```
UPDATE CustomerStage
SET CustomerName = CustomerName
WHERE 0 = 1
```

This Execute SQL task is simply holding a spot for a more complex logging and error handling statement, which you will implement in Chapter 8.

3   Click OK to save this Execute SQL task.

You have successfully created three branching global variables, two branching steps, branching tasks, and logging steps in the *UpdateCustomerDim* package.

Configuring Steps and Execution Order in the *UpdateCustomerDim* Package

In the following procedures, you will configure user-friendly names for each of the steps in the *UpdateCustomerDim* package to make it easier to understand errors that appear in the log files and then ensure that each step executes in the proper order. Before you change the name of a step that has an existing precedence constraint, you must delete all existing constraints to avoid corrupting a package.

Delete existing precedence constraints and then create user-friendly names for each step in the *UpdateCustomerDim* package

1 On the design sheet, delete all six On Success constraints in the package and then arrange the steps on the design sheet according to their execution flow.

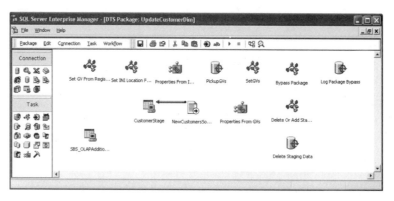

▶ **Important** You must delete all constraints that reference a step in a package before renaming the step, or the package could become corrupt.

2 On the Package menu, click Disconnected Edit.

3 In the left pane, expand Steps (make sure you expand Steps and not Tasks) and then click DTSStep_DTSDataPumpTask_1.

4 In the right pane, double-click Name in the right pane, type **LoadCustomerStageTable** in the Value box (replacing the displayed name DTSStep_DTSDataPumpTask_1), and then click OK.

5 In the left pane, click DTSStep_DTSDynamicPropertiesTask_1.

6 In the right pane, double-click Name, type **PropertiesFromINIFile** in the Value box in place of DTSStep_DTSDynamicPropertiesTask_1, and then click OK.

7 In the left pane, click DTSStep_DTSExecuteSQLTask_1.

8 In the right pane, double-click Name, type **PickupGVs** in the Value box in place of DTSStep_DTSExecuteSQLTask_1, and then click OK.

9 In the left pane, click DTSStep_DTSActiveScriptTask_1.

10 In the right pane, double-click Name, type **SetGVs** in the Value box in place of DTSStep_DTSActiveScriptTask_1, and then click OK.

11 In the left pane, click DTSStep_DTSDynamicPropertiesTask_2.

12 In the right pane, double-click Name, type **PropertiesFromGVs** in the Value box in place of DTSStep_DTSDynamicPropertiesTask_2, and then click OK.

13 In the left pane, click DTSStep_DTSActiveScriptTask_2.

14 In the right pane, double-click Name, type **SetGVFromRegistry** in the Value box in place of DTSStep_DTSActiveScriptTask_2, and then click OK.

15 In the left pane, click DTSStep_DTSActiveScriptTask_3.

16 In the right pane, double-click Name, type **SetINILocationFromGV** in the Value box in place of DTSStep_DTSActiveScriptTask_3, and then click OK.

17 In the left pane, click DTSStep_DTSActiveScriptTask_4.

18 In the right pane, double-click Name, type **DeleteOrAddStagingData** in the Value box in place of DTSStep_DTSActiveScriptTask_4, and then click OK.

19 In the left pane, click DTSStep_DTSExecuteSQLTask_2.

20 In the right pane, double-click Name, type **DeleteStagingData** in the Value box in place of DTSStep_DTSExecuteSQLTask_2, and then click OK.

21 In the left pane, click DTSStep_DTSActiveScriptTask_5.

22 In the right pane, double-click Name, type **BypassPackage** in the Value box in place of DTSStep_DTSActiveScriptTask_5, and then click OK.

23 In the left pane, click DTSStep_DTSExecuteSQLTask_3.

24 In the right pane, double-click Name, type **LogPackageBypass** in the Value box in place of DTSStep_DTSExecuteSQLTask_3, and then click OK.

25 Click Close.

Now that you have configured user-friendly names for the steps in this package, you are ready to configure the appropriate precedence constraints in the *UpdateCustomerDim* package.

Ensure package steps execute in the proper order by configuring precedence constraints in the *UpdateCustomerDim* package

1   On the design sheet, click the Set GVs From Registry step, and then hold down the Ctrl key and click the Set INI Location From GV step.

2   On the Workflow menu, click On Success.

3   On the design sheet, click the Set INI Location From GV step, and then hold down the Ctrl key and click the Properties From INI File step.

4   On the Workflow menu, click On Success.

5   On the design sheet, click the Properties From INI File step, and then hold down the Ctrl key and click the PickupGVs step.

6   On the Workflow menu, click On Success.

7   On the design sheet, click the PickupGVs step, and then hold down the Ctrl key and click the SetGVs step.

8   On the Workflow menu, click On Success.

9 On the design sheet, click the SetGVs step, and then hold down the Ctrl key and click the Bypass Package step.

The Bypass step is the first branching step in the *UpdateCustomer-Dim* package. This step determines, based on the value of the *gbBypassPackage* global variable, whether the package workflow continues and additional tasks execute or whether only the *Log Package Bypass* step is executed.

10 On the Workflow menu, click On Success.

11 On the design sheet, click the Bypass Package step, and then hold down the Ctrl key and click the Log Package Bypass step.

12 On the Workflow menu, click On Success.

The *Log Package Bypass* step will execute only if the *Bypass Package* step does not disable the *Log Package Bypass* step based on the value of the *gbBypassPackage* global variable. With a default value of 0, the *Log Package Bypass* step is disabled by the *Bypass Package* step.

13 On the design sheet, click the Bypass Package step, and then hold down the Ctrl key and click the Delete Or Add Staging Data step.

If the *Bypass Package* step directs the package workflow to the *Delete Or Add Staging Data* step, this step determines whether the *Delete Staging Data* step executes or the remaining steps in the package execute, based on the value of the *gbDeleteOrAdd* global variable value.

14 On the Workflow menu, click On Success.

Notice that there are two success paths out of the *Bypass Package* step. Only one of these two paths out of the ActiveX Script task will actually execute, although by looking at the design sheet it appears as if both steps will execute.

▶ **Tip**   To clearly indicate to someone looking at a package for the first time that a step is a branching step, use a descriptive name for the step. The design sheet makes it appear that both tasks constrained by the branch step will execute when the branching step completes. The logic of the ActiveX Script task called by the branching step actually determines which of the two tasks will execute.

15 On the design sheet, click the Delete Or Add Staging Data step, and then hold down the Ctrl key and click the Delete Staging Data step.

16 On the Workflow menu, click On Success.

The *Delete Staging Data* step will execute only if the *Delete or Add Staging Data* step does not disable the *Delete Staging Data* step based on the value of the *gbDeleteOrAdd* global variable. With a default value of 0, the *Delete Staging Data* step is disabled by the *Delete Or Add Staging Data* step.

17 On the design sheet, click the Delete Or Add Staging Data step, and then hold down the Ctrl key and click the Properties From GVs step.

18 On the Workflow menu, click On Success.

The *Properties From GVs* step will execute if the value of the *gbBypassPackage* global variable is 0 and the value of the *gbDeleteOrAdd* global variable is also 0.

19 On the design sheet, click the Properties From GVs step, and then hold down the Ctrl key and click the NewCustomersSource connection object.

20 On the Workflow menu, click On Success.

21 On the toolbar, click Save and then close the UpdateCustomerDim package.

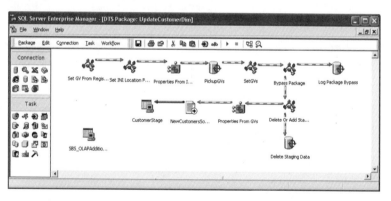

You have successfully configured two branching steps in the *UpdateCustomer-Dim* package and configured user-friendly names for each step in the package. Next you will add branching steps to the *UpdateProductDim* package.

Adding Branching Steps to *UpdateProductDim* Package

In the following procedures, you will create the *gbDeleteOrAdd*, the *gbBypass-Package*, and the *gbBypassLoadDimensionTable* global variables in the *UpdateProductDim* package. You will then create a delete or add staging data step, a bypass package step, and a bypass load dimension table step in this package. You will create ActiveX Script tasks in each package to read these variable values and determine the appropriate steps in the workflow of each package based on the values of the these global variables. By default, the package bypass step will simply call the next step in the package unless the value of the bypass global variable is changed from 0 to 1. If it is changed to 1, the package bypass step will call a logging step that will log the fact that the remaining steps in the package were bypassed. By default, the delete or add staging data step will simply call the load staging table step unless the value of the bypass global variable is changed from 0 to 1. If it is changed to 1, the delete or add staging data step will call a delete staging data step, which in turn will call a logging step that will log the fact that the delete staging data step executed. The bypass load dimension table step will simply call the load dimension table step unless the value of the global variable is changed from 0 to 1. If it is changed to 1, the bypass load dimension table step will call a logging step that will log the fact that the load dimension table step was bypassed.

Add global variables to the *UpdateProductDim* package

1   Switch to the console root in SQL Server Enterprise Manager, and then right-click Data Transformation Services in your local instance.

2   Click Open Package and then open the most recent version of the UpdateProductDim package in the C:\Microsoft Press\SQL DTS SBS\DataMovementApplication folder using a password of **mypassword**.

3   Click Properties on the Package menu, and then click the Global Variables tab.

4   In the first empty line in the Name column, type **gbDeleteOrAdd**, select Boolean in the Type list, and then type **0** in the Value list.

This global variable with a default value of 0 will indicate that new data will be added to the *ProductStage* table. A value of 1 will indicate that all existing data in this table will be deleted. This global variable value is passed from the *MasterUpdate* package, but it might be overwritten by a value retrieved from the *PackageGVs* table for this package.

5 In the next empty line in the Name column, type **gbBypassPackage**, select Boolean in the Type list, and then type 0 in the Value list.

This global variable with a default value of 0 will indicate that the tasks in this package after the branching step will be executed for a particular execution of the data movement application. A value of 1 will indicate that the tasks in this package after the branching step should not be executed for a particular execution of the data movement application. A value for this global variable in the *PackageGVs* table for this package will override the default value.

6 Type **gbBypassLoadDimensionTable** in the next empty line in the Name column, select Boolean in the Type list, type 0 in the Value list, and then click OK.

This global variable with a default value of 0 will indicate that the data in the staging table should be inserted into or update existing data in the *ProductDim* table. A value of 1 will indicate that after data has been added to the *ProductStage* table, the package will terminate without inserting or updating data in the *ProductDim* table.

Now that you have created these global variables in the *UpdateProductDim* package, you will add branching steps that will use these global variables.

Add a delete or add staging data branching step to the *UpdateProductDim* package by creating an ActiveX Script task

1 On the Task menu, click ActiveX Script Task, and then type **Delete Or Add Staging Data** in the Description box.

2 Click Browse, navigate to C:\Microsoft Press\SQL DTS SBS\Ch7\ChapterFiles, and then double-click DeleteOrAddStaging-Data.bas.

This script is identical to the script used in the *UpdateCustomerDim* package because it performs the same task in this package. By configuring user-friendly names for all steps, you can ensure that the step names are accurate. If you use the step names generated by DTS (which are partially based on the order in which steps were created), you might have to modify each script to match the names generated by DTS.

3 Click OK to save this ActiveX Script task.

Now that you have created the *Delete Or Add Staging Data* branching step, you will add a delete staging data step to this package. This step will call an Execute SQL task to delete all data in the *ProductStage* table when the value of the *gbDeleteOrAdd* global variable is set to 1.

Add a delete staging data step to the *UpdateProductDim* package by creating an Execute SQL task

1   On the Task menu, click Execute SQL Task, and then type **Delete Staging Data** in the Description box.

2   In the Existing Connection list, select SBS_OLAPAdditionalConnection.

3   In the SQL Statement box, type **TRUNCATE TABLE ProductStage**, and then click OK to save the Execute SQL task.

Now that you have created the *Delete Staging Data* step, you will add a bypass package step to this package.

Add a bypass package step to the *UpdateProductDim* package by creating an ActiveX Script task

1   On the Task menu, click ActiveX Script Task, and then type **Bypass Package** in the Description box.

2   Click Browse, navigate to C:\Microsoft Press\SQL DTS SBS\Ch7\ChapterFiles, and then double-click BypassPackage.bas.

This script is identical to the script used in the *UpdateCustomerDim* package because it performs the same task in this package.

3   Click OK to save this ActiveX Script task.

Now that you have created the *Bypass Package* step, you will add a log package bypass step to this package.

Add a log package bypass step to the *UpdateProductDim* package by creating an Execute SQL task

1   On the Task menu, click Execute SQL Task, and then type **Log Package Bypass** in the Description box.

2 Select SBS_OLAPAdditionalConnection in the Existing Connection list, and then type the following Transact-SQL statement in the SQL Statement box:

```
UPDATE ProductStage
SET ProductName = ProductName
WHERE 0 = 1
```

This Execute SQL task is simply holding a spot for a more complex logging and error handling statement, which you will implement in Chapter 8.

3 Click OK to save this Execute SQL task.

Now that you have created the *Log Package Bypass* step, you will add a bypass load dimension table step to this package.

Add a bypass load dimension table step to the UpdateProductDim package by creating an ActiveX Script task

1 On the Task menu, click ActiveX Script Task, and then type **Bypass Load Dimension Table** in the Description box.

2 Click Browse, navigate to C:\Microsoft Press\SQL DTS SBS\Ch7\ChapterFiles, and then double-click BypassLoadDimensionTable.bas.

This script is very similar to the previous scripts you used to create branching tasks.

3 Click OK to save this ActiveX Script task.

Now that you have created the *Bypass Load Dimension Table* step, you will add a log load dimension table bypass step to this package.

Add a log load dimension table bypass step to the *UpdateProductDim* package by creating an Execute SQL task

1 On the Task menu, click Execute SQL Task, and then type **Log Load Dimension Table Bypass** in the Description box.

2 Select SBS_OLAPAdditionalConnection in the Existing Connection list, and then type the following Transact-SQL statement in the SQL Statement box:

```
UPDATE ProductStage
SET ProductName = ProductName
WHERE 0 = 1
```

This Execute SQL task is simply holding a spot for a more complex logging and error handling statement, which you will implement in Chapter 8.

3 Click OK to save this Execute SQL task.

You have successfully created three branching global variables, three branching steps, branching tasks, and logging steps in the *UpdateProductDim* package.

Configuring Steps and Execution Order in the *UpdateProductDim* Package

In the following procedures, you will configure user-friendly names for each of the steps in the *UpdateProductDim* package to make it easier to understand errors that appear in the log files and then ensure that each step executes in the proper order. Before you change the name of a step that has an existing precedence constraint, you must delete all existing constraints to avoid corrupting a package.

Delete existing precedence constraints and then create user-friendly names for each step in the *UpdateProductDim* package

1 On the design sheet, delete all six On Success constraints and the one On Completion constraint in the package and arrange the steps on the design sheet according to their execution flow.

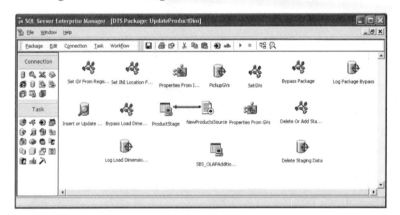

2 On the Package menu, click Disconnected Edit.

3 In the left pane, expand Steps (again, make sure you expand Steps and not Tasks) and then click DTSStep_DTSDataPumpTask_1.

4 In the right pane, double-click Name, type **LoadProductStageTable** in the Value box (replacing the displayed name DTSStep_DTSDataPumpTask_1), and then click OK.

5 In the left pane, click DTSStep_DTSDataDrivenQueryTask_1.

6 In the right pane, double-click Name, type **InsertOrUpdateProductDimTable** in the Value box in place of DTSStep_DTSDataDrivenQueryTask_1, and then click OK.

7 In the left pane, click DTSStep_DTSDynamicPropertiesTask_1.

8 In the right pane, double-click Name, type **PropertiesFromINIFile** in the Value box in place of DTSStep_DTSDynamicPropertiesTask_1, and then click OK.

9 In the left pane, click DTSStep_DTSExecuteSQLTask_1.

10 In the right pane, double-click Name, type **PickupGVs** in the Value box in place of DTSStep_DTSExecuteSQLTask_1, and then click OK.

11 In the left pane, click DTSStep_DTSActiveScriptTask_1.

12 In the right pane, double-click Name, type **SetGVs** in the Value box in place of DTSStep_DTSActiveScriptTask_1, and then click OK.

13 In the left pane, click DTSStep_DTSDynamicPropertiesTask_2.

14 In the right pane, double-click Name, type **PropertiesFromGVs** in the Value box in place of DTSStep_DTSDynamicPropertiesTask_2, and then click OK.

15 In the left pane, click DTSStep_DTSActiveScriptTask_2.

16 In the right pane, double-click Name, type **SetGVFromRegistry** in the Value box in place of DTSStep_DTSActiveScriptTask_2, and then click OK.

17 In the left pane, click DTSStep_DTSActiveScriptTask_3.

18 In the right pane, double-click Name, type **SetINILocationFromGV** in the Value box in place of DTSStep_DTSActiveScriptTask_3, and then click OK.

19 In the left pane, click DTSStep_DTSActiveScriptTask_4.

20 In the right pane, double-click Name, type **DeleteOrAddStagingData** in the Value box in place of DTSStep_DTSActiveScriptTask_4, and then click OK.

21 In the left pane, click DTSStep_DTSExecuteSQLTask_2.

22 In the right pane, double-click Name, type **DeleteStagingData** in the Value box in place of DTSStep_DTSExecuteSQLTask_2, and then click OK.

23 In the left pane, click DTSStep_DTSActiveScriptTask_5.

24 In the right pane, double-click Name, type **BypassPackage** in the Value box in place of DTSStep_DTSActiveScriptTask_5, and then click OK.

25 In the left pane, click DTSStep_DTSExecuteSQLTask_3.

26 In the right pane, double-click Name, type **LogPackageBypass** in the Value box in place of DTSStep_DTSExecuteSQLTask_3, and then click OK.

27 In the left pane, click DTSStep_DTSActiveScriptTask_6.

28 In the right pane, double-click Name, type **BypassLoadDimensionTable** in the Value box in place of DTSStep_DTSActiveScriptTask_6, and then click OK.

29 In the left pane, click DTSStep_DTSExecuteSQLTask_4.

30 In the right pane, double-click Name, type **LogLoadDimensionTableBypass** in the Value box in place of DTSStep_DTSExecuteSQLTask_4, and then click OK.

31 Click Close.

Now that you have configured user-friendly names for the steps in this package, you are ready to configure the appropriate precedence constraints in the *UpdateProductDim* package.

Ensure package steps execute in the proper order by configuring precedence constraints in the *UpdateProductDim* package

1 On the design sheet, click the Set GVs From Registry step, and then hold down the Ctrl key and click the Set INI Location From GV step.

2 On the Workflow menu, click On Success.

3 On the design sheet, click the Set INI Location From GV step, and then hold down the Ctrl key and click the Properties From INI File step.

4 On the Workflow menu, click On Success.

5 On the design sheet, click the Properties From INI File step, and then hold down the Ctrl key and click the PickupGVs step.

6 On the Workflow menu, click On Success.

7 On the design sheet, click the PickupGVs step, and then hold down the Ctrl key and click the SetGVs step.

8   On the Workflow menu, click On Success.

9   On the design sheet, click the SetGVs step, and then hold down the Ctrl key and click the Bypass Package step.

10 On the Workflow menu, click On Success.

11 On the design sheet, click the Bypass Package step, and then hold down the Ctrl key and click the Log Package Bypass step.

12 On the Workflow menu, click On Success.

13 On the design sheet, click the Bypass Package step, and then hold down the Ctrl key and click the Delete Or Add Staging Data step.

14 On the Workflow menu, click On Success.

15 On the design sheet, click the Delete Or Add Staging Data step, and then hold down the Ctrl key and click the Delete Staging Data step.

16 On the Workflow menu, click On Success.

17 On the design sheet, click the Delete or Add Staging Data step, and then hold down the Ctrl key and click the Properties From GVs step.

18 On the Workflow menu, click On Success.

19 On the design sheet, click the Properties From GVs step, and then hold down the Ctrl key and click the NewProductsSource connection object.

20 On the Workflow menu, click On Success.

21 On the design sheet, click the ProductStage connection object, and then hold down the Ctrl key and click the Bypass Load Dimension Table step.

22 On the Workflow menu, click On Completion.

> ▶ **Tip**   By configuring the phase of this package that loads data from the *ProductStage* table into the *ProductDim* table to execute regardless of the success or failure of the previous steps in the package, you can execute the *Insert Or Update Dimension Table* step after the failure of the *Load ProductStage Table* step. For example, this step might fail because no source file is provided. You might not provide a source file because you have already loaded this source data into the *ProductStage* table in a previous execution of this package or because no new dimension data needs to be added to the *ProductStage* table for the current time period.

23 On the design sheet, click the Bypass Load Dimension Table step, and then hold down the Ctrl key and click the Log Load Dimension Table Bypass step.

ActiveX Script Tasks

24 On the Workflow menu, click On Success.

25 On the design sheet, click the Bypass Load Dimension Table step, and then hold down the Ctrl key and click the Insert Or Update ProductDim Table step.

26 On the Workflow menu, click On Success.

27 On the toolbar, click Save. Do not close the UpdateProductDim package.

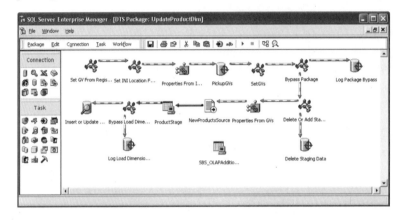

You have successfully configured two branching steps in the *UpdateCustomerDim* package and the three branching steps in the *UpdateProductDim* package. You have also configured the *MasterUpdate* package to pass the value of *gbDeleteOrUpdate* global variable to these subpackages.

Creating Delete Configurations to Execute the Branches in the Subpackages

In the following procedures, you will add global variable configuration values to the *PackageGVs* table to create three separate delete configurations in the *PackageGVs* table and then execute the data movement application packages using these new configurations.

Create delete configurations in the *PackageGVs* table

1 Switch to SQL Query Analyzer and then click Load SQL Script on the toolbar.

2   Navigate to C:\Microsoft Press\SQL DTS SBS\Ch7\ChapterFiles in the Look In list and then double-click DeleteConfigs.sql.

This script adds three configurations to the *PackageGVs* table. The first configuration sets the value of the *gbDeleteOrAdd* global variable to 1 in the *MasterUpdate* package. Since no other value is set in either of the subpackages and since the value of the *gbBypassPackage* global variable is not changed, the delete phase of each subpackage will execute if the *MasterUpdate* package is run using a *giConfigID* value of 3. The second configuration sets the value of the *gbDeleteOrAdd* global variable to 1 in the *UpdateCustomerDim* package and sets the value of the *gbBypassPackage* global variable to 1 in the *UpdateProductDim* package. When the *MasterUpdate* package is run using a *giConfigID* value of 4, the delete phase of the *UpdateCustomerDim* package is executed and the bypass phase of the *UpdateProductDim* package is executed. The third configuration is the reverse of the second configuration, enabling you to delete data in the *ProductStage* table without deleting data in the *CustomerStage* table.

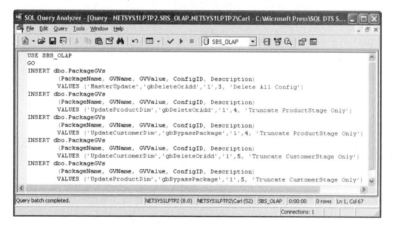

3   On the toolbar, click Execute to add these entries to the PackageGVs table and then close SQL Query Analyzer.

You have now created three new global variable configurations in the *PackageGVs* table and are ready to begin testing the branching steps using these configurations of global variables.

Test package execution using different configuration values

1   Switch to the UpdateProductDim package in DTS Designer, and then click Execute on the toolbar.

The package completes successfully.

2   Click OK and then in the Status window, review the steps that did not execute.

Notice that three steps did not execute: the *Delete Staging Data* step, the *Log Package Bypass* step, and the *Log Load Dimension Table Bypass* step. Since the *UpdateProductDim* package executed using a *giConfigID* value of 1, none of the non-default steps in this package executed.

3   Click Done.

4   On the Package menu, click Properties.

5   On the Global Variables tab, change the value for the gbDelete-OrAdd global variable to **1** and then click OK.

> ▶ **Tip**   The only valid values for a Boolean type global variable are 0 or –1. If you set the value to anything other than 0 and save it, you will discover that its value was changed to –1 the next time you open the package properties. 0 indicates *False*, and anything other than 0 becomes –1, which indicates *True*.

6 On the toolbar, click Execute.

The package completes successfully.

7 Click OK and then in the Status window, review the steps that executed.

Notice that the *Delete Staging Data* step executed after the *Delete Or Add Staging Data* step because the value of the *gbDeleteOrAdd* global variable was changed from 0 to 1.

8 Click Done.

9 On the Package menu, click Properties.

10 On the Global Variables tab, change the value of the giConfigID global variable to 5, and then click OK.

11 On the toolbar, click Execute.

The package completes successfully.

12 Click OK and then in the Status window, review the steps that executed.

Notice that the *Log Package Bypass* step executed after the *Bypass Package* step because a non-default *gbBypassPackage* global variable value was retrieved from the *PackageGVs* table by the *PickUpGVs* step and then updated in the package by the *SetGVs* step.

13 Click Done.

14 On the Package menu, click Properties and then click the Global Variables tab.

Notice that the value of the *gbBypassPackage* global variable was changed to -1.

15 Click OK and then close the UpdateProductDim package in DTS Designer. Do not save any changes.

16 Close SQL Server Enterprise Manager.

17 Using Windows Explorer, navigate to the C:\Microsoft Press\SQL DTS SBS\DataMovementApplication folder, right-click Master-UpdateDefaultConfig.cmd, and click Edit.

18 Change the value of the giConfigID global variable parameter from 1 to **3**, and then click Save As on the File menu.

19 Type **DeleteAllStagingData.cmd** in the File Name box, select All Files in the Save As Type list, click Save, and then close Notepad.

20 Double-click DeleteAllStagingData.cmd in the DataMovementApplication folder to delete all staging data in the ProductStage and the CustomerStage tables in the SBS_OLAP database.

21 After the batch completes, open the UpdateProductDimPackageError-
Log.txt file and then scroll to the end of the file to verify that the
DeleteStagingData step executed.

The steps in the log file are easier to interpret because you changed
the DTS-generated step names to user-friendly names. Notice also
that each step that did not execute is displayed in this log file along
with each step that did execute. If you review the log saved to SQL
Server, you will see that only the steps that executed successfully are
logged to SQL Server.

22 Close the UpdateProductDimPackageErrorLog.txt file in Notepad
and then open the UpdateCustomerDimPackageErrorLog.txt file to
verify that the DeleteStagingData step executed and then close
Notepad.

Chapter Summary

In this chapter, you learned how to use the ActiveX Script task to enable the packages in the data movement application to retrieve parameters from the Windows registry and update global variable values retrieved from the Windows registry and from a SQL table. As a result of the steps you performed in this chapter, as well as the steps you performed in the previous chapters, you are now able to change the names and locations of the data source files, change the database used for source and destination data, and change the folders used for logging, all without having to open or edit a single package. When your data movement application comprises dozens of packages, not having to open and edit the packages will save you time when you migrate the application from the development environment to the production environment.

You also learned how to add branching to the data movement application. You enabled individual packages to be bypassed for a particular execution. You also enabled individual packages to perform a dual function: each dimension package can either add data to its corresponding staging table or delete data from that table. Finally, you enabled a package to add data to its corresponding staging table without necessarily also inserting or updating data in the corresponding dimension table during the same execution.

Chapter 8

Incorporating Error Handling into DTS Packages

In this chapter, you will learn how to:

- Add batch control
- Create step and package success and error logging tasks
- Record the number of rows transformed and the number of rows with errors

In this chapter, you will learn how to add batch control to the data movement application, which enables you to identify the rows affected by a particular execution of the application. In the absence of transaction control, you might run into a situation in which some subpackages succeed and some fail. Currently, you're able to fix the problem that caused the error and re-execute selected packages. However, on some occasions, you might need to roll back some or all of the data added by the execution of a particular package. The addition of batch control lets you to accomplish this by generating and then recording a batch ID value with each inserted or updated row in each dimension table.

In this chapter, you will also learn how to use Execute SQL tasks to log package starts, package branching, package completion, and package step errors into a single SQL Server table. Logging all this information into a single table creates an audit trail of the execution history for the data movement application and supplements the logging options provided by DTS. After you execute the data movement application, you can review this table to quickly determine the steps in each package that actually executed without having to parse through each error log. You can easily locate package steps with errors that require closer examination to determine the causes of the errors. In many cases, you will be able to fix the error and re-execute one or more packages in the data movement application to complete the data import without having to roll back the application's entire execution.

Finally, you will learn how to create package steps to record the number of rows transformed and the number of error rows encountered by a given task. By recording this information in the audit table along with step and package execution and error information, you can see a more complete picture of the actions taken by the data movement application for a particular execution. By recording the number of rows with errors, you can easily determine whether you have data that must be cleaned and resubmitted before you process the new data in the data warehouse.

Adding Batch Control

Batch control enables you to identify the rows affected by a particular execution of the data movement application. You will implement batch control by adding a task to the *MasterUpdate* package that generates a new batch ID value each time the *MasterUpdate* package is executed. You will then pass the generated batch ID value to each subpackage, which will record the batch ID value with each row it inserts into a dimension table from one of the staging tables.

▶ **Note**   If you skipped Chapter 7, execute the IfYouSkippedChapter7.cmd batch file in the C:\Microsoft Press\SQL DTS SBS\Ch8\SkippedChapterFiles folder before you begin these procedures. This batch file restores the SBS_OLTP and SBS_OLAP databases and copies the DTS packages that would have been created in Chapters 1 through 7 into the appropriate folders. It also records the location of the Config.ini initialization file in the Windows registry. If you do not want this batch file to overwrite any packages that you created in Chapters 1 through 7, you must move them or rename them before you execute this batch file.

Modifying SQL Server Objects to Support Batch Control

In the following procedure, you will create a table and stored procedure in SQL Server that will generate a new batch ID value in the table each time the stored procedure is executed. In a subsequent procedure, you will create an Execute SQL task in the *MasterUpdate* package that will call this stored procedure and then store the new batch ID value in a global variable for that execution of the data movement application. You will then add a column to each dimension table to store the batch ID value for each record added to the dimension table by the corresponding subpackage.

Create the *BatchIDValues* table and the *GenBatchID* stored procedure

1 Open SQL Query Analyzer and connect to your local SQL Server instance as a system administrator.

2 On the File menu, click Open.

3 In the Look In list, navigate to C:\Microsoft Press\SQL DTS SBS\Ch8\ChapterFiles, and then open the BatchID.sql script.

This script creates the *BatchIdValues* table containing a *BatchID* column, which is defined using the *IDENTITY* property, and a *BatchName* column. This script also creates a *GenBatchID* stored procedure, which inserts a batch name provided as an input parameter into the *BatchIdValues* table, and returns the *BatchID* value generated by the *IDENTITY* property. This stored procedure will be called by an Execute SQL task that you will create in the *Master-Update* package.

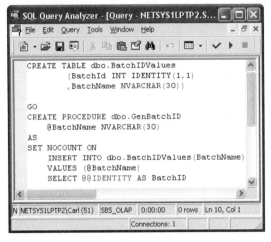

4 Execute the BatchID.sql script to create this table and stored procedure.

Now that you have created the infrastructure to generate a new *BatchID* value as needed, you must add a column to each dimension table to hold this *BatchID* value along with the data that is added to each dimension table from the corresponding staging table.

Add the *BatchID* column to each dimension table

1   On the toolbar, click Load SQL Script.

2   In the Look In list, navigate to C:\Microsoft Press\SQL DTS SBS\Ch8\ChapterFiles and then open the AddColumnsToDim-Tables.sql script.

This script adds the *BatchID* column to the *CustomerDim* and *ProductDim* dimension tables. This column will store the *BatchID* value for each row added to these tables by the *UpdateCustomerDim* and *UpdateProductDim* subpackages, respectively.

3   Execute the AddColumnsToDimTables.sql script to add this column to each of these tables.

Now that you have created the infrastructure to store the generated *BatchID* value in each row added to a dimension table, you are ready to add a step to the *MasterUpdate* package to generate a *BatchID* value each time the data movement application is executed.

Generating a *BatchID* Value, Storing It in the *MasterUpdate* Package, and Then Passing It to Subpackages

In the following procedures, you will create an Execute SQL task in the *MasterUpdate* package that calls the *GenBatchID* stored procedure and records the generated *BatchID* value into a global variable. You will then modify the Execute Package tasks to pass this *BatchID* value to each subpackage. Finally, you will update the precedence constraints to ensure the steps in the *MasterUpdate* package execute in the proper order. The step that calls the *GenBatchID* must execute after the *Properties From INI File* step and before the steps that call the subpackages.

Add the *Generate BatchID* step to the *MasterUpdate* package by creating an Execute SQL step

1   Open SQL Server Enterprise Manager and then right-click Data Transformation Services in your local instance.

2   Click Open Package and then open the most recent version of the MasterUpdate package in the C:\Microsoft Press\SQL DTS SBS\ DataMovementApplication folder using a password of **mypassword**.

3   On the Task menu, click Execute SQL Task.

4   Type **Generate BatchID** in the Description box and then type **EXEC GenBatchID MasterUpdatePackage** in the SQL Statement box.

You will configure this task to use the existing connection object because no other task will be using this connection when this Execute SQL task needs it. You are passing the parameter value of Master-UpdatePackage to the *GenBatchID* stored procedure to identify the package that generated the new *BatchID* value. As you add complexity to the data movement application, you can call this stored procedure from a different master package and pass a different package name. This package name is stored in the *BatchIDValues* table as the *BatchName*.

5   Click Parameters and then click the Output Parameters tab.

You will store the *BatchID* value returned by this stored procedure in a global variable that you will pass to each subpackage called from the *MasterUpdate* package.

6   Click Create Global Variables, type **giBatchID** in the Name column, select Integer (small) in the Type list, type **-1** in the Value list, and then click OK.

To create a global variable with an integer data type, you must provide a default value. This default value of -1 will be overridden each time the *MasterUpdate* package is executed by the *BatchID* value returned by the *GenBatchID* stored procedure.

7   Click Row Value as the Output Parameter Type, and then select giBatchID in the Output Global Variables list in the Parameter Mapping box.

The generated *BatchID* value returned by the *GenBatchID* stored procedure will be stored in the *giBatchID* global variable and then passed to each subpackage.

8   Click OK to save the mapping of the SQL query output to a global variable and then click OK to save the Execute SQL task.

Now that you have created a package step to generate a *BatchID* value and store it in a global variable, you need to pass the value of this global variable to each subpackage.

Pass the *giBatchID* global variable to each subpackage by modifying the Execute Package tasks

1   On the design sheet, double-click the Call UpdateProductDim Sub-package step and then click the Outer Package Global Variables tab.

2   In the Variables list, select giBatchID and then click OK.

3   On the design sheet, double-click the Call UpdateCustomerDim Sub-package step and then click the Outer Package Global Variables tab.

4   In the Variables list, select giBatchID and then click OK.

You have ensured that the generated batch ID value is passed to each subpackage, so now you need to ensure that the package steps execute in the proper order.

Ensure the package steps execute in the proper order by configuring precedence constraints

1   On the design sheet, delete the On Success constraint between the SetGVs step and the Call UpdateProductDim Subpackage step.

2   On the design sheet, delete the On Success constraint between the SetGVs step and the Call UpdateCustomerDim Subpackage step.

3   On the design sheet, click the SetGVs step, and then hold down the Ctrl key and click the Generate BatchID step.

4   On the Workflow menu, click On Success.

5   On the design sheet, click the Generate BatchID step, and then hold down the Ctrl key and click the Call UpdateProductDim Subpackage step.

6   On the Workflow menu, click On Success.

7   On the design sheet, click the Generate BatchID step, and then hold down the Ctrl key and click the Call UpdateCustomerDim Subpackage step.

8   On the Workflow menu, click On Success.

Error Handling

8

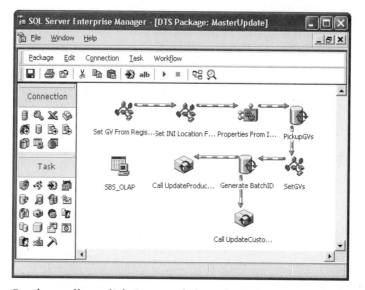

9   On the toolbar, click Save and then close the MasterUpdate package.

You have finished configuring the *MasterUpdate* package to generate a *BatchID* value and pass this value to each subpackage. Next you need to add the *giBatchID* global variable to each subpackage and then configure the appropriate tasks to add the generated *BatchID* value to each row added or updated in the corresponding dimension table.

Incorporating the *BatchID* Value into Tasks in the *UpdateProductDim* Package

In the following procedures, you will add the *giBatchID* global variable to the *UpdateProductDim* package. You will then modify the *ProductStageRowsetSP* stored procedure to accept the value of the *giBatchID* global variable as an input parameter and then return its value in the rowset generated by this stored procedure. Next you will create a binding table that matches the schema of the rowset returned by the *ProductStageRowsetSP* stored procedure for use by the DDQ task in this package. You must create a dedicated binding table because the schema returned by the rowset does not match any existing table in the SBS_OLAP database. Finally, you will modify the DDQ task in this package to read the global variable containing the *giBatchID* value, pass this value to the *ProductStageRowsetSP* stored procedure, and then use the rowset returned by the stored procedure to update existing rows and insert new values in the *ProductDim* table.

Add the *giBatchID* global variable to the *UpdateProductDim* package

1   In the SQL Server Enterprise Manager console tree, right-click Data Transformation Services in your local instance.

2   Click Open Package and then open the most recent version of the UpdateProductDim package in the C:\Microsoft Press\SQL DTS SBS\ DataMovementApplication folder using a password of **mypassword**.

3   Right-click an open area of the design sheet, and then click Package Properties.

4   Click the Global Variables tab.

5   Type **giBatchID** in the Name column, select Integer (small) in the Type list, type **-1** in the Value box, and then click OK.

Now that you have created the *giBatchID* global variable in this subpackage, you are ready to modify the DDQ task called by the *Insert Or Update Product-Dim Table* step to add the value of this global variable to each new record that it inserts and to each existing record that it updates in the *ProductDim* table. First you will modify the *ProductStageRowsetSP* stored procedure to accept the value of the *giBatchID* global variable as an input parameter and then return it in the rowset used by the DDQ task.

Add the value of the *giBatchID* global variable to the rowset returned by the *ProductStageRowsetSP* stored procedure

1   Switch to SQL Query Analyzer and then click Load SQL Script on the toolbar.

2   Navigate to C:\Microsoft Press\SQL DTS SBS\Ch8\ChapterFiles in the Look In list and then open the AlterProductStageRowsetSP.sql script.

This script modifies the *ProductStageRowsetSP* by adding the *@BatchID* variable to hold the value of an input parameter passed into this stored procedure and then include the value of the *@BatchID* variable in the rowset that it returns to the DDQ task that calls this stored procedure. The DDQ task will pass the value of the *giBatchID* global variable into this stored procedure and use this rowset to insert or update values in the *ProductDim* table.

3   Execute the AlterProductStageRowsetSP.sql script to alter this stored procedure.

Now that the *BatchID* value is being included in the rowset that is returned by the stored procedure, you need to create a binding table that the DDQ task will use. When you created the DDQ task in Chapter 4, you used the *ProductStage* table as the binding table. However, the rowset being used as the data source in the DDQ task no longer has the same schema as the *ProductStage* table. The simplest way to solve this problem is to create a binding table that has a schema that matches the source rowset.

Create the *ProductBinding* table for use in the DDQ task

1   On the SQL Query Analyzer toolbar, click Load SQL Script.

2   In the Look In list, navigate to C:\Microsoft Press\SQL DTS SBS\Ch8\ChapterFiles and then open the CreateProductBinding-Table.sql script.

This script creates a table that matches the schema of the rowset returned by the *ProductStageRowsetSP*. The schema for this table begins with the schema of the *ProductStage* table, but without the *InsertOrUpdate* column, and then adds the *BatchID* column.

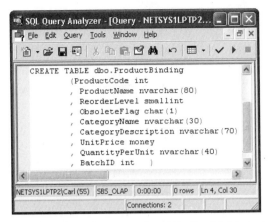

3   Execute the CreateProductBindingTable.sql script to create the ProductBinding table.

Now that you have altered the infrastructure required for the DDQ task to
use the *BatchID* value, you are ready to modify the DDQ task in the
UpdateProductDim subpackage so that it writes the *BatchID* value to the
appropriate column in the *ProductDim* table.

Update the DDQ task in the *UpdateProductDim* subpackage to use the *BatchID* value

1   Switch to the UpdateProductDim subpackage in DTS Designer and
then double-click the Insert Or Update ProductDim Table step on the
design sheet.

2   In the SQL Query box, modify the query to read:
EXEC dbo.ProductStageRowsetSP ? and then click Parameters.

3   In the Input Global Parameters list, select giBatchID and then click
OK.

4   Click the Bindings tab.
Notice that DTS does not know what table to use as the binding
table. In Chapter 4, you defined the *ProductStage* table as the
binding table. However, DTS has detected that the schema of the
ProductStage table does not match the schema of the source rowset.
As a result, DTS displays the first table in the SBS_OLAP database
(the *Authors* table).

5 On the Bindings tab, verify that SBS_OLAPAdditionalConnection is selected in the Connection list, and then select "SBS_OLAP"."dbo"."ProductBinding" in the Table Name list.

Notice that the *BatchID* column appears in the binding table to hold the *BatchID* value in the rowset returned by the *ProdStageRowsetSP* stored procedure.

6 Click the Transformations tab and then click Remove Invalid Transformations.

7 Click Select All and then click New.

8 Click ActiveX Script, click OK, and then click Properties.

9 Click Browse, navigate to C:\Microsoft Press\SQL DTS SBS\Ch8\ChapterFiles, and then double-click DDQ2.bas.

This modified ActiveX script adds the *DTSDestination("BatchID")* = *DTSSource("BatchID")* statement to the ActiveX script immediately before the *Select Case* statement.

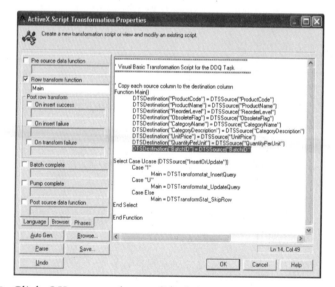

10 Click OK to save the modified ActiveX script, and then click OK to close the Transformation Options dialog box.

11 On the Queries tab, verify that Insert is selected as the query type and then modify the Insert query by adding the BatchID column to the column list and adding an additional parameter to the VALUES list. The modified query should read as follows:

```
INSERT INTO dbo.ProductDim
(ProductCode, ProductName, ReorderLevel, ObsoleteFlag, CategoryName,
CategoryDescription, UnitPrice, QuantityPerUnit, BatchID)
VALUES (?, ?, ?, ?, ?, ?, ?, ?, ?)
```

12 Click Parse/Show Parameters and then click OK.

This maps the columns in the bindings table to parameters in the VALUES list. Notice that the *BatchID* column is mapped to Parameter 9 in the VALUES list.

13 In the Query Type list, select Update and then modify the Update query by adding the BatchID column to the SET list. The modified query should read as follows:

```
UPDATE dbo.ProductDim SET
ProductName = ?,
ReorderLevel = ?,
ObsoleteFlag = ?,
CategoryName = ?,
CategoryDescription = ?,
UnitPrice = ?,
QuantityPerUnit = ?,
BatchID = ?
WHERE ProductCode = ?
```

Error Handling

8

14 Click Parse/Show Parameters and then click OK.

15 In the Destination To Parameter Mapping box, map the following parameters:

Parameter 1	ProductName
Parameter 2	ReorderLevel
Parameter 3	ObsoleteFlag
Parameter 4	CategoryName
Parameter 5	CategoryDescription
Parameter 6	UnitPrice
Parameter 7	QuantityPerUnit
Parameter 8	BatchID
Parameter 9	ProductCode

16 Click OK to save the modified DDQ task.

17 On the toolbar, click Save and then close the UpdateProductDim package.

Now that you have modified the *UpdateProductDim* subpackage to incorporate the *BatchID* value into each record inserted or modified in the *Product_Dim* table, you are ready to incorporate the *BatchID* value into the *UpdateCustomerDim* package.

Incorporating the *BatchID* Value into Tasks in the *UpdateCustomerDim* Package

In the following procedures, you will add the *giBatchID* global variable to the *UpdateCustomerDim* package. You will then create an insert and an update stored procedure that insert or update data (as the case may be) into the *CustomerDim* table from the *CustomerStage* table, while incorporating the batch ID value. These stored procedures will be called by Execute SQL tasks that you will create. You will create a bypass load dimension table task that will bypass these new steps based on the value of the *gbBypassLoadDimensionTable* global variable. Finally, you will create logging tasks for these new steps, configure user-friendly names for these new steps, and then ensure these steps execute in the proper order.

Add the *giBatchID* global variable to the *UpdateCustomerDim* package

1   In the SQL Server Enterprise Manager console tree, right-click Data Transformation Services in your local instance.

2   Click Open Package and then open the most recent version of the UpdateCustomerDim package in the C:\Microsoft Press\SQL DTS SBS\ DataMovementApplication folder using a password of **mypassword.**

3   Right-click an open area of the design sheet and then click Package Properties.

4   Click the Global Variables tab.

5   Type **giBatchID** in the Name column, select Integer (small) in the Type list, type **-1** in the Value box, and then click OK.

Now that you have created the *giBatchID* global variable in this subpackage, you are ready to create the tasks required to update the data in the *Customer-Dim* table based on the rows of data in the *CustomerStage* table, adding the *BatchID* value to each row being added or updated. However, unlike the records in the *ProductStage* table, the records in the *CustomerStage* table are not marked to indicate which values are new and which values are updates to existing values. To solve this problem, you will create separate insert and update tasks that will each use a stored procedure to update to appropriate rows and include the *BatchID* value.

Create the *Customer Insert* and *Customer Update* stored procedures

1   Switch to SQL Query Analyzer and then click Load SQL Script on the toolbar.

2   In the SQL Query Analyzer Look In list, navigate to C:\Microsoft Press\SQL DTS SBS\Ch8\ChapterFiles and then open the Customer-DimValues.sql script.

This script creates two stored procedures. The *CustomerDimUpdate-Values* stored procedure updates rows in the *CustomerDim* table, based on their *CustomerCode* key, with values from the *Customer-Stage* table. The *CustomerDimInsertValues* stored procedure inserts those records from the *CustomerStage* table into the *CustomerDim* table for which there is no matching *CustomerCode* entry. Notice that the value for the *BatchID* column is passed into each of these stored procedures as an input parameter and added to each inserted or updated record.

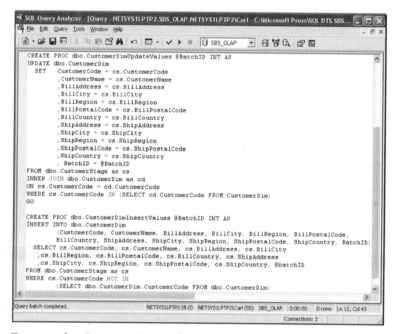

3   Execute the CustomerDimValues.sql script to create these stored procedures.

Now that you have created the stored procedures that will insert new data or update existing data, you are ready to create the tasks that call these stored procedures to perform the insert and update actions.

Call the *CustomerDimUpdateValues* stored procedure by creating an Execute SQL task in the *UpdateCustomerDim* package

1   Switch to the UpdateCustomerDim package in DTS Designer and then click Execute SQL Task on the Task menu.

2   Type **Update Data in CustomerDim Table** in the Description box, select CustomerStage in the Existing Connection list, and then type **EXEC dbo.CustomerDimUpdateValues ?** in the SQL Query box.

3   Click Parameters, select giBatchID in the Input Global Variables list, and then click OK.

4   Click OK to save the Execute SQL task.

Now that you have added a step that updates existing customer data in the *CustomerDim* table, you are ready to add a step that inserts new customer data into the *CustomerDim* table.

Call the *CustomerDimInsertValues* stored procedure by creating an Execute SQL task in the *UpdateCustomerDim* package

1   On the Task menu, click Execute SQL Task.

2   Type **Insert New Data in CustomerDim Table** in the Description box, select CustomerStage in the Existing Connection list, and then type **EXEC CustomerDimInsertValues ?** in the SQL Query box.

3   Click Parameters, select giBatchID in the Input Global Variables list, and then click OK.

4   Click OK to save the Execute SQL task.

Now that you have added the *Update Data In CustomerDim Table* and *Insert New Data In CustomerDim Table* steps to the *UpdateCustomerDim* package, you will add a bypass load dimension table step to the *UpdateCustomerDim* package to enable you to load data into the *CustomerStage* table without always loading data from the *CustomerStage* table into the *CustomerDim* table.

Add a bypass load dimension table step to the *UpdateCustomerDim* package by creating an ActiveX Script task

1   On the Task menu, click ActiveX Script Task, and then type **Bypass Load Dimension Table** in the Description box.

2   Click Browse, navigate to C:\Microsoft Press\SQL DTS SBS\Ch8\ ChapterFiles, and then double-click BypassLoadDimensionTable.bas.

This script is very similar to the previous scripts you used to create branching tasks. However, it disables two tasks if the value of the *gbBypassLoadDimensionTable* global variable is set to 1.

3   Click OK to save this ActiveX Script task.

Now that you have created the *Bypass Load Dimension Table* step, you will add a log dimension table bypass step to this package.

Add the *Log Load Dimension Table Bypass* step to the *UpdateCustomerDim* package by creating an Execute SQL task

1   On the Task menu, click Execute SQL Task, and then type **Log Load Dimension Table Bypass** in the Description box.

2   Select SBS_OLAPAdditionalConnection in the Existing Connection list, and then type the following Transact-SQL statement in the SQL Statement box:

```
UPDATE CustomerStage
SET CustomerName = CustomerName
WHERE 0 = 1
```

This Execute SQL package is simply holding a spot for a more complex logging and error handling statement, which you will implement later in this chapter.

3   Click OK to save this Execute SQL task.

Now that you have created these new steps, you are ready to change the names of the steps in this package to user-friendly names.

Create user-friendly names for the new steps in the *UpdateCustomerDim* package

1   On the Package menu, click Disconnected Edit and then expand the Steps node in the left pane.

2   In the left pane, click DTSStep_DTSExecuteSQLTask_1 and then double-click Name in the right pane.

3   In the Value box, type **UpdateCustomerDimensionData** in place of DTSStep_DTSExecuteSQLTask_1 and then click OK.

4   In the left pane, click DTSStep_DTSExecuteSQLTask_2 and then double-click Name in the right pane.

5   In the Value box, type **InsertCustomerDimensionData** in place of DTSStep_DTSExecuteSQLTask_2 and then click OK.

6   In the left pane, click DTSStep_DTSActiveScriptTask_1 and then double-click Name in the right pane.

7   In the Value box, type **BypassLoadDimensionTable** in place of DTSStep_ DTSActiveScriptTask _1 and then click OK.

8   In the left pane, click DTSStep_DTSExecuteSQLTask_3 and then double-click Name in the right pane.

9   In the Value box, type **LogLoadDimensionTableBypass** in place of DTSStep_DTSExecuteSQLTask_3 and then click OK.

10 Click Close.

Now that you have configured user-friendly names for the new steps in this package, you are ready to configure the appropriate precedence constraints in the *UpdateCustomerDim* package to ensure these steps execute in the proper order.

8

Error Handling

Ensure the package steps execute in the proper order by adding precedence constraints to the *UpdateCustomerDim* package

1 On the design sheet, click the CustomerStage connection object, and then hold down the Ctrl key and click the Bypass Load Dimension Table step.

2 On the Workflow menu, click On Completion.

If the *Load CustomerStage Table* step fails to load new data into the *CustomerStage* table, the *Bypass Load Dimension Table* step will still execute, and if the default value is not changed, the package will continue and update the *CustomerDim* table.

3 On the design sheet, click the Bypass Load Dimension Table step, and then hold down the Ctrl key and click the Log Load Dimension Table Bypass step.

4 On the Workflow menu, click On Success.

5 On the design sheet, click the Bypass Load Dimension Table step, and then hold down the Ctrl key and click the Update Data in CustomerDim Table step.

6 On the Workflow menu, click On Success.

7 On the design sheet, click the Update Data in CustomerDim Table step, and then hold down the Ctrl key and click the Insert New Data in CustomerDim Table step.

8 On the Workflow menu, click On Success.

9 On the toolbar, click Save, and then close the UpdateCustomerDim package.

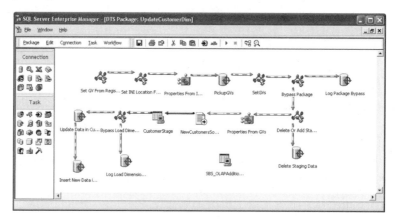

Now that you have configured these three packages to use batch ID values, you are ready to test the execution of these packages.

Testing the Steps That Generate and Add the *BatchID* Value

In the following procedure, you will test the steps that generate and add the *BatchID* value to each row inserted or updated in the dimension tables. You will begin by executing the *LoadHistoricalData* package to delete all test data from the dimension tables. You will then execute the *MasterUpdate* package and its subpackages using the delete configuration to delete all test data from the staging tables. You will then execute the *MasterUpdate* package and its sub-packages using the default configuration and query the dimension tables to observe the *BatchID* values. You will then create a new batch file that executes the *MasterUpdate* package and its subpackages using a *ConfigID* value of 2 and query the dimension tables to observe the *BatchID* values.

Test the execution of the data movement application

1 In the SQL Server Enterprise Manager console tree, right-click Data Transformation Services in your local instance and then click Open Package.

2 Navigate to the C:\Microsoft Press\SQL DTS SBS\DataMovement-Application folder and then open the most recent version of the LoadHistoricalData package using a password of **mypassword**.

3 On the toolbar, click Execute.

   Performing this step truncates all data in the dimension and fact tables, and then reloads the original historical data. By executing this task, it will be easier to observe the effect of executing the *Update-CustomerDim* and *UpdateProductDim* packages again because the test data that you have previously loaded into the dimension tables is deleted.

4 Click OK, click Done, and then switch to Windows Explorer.

5 Navigate to the C:\Microsoft Press\SQL DTS SBS\DataMovement-Application folder, and then double-click DeleteAllStagingData.cmd.

   Performing this step eliminates all data in the staging tables to make it easier to observe the effect of executing the *UpdateCustomerDim* and *UpdateProductDim* packages again because the test data that you have previously loaded into the staging tables is deleted.

6 In the DataMovementApplication folder, double-click MasterUpdate-DefaultConfig.cmd to load data from the source files into the staging tables, and then from the staging tables into the dimension tables.

7   After this batch file completes, switch to SQL Query Analyzer and then click Load SQL Script on the toolbar.

8   In the Look In list, navigate to C:\Microsoft Press\SQL DTS SBS\Ch8\ChapterFiles and then double-click TestBatchExecution.sql.

This script queries the *ProductDim* and *CustomerDim* tables to return those rows inserted or modified by the package execution with the *BatchID* value that is not equal to 0 or NULL.

9   Execute the query.

Notice that no rows were added to the *CustomerDim* table and three rows were added or updated in the *ProductDim* table by the batch with a *BatchID* value of 2. No rows were added to the *Customer-Dim* table because no rows existed in the *CustomerStage* table. No rows existed in the *CustomerStage* table because the number of rows in the source file exceeded the number of errors permitted. The *BatchID* value is 2 because the *BatchID* value of 1 was generated when the *MasterUpdate* package executed using a *ConfigID* value of 3 (which deleted all staging data).

10   Switch to Windows Explorer, right-click MasterUpdateDefault-Config.cmd in the DataMovementApplication folder and then click Edit.

11   Change the value of the *giConfigID* parameter from 1 to **2** and then click Save As on the File menu.

12   Type **Config2.cmd** in the File Name box, select All Files in the Save As Type list, and then click Save.

13   Close the Config2.cmd file in Notepad and then double-click Config2.cmd in the DataMovement Application folder.

14   After this batch file completes, switch to SQL Query Analyzer and re-execute the TestBatchExecution.sql script.

Notice that 27 rows were added to the *CustomerDim* table by the batch with a *BatchID* value of 3, but that four rows were added or updated in the *ProductDim* table (duplicating the rows added or updated by the batch with the *BatchID* value of 2). You can see why having a delete branch and a bypass package branch in each sub-package is important. Since the error in the source file affected only the *UpdateCustomerDim* package, you could have bypassed to the *UpdateProductDim* package. You will work through these scenarios in Chapter 10.

Now that you have added batch control to your data movement application, you will learn how to add logging tasks to the packages in the application to easily determine the most important steps that occurred in each package and their consequences.

Creating Task and Package Logging Steps

Adding task and package logging steps to your packages enables you to create in a single location an execution audit trail for each task and package in the data movement application rather than having information distributed throughout several logging locations.

Creating an Audit Table in SQL Server

In the following procedure, you will create an audit table in SQL Server. In subsequent procedures, you will add tasks in each package that will write entries to this table whenever a package step succeeds or fails. Using this audit trail, you will be able to quickly determine the branch of a package that executed and whether any steps failed.

Create the audit table

1   On the SQL Query Analyzer toolbar, click Load SQL Script.

2   In the Look In list, navigate to C:\Microsoft Press\SQL DTS SBS\ Ch8\ChapterFiles and then open the CreateAuditEventsTable.sql script.

This script creates a six-column table for recording audit events. It enables you to record the batch ID, package name, date and time the step executed, step name, and additional information regarding events that you choose to capture.

> ▶ **Tip**   In your production environment, you might want to create additional columns to enable you to capture additional information, such as start and finish times for each step and each package.

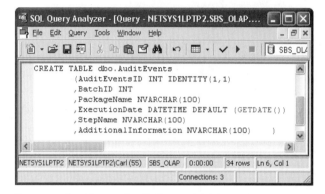

3   Execute the CreateAuditEventsTable script to create the AuditEvents table.

Now that you have created the *AuditEvents* table, you are ready to modify the package in the data movement application to write execution information to this table.

Creating Logging Steps in the *MasterUpdate* Package

In the following procedures, you will create a number of Execute SQL tasks in the *MasterUpdate* package that will write an entry to the *AuditEvents* table you just created each time a new *BatchID* value is generated and when all dimension subpackages complete their execution.

Log information about the *Generate BatchID* step by creating an Execute SQL task in the *MasterUpdate* package

1   Switch to SQL Server Enterprise Manager console tree, and then right-click Data Transformation Services in your local instance.

2   Click Open Package and then open the most recent version of the MasterUpdate package in the C:\Microsoft Press\SQL DTS SBS\ DataMovementApplication folder using a password of **mypassword**.

3   On the Task menu, click Execute SQL Task.

4   Type **Log BatchID Generation** in the Description box, and then click Browse.

5   In the Look In list, navigate to C:\Microsoft Press\SQL DTS SBS\ Ch8\ChapterFiles, and then double-click LogBatchIDGeneration.sql.

This script inserts logging information about the *Generate BatchID* step into the *AuditEvents* table.

6   Click Parameters, select giBatchID in the Input Global Variables list, and then click OK.

7   Click OK to save this Execute SQL task.

You will configure the *Log BatchID Generation* step to execute after the *Generate BatchID* step succeeds.

8   On the design sheet, click the Generate BatchID step, and then hold down the Ctrl key and click the Log BatchID Generation step.

9   On the Workflow menu, click On Success.

Now that you have added a step to log information about the generation of a new *BatchID* value for each execution of the data movement application, you will add a step that logs the successful completion of all the dimension update steps in the *MasterUpdate* package.

Log information about the completion of all dimension update subpackage steps by creating an Execute SQL task in the *MasterUpdate* package

1   On the Task menu, click Execute SQL Task.

2   Type **Log Dimensions Updated** in the Description box, and then click Browse.

3   In the Look In list, navigate to C:\Microsoft Press\SQL DTS SBS\Ch8\ChapterFiles, and then double-click LogUpdateDimensions-Complete.sql.

This script inserts information into the *AuditEvents* table that documents that all dimension update steps have completed. You will configure this step to execute after the completion of all the dimension update subpackages.

4   Click Parameters, select giBatchID in the Input Global Variables list, and then click OK.

5   Click OK to save this Execute SQL task.

6   On the design sheet, click the Call UpdateProductDim Subpackage step, and then hold down the Ctrl key and click the Log Dimensions Updated step.

7   On the Workflow menu, click On Completion.

Remember that a subpackage completes reporting success even if a task in the subpackage reports a failure. Therefore, using an On Completion constraint more accurately reflects when the subsequent step will execute.

8   On the design sheet, click Call UpdateCustomerDim Subpackage step, and then hold down the Ctrl key and click the Log Dimensions Updated step.

9   On the Workflow menu, click On Completion.

Because two precedence constraints are configured to the *Log Dimensions Updated* step, this logging step will not execute until both dimension update packages have completed. The *Call Update-SalesFact Subpackage* step, which you will add in the next chapter, requires that all dimension update subpackages complete before it executes. This *Log Dimensions Updated* step creates an entry in the *AuditEvents* table that documents that these predecessor steps completed, and when.

10   On the toolbar, click Save, and then close the MasterUpdate subpackage.

Now that you created these logging steps in the *MasterUpdate* package, you are ready to create logging steps in the *UpdateProductDim* and *UpdateCustomerDim* subpackages.

▶   **Note**   In a production environment, you should create success and failure logging steps for each step in this package to provide a complete audit log in the audit table.

Creating Logging Steps in the *UpdateCustomerDim* Package

In the following procedures, you will create a number of Execute SQL tasks in the *UpdateCustomerDim* package that will write an entry to the *AuditEvents* table whenever the step associated with the Execute SQL task succeed, fail, or execute.

Log the bypass of the *UpdateCustomerDim* package by modifying the *Log Package Bypass* step

1 In the SQL Server Enterprise Manager console tree, right-click Data Transformation Services in your local instance.

2 Click Open Package and then open the most recent version of the UpdateCustomerDim package in the C:\Microsoft Press\SQL DTS SBS\DataMovementApplication folder using a password of **mypassword**.

3 On the design sheet, double-click the Log Package Bypass step.

4 Click Browse.

5 In the Look In list, navigate to C:\Microsoft Press\SQL DTS SBS\Ch8\ChapterFiles, and then double-click LogUpdateCustomerDimPackageBypassed.sql.

   This script inserts logging information into the *AuditEvents* table to log the bypass of the *UpdateCustomerDim* package. This step executes if the *Bypass Package* step enables the *Log Package Bypass* step and disables the *Delete Or Add Staging Data* step, which disables the remaining steps in the *UpdateCustomerDim* package.

6 Click Parameters, select giBatchID in the Input Global Variables list, and then click OK.

7 Click OK to save the modifications to this Execute SQL task.

Now that you can log the bypass of this package if it occurs, you will create a logging step to log whether the delete branch or the add staging data branch of the *UpdateCustomerDim* package executes.

Log the execution of the delete branch of the *UpdateCustomerDim* package by creating an Execute SQL task

1 On the Task menu, click Execute SQL Task.

2 Type **Log Delete Branch Executed** in the Description box, select SBS_OLAPAdditionalConnection in the Existing Connection list, and then click Browse.

3   In the Look In list, navigate to C:\Microsoft Press\SQL DTS SBS\Ch8\ChapterFiles, and then double-click LogUpdateCustomer-DimDeleteBranchExecuted.sql.

This script inserts logging information into the *AuditEvents* table to document that the delete branch of the *UpdateCustomerDim* package executed. You will configure this step to execute after the completion of the *Delete Staging Data* step.

4   Click Parameters, select giBatchID in the Input Global Variables list, and then click OK.

5   Click OK to save this Execute SQL task.

6   Right-click an open area of the design sheet, and click Disconnected Edit.

7   In the left pane, expand the Steps node and then click DTSStep_DTSExecuteSQLTask_1.

8   In the right pane, double-click Name and then type **LogDeleteBranchExecuted** in the Value box in place of DTSStep_DTSExecuteSQLTask_1.

9   Click OK and then click Close.

10 On the design sheet, click the Delete Staging Data step, and then hold down the Ctrl key and click the Log Delete Branch Executed step.

11 On the Workflow menu, click On Completion.

You are using an On Completion precedence constraint because you are merely creating a log entry to document that this branch of the package executed, not whether the *Delete Staging Data* step actually succeeded or failed.

You have created a step to log when the delete branch of the *UpdateCustomer-Dim* package executes. Next you will create a step to log the success of the *Load CustomerStage Table* step.

Log the successful execution of the *Load CustomerStage Table* step in the *UpdateCustomerDim* package by adding an Execute SQL task

1   On the Task menu, click Execute SQL Task.

2   Type **Log Load CustomerStage Table Success** in the Description box, select SBS_OLAPAdditionalConnection in the Existing Connection list, and then click Browse.

3   In the Look In list, navigate to C:\Microsoft Press\SQL DTS SBS\Ch8\ChapterFiles, and then double-click LogUpdateCustomer-DimLoadCustomerStageTableSuccess.sql.

This script inserts logging information into the *AuditEvents* table to document when the *Load CustomerStage Table* step completes successfully. You will configure this step to execute after the success of the *Load CustomerStage Table* step.

> ▶ **Note**   Remember that the setting you use for the *MaximumErrorCount* property will determine the number of errors permissible before a step fails.

4   Click Parameters, select giBatchID in the Input Global Variables list, and then click OK.

5   Click OK to save this Execute SQL task.

6   Right-click an open area of the design sheet, and click Disconnected Edit.

7   In the left pane, expand the Steps node and then click DTSStep_DTSExecuteSQLTask_1.

8   In the right pane, double-click Name and then type **LogLoadCustomerStageTableSuccess** in the Value box in place of DTSStep_DTSExecuteSQLTask_1.

9   Click OK and then click Close.

10   On the design sheet, click the CustomerStage connection object and then hold down the Ctrl key and click the Log Load CustomerStage Table Success step.

11   On the Workflow menu, click On Success.

You have added a step that creates a log entry in the *AuditEvents* table when the *Load CustomerStage Table* step completes successfully. Now you will add a step that creates a log entry in the *AuditEvents* table when the *Load CustomerStage Table* step fails to complete successfully.

Log the failure of the *Load CustomerStage Table* step in the *UpdateCustomerDim* package by adding an Execute SQL task

1   On the Task menu, click Execute SQL Task.

2   Type **Log Load CustomerStage Table Failure** in the Description box, select SBS_OLAPAdditionalConnection in the Existing Connection list, and then click Browse.

3   In the Look In list, navigate to C:\Microsoft Press\SQL DTS SBS\Ch8\ChapterFiles, and then double-click LogUpdateCustomer-DimLoadCustomerStageTableFailure.sql.

This script inserts logging information into the *AuditEvents* table to document when the *Load CustomerStage Table* step does not complete successfully. You will configure this step to execute after the failure of the *Load CustomerStage Table* step.

4   Click Parameters, select giBatchID in the Input Global Variables list, and then click OK.

5   Click OK to save this Execute SQL task.

6   Right-click an open area of the design sheet, and click Disconnected Edit.

7   In the left pane, expand the Steps node and then click DTSStep_DTSExecuteSQLTask_1.

8   In the right pane, double-click Name and then type **LogLoadCustomerStageTableFailure** in the Value box in place of DTSStep_DTSExecuteSQLTask_1.

9   Click OK and then click Close.

10   On the design sheet, click the CustomerStage connection object, and then hold down the Ctrl key and click the Log Load CustomerStage Table Failure step.

11   On the Workflow menu, click On Failure.

You have added steps to log the success or failure of the *Load CustomerStage Table* step in the *UpdateCustomerDim* package to the *AuditEvents* table. Next you will modify the *Log Load Dimension Table Bypass* step that you added earlier in the chapter but did not configure.

Log the bypass of the load dimension table steps in the *UpdateCustomerDim* package by editing the *Log Load Dimension Table Bypass* step

1   On the design sheet, double-click the *Log Load Dimension Table Bypass* step and then click Browse.

2   In the Look In list, navigate to C:\Microsoft Press\SQL DTS SBS\Ch8\ChapterFiles, and then double-click LogUpdateCustomer-DimInsertAndUpdateDimTableBypassed.sql.

This script inserts logging information into the *AuditEvents* table to document when the *Update Data in CustomerDim Table* step and the *Insert New Data in CustomerDim Table* step are bypassed.

3   Click Parameters, select giBatchID in the Input Global Variables list, and then click OK.

4   Click OK to save the modification of this Execute SQL task.

You have created a step that will create a log entry in the *AuditEvents* table when the steps that insert and update data in the *CustomerDim* table are bypassed. Next you will create steps to log the success or failure of the steps that insert and update data from the *CustomerStage* table to the *CustomerDim* table.

Log the success of the *Update Data In CustomerDim Table* step in the *UpdateCustomerDim* package by adding an Execute SQL task

1   On the Task menu, click Execute SQL Task.

2   Type **Log Update Data in CustomerDim Table Success** in the Description box, select SBS_OLAPAdditionalConnection in the Existing Connection list, and then click Browse.

3   In the Look In list, navigate to C:\Microsoft Press\SQL DTS SBS\Ch8\ChapterFiles, and then double-click LogUpdateCustomer-DimUpdateCustomerDimTableSuccess.sql.

   This script inserts logging information into the *AuditEvents* table to document that the dimension data in the *CustomerDim* table was successfully updated by the *Update Data In CustomerDim Table* step. You will configure this step to execute after the success of the *Update Data In CustomerDim Table* step.

4   Click Parameters, select giBatchID in the Input Global Variables list, and then click OK.

5   Click OK to save this Execute SQL task.

6   Right-click an open area of the design sheet, and click Disconnected Edit.

7   In the left pane, expand the Steps node and then click DTSStep_DTSExecuteSQLTask_1.

8   In the right pane, double-click Name and then type **LogUpdateDataInCustomerDimTableSuccess** in the Value box in place of DTSStep_DTSExecuteSQLTask_1.

9   Click OK and then click Close.

10 On the design sheet, click the Update Data In CustomerDim Table step, and then hold down the Ctrl key and click the Log Update Data In CustomerDim Table Success step.

11 On the Workflow menu, click On Success.

Now that you have added the step to create a log entry when dimension data in the *CustomerDim* table is successfully updated by the *Update Data In CustomerDim Table* step, you will add a step to create a log entry when this step fails.

Log the failure of the *Update Data In CustomerDim Table* step in the *UpdateCustomerDim* package by adding an Execute SQL task

1   On the Task menu, click Execute SQL Task.

2   Type **Log Update Data in CustomerDim Table Failure** in the Description box, select SBS_OLAPAdditionalConnection in the Existing Connection list, and then click Browse.

3   In the Look In list, navigate to C:\Microsoft Press\SQL DTS SBS\Ch8\ChapterFiles, and then double-click LogUpdateCustomer-DimUpdateCustomerDimTableFailure.sql.

    This script inserts logging information into the *AuditEvents* table to document that the dimension data in the *CustomerDim* table was not successfully updated by the *Update Data In CustomerDim Table* step. You will configure this step to execute after the failure of the *Update Data In CustomerDim Table* step.

4   Click Parameters, select giBatchID in the Input Global Variables list, and then click OK.

5   Click OK to save this Execute SQL task.

6   Right-click an open area of the design sheet, and click Disconnected Edit.

7   In the left pane, expand the Steps node and then click DTSStep_DTSExecuteSQLTask_1.

8   In the right pane, double-click Name and then type **LogUpdateDataInCustomerDimTableFailure** in the Value box in place of DTSStep_DTSExecuteSQLTask_1.

9   Click OK and then click Close.

10 On the design sheet, click the Update Data in CustomerDim Table step, and then hold down the Ctrl key and click the Log Update Data In CustomerDim Table Failure step.

11 On the Workflow menu, click On Failure.

You have added the steps to log whether the *Update Data in CustomerDim Table* step succeeded or failed. Next you will add the steps to log whether the *Insert New Data in CustomerDim Table* step succeeds or fails.

Log the success of the *Insert New Data In CustomerDim Table* step in the *UpdateCustomerDim* package by adding an Execute SQL task

1 On the Task menu, click Execute SQL Task.

2 Type **Log Insert New Data in CustomerDim Table Success** in the Description box, select SBS_OLAPAdditionalConnection in the Existing Connection list, and then click Browse.

3 In the Look In list, navigate to C:\Microsoft Press\SQL DTS SBS\Ch8\ChapterFiles, and then double-click LogUpdateCustomer-DimInsertCustomerDimTableSuccess.sql.

This script inserts logging information into the *AuditEvents* table to document that new dimension data in the *CustomerStage* table was successfully inserted into the *CustomerDim* table by the *Insert New Data In CustomerDim Table* step. You will configure this step to execute after the success of the *Insert New Data In CustomerDim Table* step.

4 Click Parameters, select giBatchID in the Input Global Variables list, and then click OK.

5 Click OK to save this Execute SQL task.

6 Right-click an open area of the design sheet, and click Disconnected Edit.

7 In the left pane, expand the Steps node and then click DTSStep_DTSExecuteSQLTask_1.

8 In the right pane, double-click Name and then type **LogInsertNewDataInCustomerDimTableSuccess** in the Value box in place of DTSStep_DTSExecuteSQLTask_1.

9 Click OK and then click Close.

10 On the design sheet, click the Insert New Data In CustomerDim Table step, and then hold down the Ctrl key and click the Log Insert New Data In CustomerDim Table Success step.

11 On the Workflow menu, click On Success.

You have added the step to create a log entry when new dimension data is successfully inserted into the *CustomerDim* table by the *Insert New Data In CustomerDim Table* step. Now you will add a step to create a log entry when the *Insert New Data In CustomerDim Table* step fails to insert new dimension data into the *CustomerDim* table.

Log the Failure of the *Insert New Data In CustomerDim Table* step in the *UpdateCustomerDim* package by adding an Execute SQL task

1 On the Task menu, click Execute SQL Task.

2 Type **Log Insert New Data in CustomerDim Table Failure** in the Description box, select Cust Stage Dest in the Existing Connection list, and then click Browse.

3 In the Look In list, navigate to C:\Microsoft Press\SQL DTS SBS\Ch8\ChapterFiles, and then double-click LogUpdateCustomer-DimInsertCustomerDimTableFailure.sql.

This script inserts logging information into the *AuditEvents* table to document that new dimension data in the *CustomerStage* table was not successfully inserted into the *CustomerDim* table by the *Insert New Data In CustomerDim Table* step. You will configure this step to execute after the failure of the *Insert New Data In CustomerDim Table* step.

4 Click Parameters, select giBatchID in the Input Global Variables list, and then click OK.

5 Click OK to save this Execute SQL task.

6 Right-click an open area of the design sheet, and click Disconnected Edit.

7 In the left pane, expand the Steps node and then click DTSStep_DTSExecuteSQLTask_1.

8 In the right pane, double-click Name and then type **LogInsertNewDataInCustomerDimTableFailure** in the Value box in place of DTSStep_DTSExecuteSQLTask_1.

9 Click OK and then click Close.

10 On the design sheet, click the Insert New Data In CustomerDim Table step, and then hold down the Ctrl key and click the Log Insert New Data In CustomerDim Table Failure step.

11 On the Workflow menu, click On Failure.

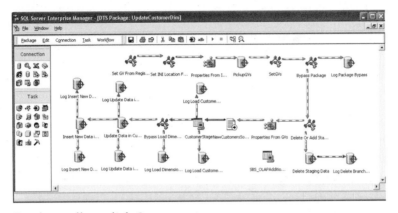

12 On the toolbar, click Save.

13 Close the UpdateCustomerDim package in DTS Designer.

Now that you have added logging steps to the *UpdateCustomerDim* package, you are ready to add similar steps to the *UpdateProductDim* package.

Creating Logging Steps in *UpdateProductDim* Package

In the following procedures, you will create a number of Execute SQL tasks in the *UpdateProductDim* package that will each write an entry to the *AuditEvents* table whenever the step associated with the Execute SQL task succeeds, fails, or executes.

Edit the *LogBypass* step in the *UpdateProductDim* package

1 In the SQL Server Enterprise Manager console tree, right-click Data Transformation Services in your local instance.

2 Click Open Package and then open the most recent version of the UpdateProductDim package in the C:\Microsoft Press\SQL DTS SBS\ DataMovementApplication folder using a password of **mypassword**.

3 On the design sheet, double-click the Log Package Bypass step.

4 Click Browse.

5   In the Look In list, navigate to C:\Microsoft Press\SQL DTS SBS\Ch8\ChapterFiles, and then double-click LogUpdateProduct-DimPackageBypassed.sql.

This script inserts logging information into the *AuditEvents* table to log the bypass of the *UpdateProductDim* package. This step executes if the *Bypass Package* step enables the *Log Package Bypass* step and disables the *Delete or Add Staging Data* step, which disables the remaining steps in the *UpdateProductDim* package.

6   Click Parameters, select giBatchID in the Input Global Variables list, and then click OK.

7   Click OK to save the modifications to this Execute SQL task.

Now that you can log the bypass of this package if it occurs, you will create a logging step to log whether the delete branch or the add staging data branch of the *UpdateProductDim* package executes.

Log the execution of the delete branch of the *UpdateProduct-Dim* package by creating an Execute SQL task

1   On the Task menu, click Execute SQL Task.

2   Type **Log Delete Branch Executed** in the Description box, select SBS_OLAPAdditionalConnection in the Existing Connection list, and then click Browse.

3   In the Look In list, navigate to C:\Microsoft Press\SQL DTS SBS\Ch8\ChapterFiles, and then double-click LogUpdateProduct-DimDeleteBranchExecuted.sql.

This script inserts logging information into the *AuditEvents* table to document that the deleted branch of the *UpdateProductDim* package executed. You will configure this step to execute after the completion of the *Delete Staging Data* step.

4   Click Parameters, select giBatchID in the Input Global Variables list, and then click OK.

5   Click OK to save this Execute SQL task.

6   Right-click an open area of the design sheet, and click Disconnected Edit.

7   In the left pane, expand the Steps node and then click DTSStep_DTSExecuteSQLTask_1.

8   In the right pane, double-click Name and then type **LogDeleteBranchExecuted** in the Value box in place of DTSStep_DTSExecuteSQLTask_1.

9 Click OK and then click Close.

10 On the design sheet, click the Delete Staging Data step, and then hold down the Ctrl key and click the Log Delete Branch Executed step.

11 On the Workflow menu, click On Completion.

Now that you have added a step to log when the delete branch of the *UpdateProductDim* package executes, you will add a step to log the success of the *Load ProductStage Table* step.

Log the successful execution of the *Load ProductStage Table* step in the *UpdateProductDim* package by adding an Execute SQL task

1 On the Task menu, click Execute SQL Task.

2 Type **Log Load ProductStage Table Success** in the Description box, select SBS_OLAPAdditionalConnection in the Existing Connection list, and then click Browse.

3 In the Look In list, navigate to C:\Microsoft Press\SQL DTS SBS\Ch8\ChapterFiles, and then double-click LogUpdateProduct-DimLoadProductStageTableSuccess.sql.

   This script inserts logging information into the *AuditEvents* table to document when new data is successfully added to the *ProductStage* table. You will configure this step to execute after the success of the *Load ProductStage Table* step.

4 Click Parameters, select giBatchID in the Input Global Variables list, and then click OK.

5 Click OK to save this Execute SQL task.

6 Right-click an open area of the design sheet, and click Disconnected Edit.

7 In the left pane, expand the Steps node and then click DTSStep_DTSExecuteSQLTask_1.

8 In the right pane, double-click Name and then type **LogLoadProductStageTableSuccess** in the Value box in place of DTSStep_DTSExecuteSQLTask_1.

9 Click OK and then click Close.

10 On the design sheet, click the ProductStage connection object, and then hold down the Ctrl key and click the Log Load ProductStage Table Success step.

11 On the Workflow menu, click On Success.

You have added a step that creates a log entry in the *AuditEvents* table when the *Load ProductStage Table* step completes successfully. Now you will add a step that creates a log entry in the *AuditEvents* table when the *Load Product-Stage Table* step fails to complete successfully.

Log the failure of the *Load ProductStage Table* step in the *UpdateProductDim* package by adding an Execute SQL task

1   On the Task menu, click Execute SQL Task.

2   Type **Log Load ProductStage Table Failure** in the Description box, select SBS_OLAPAdditionalConnection in the Existing Connection list, and then click Browse.

3   In the Look In list, navigate to C:\Microsoft Press\SQL DTS SBS\Ch8\ChapterFiles, and then double-click LogUpdateProduct-DimLoadProductStageTableFailure.sql.

   This script inserts logging information into the *AuditEvents* table to document when the *Load ProductStage Table* step does not complete successfully. You will configure this step to execute after the failure of the *Load ProductStage Table* step.

4   Click Parameters, select giBatchID in the Input Global Variables list, and then click OK.

5   Click OK to save this Execute SQL task.

6   Right-click an open area of the design sheet, and click Disconnected Edit.

7   In the left pane, expand the Steps node and then click DTSStep_DTSExecuteSQLTask_1.

8   In the right pane, double-click Name and then type **LogLoadProductStageTableFailure** in the Value box in place of DTSStep_DTSExecuteSQLTask_1.

9   Click OK and then click Close.

10   On the design sheet, click the ProductStage connection object, and then hold down the Ctrl key and click the Log Load ProductStage Table Failure step.

11   On the Workflow menu, click On Failure.

You have added steps to log the success or failure of the *Load ProductStage Table* step in the *UpdateProductDim* package to the *AuditEvents* table. Next you will modify the *Log Load Dimension Table Bypass* step that you added in Chapter 7 but did not configure.

Log the bypass of the *Insert Or Update ProductDim Table* step in the *UpdateProductDim* package by editing the *Log Load Dimension Table Bypass* step

1. On the design sheet, double-click the *Log Load Dimension Table Bypass* step and then click Browse.

2. In the Look In list, navigate to C:\Microsoft Press\SQL DTS SBS\Ch8\ChapterFiles, and then double-click LogUpdateProductDimInsertAndUpdateDimTableBypassed.sql.

   This script inserts logging information into the *AuditEvents* table to document when the *Insert Or Update ProductDim Table* step is bypassed.

3. Click Parameters, select giBatchID in the Input Global Variables list, and then click OK.

4. Click OK to save the modification of this Execute SQL task.

You have created a step that will create a log entry in the *AuditEvents* table when the *Insert Or Update ProductDim Table* step is bypassed. Next you will create steps to log the success or failure of the *Insert Or Update ProductDim Table* step.

Log the success of the *Insert Or Update ProductDim Table* step in the *UpdateProductDim* package by adding an Execute SQL task

1. On the Task menu, click Execute SQL Task.

2. Type **Log Insert Or Update ProductDim Table Success** in the Description box, select SBS_OLAPAdditionalConnection in the Existing Connection list, and then click Browse.

3. In the Look In list, navigate to C:\Microsoft Press\SQL DTS SBS\Ch8\ChapterFiles, and then double-click LogUpdateProductDimInsertOrUpdateProductDimTableSuccess.sql.

   This script inserts logging information into the *AuditEvents* table to document that the dimension data in the *ProductDim* table was successfully updated by the *Insert Or Update ProductDim Table* step. You will configure this step to execute after the success of the *Insert Or Update ProductDim Table* step.

4. Click Parameters, select giBatchID in the Input Global Variables list, and then click OK.

5 Click OK to save this Execute SQL task.

6 Right-click an open area of the design sheet, and click Disconnected Edit.

7 In the left pane, expand the Steps node and then click DTSStep_DTSExecuteSQLTask_1.

8 In the right pane, double-click Name and then type **LogInsertOrUpdateProductDimTableSuccess** in the Value box in place of DTSStep_DTSExecuteSQLTask_1.

9 Click OK and then click Close.

10 On the design sheet, click the Insert Or Update ProductDim Table step, and then hold down the Ctrl key and click the Log Insert Or Update ProductDim Table Success step.

11 On the Workflow menu, click On Success.

Now that you have added the step to create a log entry when the *Insert Or Update ProductDim Table* step completes successfully, you will add a step to create a log entry when this step fails.

Log the failure of the *Insert Or Update ProductDim Table* step in the *UpdateProductDim* package by adding an Execute SQL task

1 On the Task menu, click Execute SQL Task.

2 Type **Log Insert Or Update ProductDim Table Failure** in the Description box, select SBS_OLAPAdditionalConnection in the Existing Connection list, and then click Browse.

3 In the Look In list, navigate to C:\Microsoft Press\SQL DTS SBS\Ch8\ChapterFiles, and then double-click LogUpdateProductDimInsertOrUpdateProductDimTableFailure.sql.

This script inserts logging information into the *AuditEvents* table to document that the *Insert Or Update ProductDim Table* step was unsuccessful in updating dimension data in the *ProductDim* table. You will configure this step to execute after the success of the *Insert Or Update ProductDim Table* step.

4 Click Parameters, select giBatchID in the Input Global Variables list, and then click OK.

5 Click OK to save this Execute SQL task.

6   Right-click an open area of the design sheet, and click Disconnected Edit.

7   In the left pane, expand the Steps node and then click DTSStep_DTSExecuteSQLTask_1.

8   In the right pane, double-click Name and then type **LogInsertOrUpdateProductDimTableFailure** in the Value box in place of DTSStep_DTSExecuteSQLTask_1.

9   Click OK and then click Close.

10 On the design sheet, click the Insert Or Update ProductDim Table step, and then hold down the Ctrl key and click Log Insert Or Update ProductDim Table Failure.

11 On the Workflow menu, click On Failure.

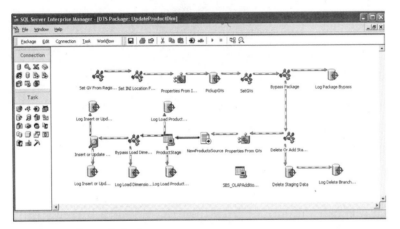

12 On the toolbar click Save.

13 Close the UpdateProductDim package in DTS Designer.

You have added logging steps to the *UpdateProductDim* package, so now you are ready to test the execution of the data movement application and view the contents of the *AuditEvents* table.

Testing the Use of the *AuditEvents* Table

In the following procedure, you will execute the *MasterUpdate* package and its subpackages using the default configuration and the delete all configuration. You will then query the *AuditEvents* table to observe the log entries that were written to the *AuditEvents* table when the *MasterUpdate* package and its subpackages executed with different *ConfigID* values.

Test package execution

1 Using Windows Explorer, navigate to C:\Microsoft Press\SQL DTS
SBS\DataMovementApplication, and then double-click Master-
UpdateDefaultConfig.cmd.

2 After the batch file completes its execution, switch to SQL Query
Analyzer and click Clear Window on the toolbar.

3 In the query pane, type **SELECT * FROM
SBS_OLAP.dbo.AuditEvents ORDER BY PackageName**, and then
click Execute on the toolbar.

This query returns the steps in each package that executed, sorted by
the *PackageName*. Notice that you can quickly determine which
packages in the data movement application executed for a particular
batch and which steps in each package succeeded or failed. Notice
that the steps in the *UpdateCustomerDim* package are executing in
parallel with the steps in the *UpdateProductDim* package.

4 Switch to Windows Explorer and then double-click Config2.cmd in
the DataMovementApplication folder.

5 After the batch file completes its execution, switch to SQL Query
Analyzer and change the query to read **SELECT * FROM
SBS_OLAP.dbo.AuditEvents WHERE BatchID = 5 ORDER BY
AuditEventsID**, and then click Execute on the toolbar.

Notice that the *Load CustomerStage Table* step, which has two
errors in the source file and failed in the previous execution, now
reports success because the number of errors does not exceed the
MaximumErrorCount value associated with *ConfigID* 2.

6   Switch to Windows Explorer and then double-click DeleteAllStaging-Data.cmd in the DataMovementApplication folder.

7   After the batch file completes its execution, switch to SQL Query Analyzer and change the query to read **SELECT * FROM SBS_OLAP.dbo.AuditEvents WHERE BatchID = 6 ORDER BY AuditEventsID,** and then click Execute on the toolbar.

Notice that you are easily able to determine that for *BatchID* 6, the delete branches of the *UpdateProductDim* and the *UpdateCustomer-Dim* packages executed.

You have successfully created an audit and error detection table for the data movement application and created steps in the data movement application packages to record execution information. However, the information recorded in the *AuditEvents* table is not as complete as needed to fully understand the actions performed by each step in the packages.

Recording Completed Rows and Rows with Errors

To more completely understand the actions performed by package tasks, you can record additional information in the audit table, such as the number of rows completed or transformed and the number of rows with errors. To record this information in the *AuditEvents* table about actions performed by the Transform Data or Data Driven Query tasks, you need to query the *DataPumpTask2* object and the *DataDrivenQueryTask2* object through the DTS object model. Among the properties of these objects are *RowsComplete* and *RowsInError*. The *RowsComplete* property returns the count of transformed rows, and the *RowsInError* property returns the number of transformation error rows. To record information about the actions performed by Execute SQL tasks, you can have the Execute SQL task write directly to the *AuditEvents* table

Modifying the *AuditEvents* Table to Record Row Processing Information

In the following procedures, you will add columns to the *AuditEvents* table to store number of rows completed and then the number of rows with errors. In the subsequent procedures, you will modify tasks in the *UpdateProductDim* and *UpdateCustomerDim* packages to record row processing information to the *AuditEvents* table.

Enable rows added and rows with errors to be recorded by adding columns to the *AuditEvents* table

1   Switch to SQL Query Analyzer and then click New Query on the toolbar.

2   Click Load SQL Script on the toolbar, navigate to C:\Microsoft Press\SQL DTS SBS\Ch8\ChapterFiles, and then open the Add-ColumnsToAuditEventsTable.sql script.

    This script adds the *RowsComplete* and *RowsInError* columns to the *AuditEvents* table. These columns will store the values for the *RowsComplete* and *RowsInError* properties of the *DataPumpTask2* and the *DataDrivenQueryTask2* objects.

3   Execute the AddColumnsToAuditEventsTable.sql script to add these columns to the AuditEvents table.

Now that you have created the infrastructure to store the values for the *RowsComplete* and *RowsInError* properties of the *DataPumpTask2* and *DataDrivenQueryTask2* objects, you are ready to add a global variable to the *UpdateProductDim* package to record the file location for the SBS_OLAP.udl file.

Reporting Row Processing Information by *UpdateProductDim* Package Tasks

In the following procedures, you will create a global variable in the *Update-ProductDim* package to store the file location for the SBS_OLAP.udl file. You will then create an ActiveX Script task that will record directly the values for the *RowsComplete* and *RowsInError* properties for the *DataPumpTask2* object (the *Load ProductStage Table* step) and for the *DataDrivenQueryTask2* object (the *Insert Or Update ProductDim Table* step) directly into the *AuditEvents* table.

Store the location of the SBS_OLAP.UDL file in a global variable in the *UpdateProductDim* package

1   Switch to SQL Enterprise Manager, and then right-click Data Transformation Services in your local instance.

2   Click Open package and then open the most recent version of the UpdateProductDim package in the C:\Microsoft Press\SQL DTS SBS\ DataMovementApplication folder using a password of **mypassword**.

3   Right-click an open area on the design sheet, and then click Package Properties.

4   On the Global Variables tab, type **gsSBS_OLAP_UDL** in the Name column, select String in the Type column, type **C:\Microsoft Press\SQL DTS SBS\DataMovementApplication\SBS_OLAP.udl** in the Value column, and then click OK.

You have added a global variable to the *UpdateProductDim* package that points to the SBS_OLAP.udl file. You will create an ActiveX Script task that will use this global variable to connect directly to the SBS_OLAP database. You are now ready to add steps to the *UpdateProductDim* package that will insert the rows completed and rows in error values into the *AuditEvents* table.

▶ **Tip**   Since you will be logging the *RowsComplete* and *RowsInError* values to the *AuditEvents* table using an ActiveX Script task, you cannot directly take advantage of the *SBSOLAP_AdditionalConnection* connection object to connect to the SBS_OLAP database. That is why the *gsSBS_OLAP* global variable was added to provide the path to the SBS_OLAP.udl file. To centralize the configuration of this path, you could add an entry for *gsSBS_OLAP* to the *PackageGVs* table, or you could modify the ActiveX Script task to read the path to the SBS_OLAP.udl file from the *UDLPath* property of the *SBSOLAP_AdditionalConnection* connection object.

Record the number of rows completed and rows with errors by the *Load ProductStage Table* step by adding an ActiveX Script task to the *UpdateProductDim* package

1   On the Task menu, click ActiveX Script Task.

2   In the Description box, type **Log Load ProductStage Table Load Rows**, and then click Browse.

3   In the Look In list, navigate to C:\Microsoft Press\SQL DTS SBS\Ch8\ChapterFiles, and then double-click LogUpdateProductDimLoadProductStageTableLoadRows.bas.

This script queries the *RowsComplete* and *RowsInError* properties of the *DTSTask_DTSDataPumpTask_1* task (the *Load ProductStage Table* step) and places these values into variables. Next this script creates a SQL script to insert the appropriate values into the *AuditEvents* table and then executes this script.

4   Click OK to save this ActiveX Script task.

5   On the design sheet, click the ProductStage connection object, and then hold down the Ctrl key and click the Log Load ProductStage Table Load Rows step.

6   On the Workflow menu, click On Completion.

Now that you have added a step to record into the *AuditEvents* table the rows completed and rows in error for the *Load ProductStage Table* step, you are ready to add a similar step for the *Insert Or Update ProductDim Table* step.

Record the number of rows completed and rows with errors by the *Insert Or Update ProductDim Table* step by adding an ActiveX Script task to the *UpdateProductDim* package

1   On the Task menu, click ActiveX Script Task.

2   In the Description box, type **Log Insert or Update ProductDim Table LoadRows** and then click Browse.

3   In the Look In list, navigate to C:\Microsoft Press\SQL DTS SBS\Ch8\ChapterFiles, and then double-click LogUpdateProductDimInsertOrUpdateProductDimLoadRows.bas.

  This script queries the *RowsComplete* and *RowsInError* properties of the *DTSTask_DTSDataDrivenQueryTask_1* task (the *Insert Or Update ProductDim Table* step) and places these values into variables. Next this script creates a SQL script to insert the appropriate values into the *AuditEvents* table, and then executes this script.

4   Click OK to save this ActiveX Script task.

5   On the design sheet, click the Insert Or Update ProductDim Table step, and then hold down the Ctrl key and click the Log Insert Or Update ProductDim Table Load Rows step.

6   On the Workflow menu, click On Completion.

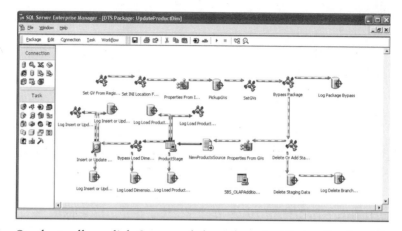

7   On the toolbar, click Save, and then close the UpdateProductDim package.

Now that you have added steps to record the rows completed and rows in error for the data load into the *ProductStage* and *ProductDim* tables, you are ready to add similar steps for the data load into the *CustomerStage* and *CustomerDim* tables.

Reporting Row Processing Information by *UpdateCustomerDim* Package Tasks

In the following procedures, you will create a global variable in the *Update-CustomerDim* packages to store the file location for the SBS_OLAP.udl file. You will then create an ActiveX Script task that will record directly the values for the *RowsComplete* and *RowsInError* properties for the *DataPumpTask1* object (the *Load CustomerStage Table* step). You will then modify the stored procedures that insert and update data in the *CustomerDim* table to query and report the number of rows updated or inserted by the stored procedure to the *AuditEvents* table.

Store the location of the SBS_OLAP UDL file in a global variable in the *UpdateCustomerDim* package

1   In the SQL Enterprise Manager console tree, right-click Data Transformation Services in your local instance.

2   Click Open Package and then open the most recent version of the UpdateCustomerDim package in the C:\Microsoft Press\SQL DTS SBS\DataMovementApplication folder using a password of **mypassword**.

3   Right-click an open area on the design sheet, and then click Package Properties.

4   On the Global Variables tab, type **gsSBS_OLAP_UDL** in the Name column, select String in the Type column, type **C:\Microsoft Press\SQL DTS SBS\DataMovementApplication\SBS_OLAP.udl** in the Value column, and then click OK.

You have added a global variable to the *UpdateCustomerDim* package that points to the SBS_OLAP.udl file. You will create an ActiveX Script task that will use this global variable to connect directly to the SBS_OLAP database. You are now ready to add steps to the *UpdateCustomerDim* package that will insert the rows completed and rows in error values into the *AuditEvents* table.

Record the number of rows completed and rows with errors by the *Load CustomerStage Table* step by adding an ActiveX Script task to the *UpdateCustomerDim* package

1   On the Task menu, click ActiveX Script Task.

2   In the Description box, type **Log Load CustomerStage Table Load Rows,** and then click Browse.

3   In the Look In list, navigate to C:\Microsoft Press\SQL DTS SBS\Ch8\ChapterFiles, and then double-click LogUpdateCustomer-DimLoadCustomerStageTableLoadRows.bas.

This script queries the *RowsComplete* and *RowsInError* properties of the *DTSTask_DTSDataPumpTask_1* task (the *Load Customer-Stage Table* step) and places these values into variables. Next this script creates a SQL script to insert the appropriate values into the *AuditEvents* table, and then executes this script.

4   Click OK to save this ActiveX Script task.

5   On the design sheet, click the CustomerStage connection object, and then hold down the Ctrl key and click the Log Load CustomerStage Table Load Rows step.

6   On the Workflow menu, click On Completion.

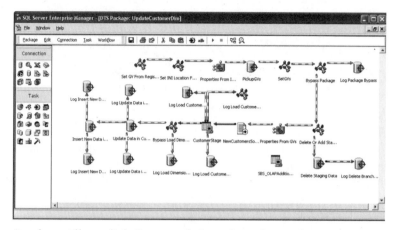

7   On the toolbar, click Save, and then close the UpdateCustomerDim package.

Now that you have added a task to record the rows completed and rows in error for the data load into the *CustomerStage* table from the source files, you are ready to add a similar task for the data load into the *CustomerDim* table from the *CustomerStage* table. However, because these inserts and updates are performed by stored procedures called by Execute SQL tasks, you cannot query the DTS object model for this information. Rather, you must use traditional Transact-SQL methods to count the number of rows inserted or updated and have the stored procedures insert this value directly into the *AuditEvents* table.

Report the number of rows inserted or updated by modifying the *CustomerDimUpdateValues* and *CustomerDimInsertValues* stored procedures

1   Switch to SQL Query Analyzer and then click Load SQL Script on the toolbar.

2   In the Look In list, navigate to C:\Microsoft Press\SQL DTS SBS\Ch8\ChapterFiles, and then double-click AlterCustomerDimValues.sql.

     This script alters the *CustomerDimUpdateValues* and *CustomerDim-InsertValues* stored procedures by adding an *INSERT* statement to each that adds a row into the *AuditEvents* table. This *INSERT* statement includes a query of the @@*ROWCOUNT* counter to report the number of rows affected by the previous *UPDATE* or *INSERT* statement.

▶ **Tip** When a Transact-SQL *INSERT* or *UPDATE* statement encounters an error, the statement aborts. As a result, counting the errors encountered by a Transact-SQL *INSERT* or *UPDATE* statement cannot be done. To avoid errors from terminating an *INSERT* or *UPDATE* statement contained in an Execute SQL task, you can add a step before the *INSERT* or *UPDATE* statement to detect and correct errors before the insertion or update occurs. For example, rows with errors can be moved to an error table before the remaining rows are added to the dimension table. You can then correct the rows with errors at a later time and resubmit the corrected error rows as a separate batch.

3   Execute the AlterCustomerDimValues.sql script to modify these stored procedures.

4   Close this query window in SQL Query Analyzer, but do not close SQL Query Analyzer.

Now that you have modified these stored procedures and added steps to the *UpdateCustomerDim* and *UpdateProductDim* packages to record in the *AuditEvents* table the number of rows completed and the number of rows in error, you are ready to test the execution of the data movement application.

Testing the Recording of Row Processing Information

In the following procedure, you will execute the *LoadHistoricalData* package to delete all test data from the dimension tables. You will then execute the *MasterUpdate* package and its subpackages using the delete all configuration to delete all staging data from the staging tables. Finally, you will execute the *MasterUpdate* package and its subpackages using the default configuration and then query the *AuditEvents* table to determine the number of rows inserted into the staging and dimension tables.

Test package execution

1 In the SQL Server Enterprise Manager, switch to the LoadHistorical-Data package in DTS Designer and the click Execute on the toolbar.

   Performing this step truncates all data in the dimension and fact tables, and then reloads the original historical data. By executing this task, it will be easier to observe the effect of executing the *Update-CustomerDim* and *UpdateProductDim* packages again because the test data that you have previously loaded into the dimension tables is deleted.

2 Click OK and then click Done.

3 Close the LoadHistoricalData package in DTS Designer and then switch to Windows Explorer.

4 Navigate to C:\Microsoft Press\SQL DTS SBS\DataMovementAppli-cation, and then double-click Config2.cmd.

5 After this batch file completes, switch to SQL Query Analyzer.

6 Change the query to read **SELECT * FROM SBS_OLAP.dbo.AuditEvents WHERE BatchID = 7 ORDER BY PackageName, ExecutionDate**, and then click Execute on the toolbar.

   This query returns the steps in each package that executed, sorted by *PackageName* and then by *ExecutionDate*. You can now quickly determine the number of rows affected by each package as well as the number of error rows. Notice that the *Load CustomerStage Table* step in the *UpdateCustomerDim* package encountered two rows with errors. To determine the cause of these errors, you can review the LoadCustomerStageTableExceptionFile.txt, the LoadCustomer-StageTableExceptionFile.txt.Source, and the LoadCustomerStage-TableExceptionFile.txt.Dest logs in the file system. No errors were encountered loading data in the *ProductStage* table. In addition, all 27 of the rows in the *CustomerStage* table were successfully inserted into the *CustomerDim* table and the three rows in the *ProductStage* table were successfully inserted or updated in the *ProductDim* table.

7   Close SQL Query Analyzer without saving any modified scripts and then close SQL Server Enterprise Manager.

You have successfully queried the DTS Object Model to return information about rows completed and rows affected, as well as used traditional Transact-SQL techniques to return information about rows inserted and updated.

Chapter Summary

In this chapter, you learned a number of techniques for incorporating error handling into DTS packages. You added batch control to your packages to enable you to differentiate between executions of the data movement application. You added success and error logging steps into the packages, which record the batch ID value with each log entry into an audit table. Finally, you captured information about the number of rows transformed and the number of rows with errors for each step in each package that modified rows. These techniques enable you to capture additional error information and quickly determine whether you need to review the error logs in detail for any particular execution of the data movement application.

Chapter 9

Completing the Data Movement Application

In this chapter, you will learn how to:

■ Create a starter DTS package

■ Add a fact table subpackage

■ Add an Analysis Services Processing task to a package

In this chapter, you will complete your prototype of a data movement application. You will begin by creating a DTS package (the *StarterDTS* package) that is based on the subpackages you have already created. You can use this package as a template for all future packages that you create for the data movement application. This template package will include the initial configuration steps for dynamically setting package properties at run time. You will then use this template package as the starting point for creating the *UpdateSalesFacts* subpackage. This package will load sales data from a delimited text file into the *SalesStage* table and then load data from the *SalesStage* table into the *SalesFact* table, joining it with data from the *ProductDim*, *CustomerDim*, and *TimeDim* tables. The *UpdateSalesFacts* subpackage will be called by the *MasterUpdate* package after all dimension subpackages have completed executing. You will also add appropriate package bypass, delete data, and logging steps to this package.

You will complete your prototype of the data movement application by adding an Analysis Services Processing task to the *MasterUpdate* package. This task will execute after all dimension and fact subpackages have executed. It will process the data in the dimension and fact tables in the SBS_OLAP relational database into a multidimensional cube that you will restore to an instance of Analysis Services. You will also add a bypass step to the *MasterUpdate* package to enable you to execute the *MasterUpdate* package without calling the Analysis Services Processing task. Finally, you will add a logging task to the *MasterUpdate* package to create a log entry in the *AuditEvents* table that documents when the Analysis Services Processing task is bypassed.

Creating a Starter DTS Package

Now that you have learned the advantages of creating packages that can be dynamically configured at run time by using initialization files, global variables, and registry entries, you will want to create each new package for the data movement application with these same steps. The easiest way to do this is to create a template package based on one of the existing dimension subpackages. You can then use this prototype as the starting point for each new package that you add to the data movement application.

▶ **Note**   If you skipped Chapter 8, execute the IfYouSkippedChapter8.cmd batch file in the C:\Microsoft Press\SQL DTS SBS\Ch9\SkippedChapterFiles folder before you begin these procedures. This batch file restores the SBS_OLTP and SBS_OLAP databases and copies the DTS packages that would have been created in Chapters 1 through 8 into the appropriate folders. It also records the location of the Config.ini initialization file in the Windows registry. If you do not want this batch file to overwrite any packages that you created in Chapters 1 through 8, you must move them or rename them before you execute this batch file.

Create a DTS starter package based on the *UpdateProductDim* package

1   Open SQL Server Enterprise Manager and then right-click Data Transformation Services in your local instance.

2   Click Open Package and then open the most recent version of the UpdateProductDim package in the C:\Microsoft Press\SQL DTS SBS\ DataMovementApplication folder using a password of **mypassword**.

3   On the design sheet, delete the NewProductsSource connection object and then delete the following steps:

- Delete Or Add Staging Data
- Delete Staging Data
- Log Delete Branch
- Log Load ProductStage Table Success

- Log Load ProductStage Table Failure
- Log Load ProductStage Table Load Rows
- Bypass Load Dimension Table
- Log Load Dimension Table Bypass
- Insert or Update ProductDim Table
- Log Insert or Update ProductDim Table Success
- Log Insert or Update ProductDim Table Failure
- Log Insert or Update ProductDim Table Load Rows

The remaining steps and connection objects are the initial setup steps that you will use in each new package that you create and the connection objects you will need for these steps, as well as any new steps you add.

> ▶ **Tip**   The easiest way to delete a number of steps in a package is to draw a box around them on the design sheet to select them as a group.

4   Right-click an open area on the design sheet and click Disconnected Edit.

5   In the left pane, expand Connections and then click ProductStage.

6   In the right pane, double-click Name, type **SBS_OLAPConnection** in the Value box in place of ProductStage, and then click OK.

7   Click Close, double-click the ProductStage connection object on the design sheet, and then click OK

The name of this connection object is now updated to display its new generic name.

8   On the design sheet, double-click the Properties From INI File step, and then delete the following package properties from the Change list:

- DataSource property for the NewProductData connection object
- ExceptionFileName property for the Load ProductStage Table step
- ExceptionFileName property for the Insert Or Update Product-Dim Table step
- LogFileName for the UpdateProductDim package

These properties were unique to the *UpdateProductDim* package and are not needed in the template package.

9 Click the first line in the Change List and then click Edit.

An error appears because you have renamed the *ProductStage* connection object.

10 Click OK, click SBS_OLAPConnection in the left pane, double-click UDLPath in the right pane, click OK, and then click OK to save the update of this Dynamic Properties task.

11 Click OK to save the modified Dynamic Properties task.

12 On the design sheet, double-click the Bypass Package step.

The ActiveX Script task called by this step currently references the *DeleteOrAddStagingData* step, which will not be part of the *Starter-DTS* package. You will modify the script in the *Bypass Package* step to reference the *PropertiesFromGVs* step rather than the *DeleteOr-AddStagingData* step.

13 In this ActiveX script, locate each reference to the DeleteOrAddStaging-Data step, and replace it with a reference to the **PropertiesFromGVs** step. Then click OK to save the modified Bypass Package step.

14 On the design sheet, double-click the Log Package Bypass step.

15 In the SQL Statement box, replace 'UpdateProductDim' with **?** (make sure you remove the apostrophes), replace 'UpdateProductDim Package Was Bypassed' with **'Package Was Bypassed'**, and then click Parameters.

16 Click Create Global Variables, type **gsPackageName** in the Name column, select String in the Type list, type **StarterDTS** in the Value box, and then click OK.

17 In the Parameter Mapping box, select gsPackageName on the second line, mapped to Parameter 2 in the Parameters column, and then click OK.

Changing the parameter in the *INSERT* statement to a global variable and using a more generic phrase for the additional information column allows you to dynamically configure this log entry for each package you create based on this *StarterDTS* package. You will populate this global variable with the name of the package when you create a new package rather than editing the *INSERT* statement in each logging step each time you create a new package. This technique can really save you time if you add logging steps to each of the initial tasks in this package.

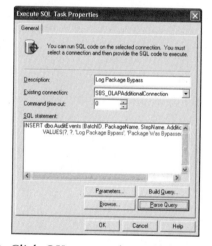

18 Click OK to save the modified Execute SQL task.

19 On the design sheet, double-click the PickupGVs step, replace 'UpdateProductDim' in the WHERE clause of the SELECT statement with ?, and then click Parameters.

20 In the Parameter Mapping box, select gsPackageName on the first line, mapped to Parameter 1, select giConfigID on the second line, mapped to Parameter 2, and then click OK.

Because the additional parameter was added to the WHERE clause before the parameter that was already mapped, you must change the mapping of the existing parameter as well as add the mapping for the additional parameter.

21 Click OK to save the modified Execute SQL task.

22 On the design sheet, click the Bypass Package step, and then hold down the Ctrl key and click the Properties From GVs step.

9

Completing the Application

23 On the Workflow menu, click On Success.

24 Right-click an open area of the design sheet and click Package Properties.

25 On the logging tab, delete the entry in the Error File box and then click OK.

By default, each new package based on this *StarterDTS* package will log its execution to SQL Server. If you want each new package to also log its execution to a text file, you can add the LogFileName property to the Properties From INI File step and then add the appropriate entry to the Config.ini initialization file.

26 On the design sheet, double-click the Properties From GVs step, click Delete to delete the MaximumErrorCount property, click Delete again to delete the InsertCommitSize property, and then click OK.

These entries in the Change List referred to a task that has been deleted. In the *StarterDTS* package, you will not dynamically set any task properties from global variables until you create the tasks. However, by leaving the *Properties From GVs* step as the final step in the *StarterDTS* package, you can add dynamically configured properties for the tasks that you add to a package created based on the *Starter-DTS* package. However, you will leave the *giMaxErrorCount* and *giInsertCommitSize* global variables in the *StarterDTS* package for use by tasks that you add to packages based on this package.

27 On the Package menu, click Save As.

28 In the Package Name box, type **StarterDTS**, verify that Structured Storage File is selected in the Location list, type **C:\Microsoft Press\SQL DTS SBS\DataMovementApplication\StarterDTS.dts** in the File Name box, and then click OK.

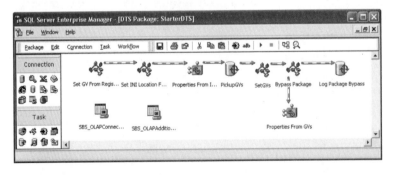

Now that you have successfully created the *StarterDTS* package, you are ready to create a subpackage based on it.

Creating and Calling a Package That Populates the *SalesFact* Table

The data movement application currently includes the steps required to update the dimension tables but not the fact table. In a data warehouse, you will need to periodically add new fact data, as it becomes available, to the fact table. For example, every month you might want to add new sales data from your production database to the data warehouse. The new fact data is generally loaded into a staging table where it can be scrubbed before it is loaded into the fact table for the Analysis Services cube. The fact table can be loaded only after all dimension data has been updated, and the fact data in the staging table must be deleted before new fact data is loaded to avoid duplicate data entry.

Creating the Steps That Load Data into the *SalesStage* and *SalesFact* Tables

In the following procedures, you will create the *UpdateSalesFacts* subpackage using the *StarterDTS* package as a template. You will add a Bulk Insert task to this package that inserts new sales data from a delimited text file into the *SalesStage* table. You can change the data in this delimited text file on a weekly or monthly basis to include the sales data for the previous week or month. Next you will add a column to the *SalesFact* table to hold the *BatchID* value passed to the *UpdateSalesFacts* package from the *MasterUpdate* package. You will then add an Execute SQL task to this package that joins data from the *SalesStage*, *ProductDim*, *CustomerDim*, and *TimeDim* tables and inserts this data into the *SalesFact* table.

Create the *UpdateSalesFacts* subpackage based on the *StarterDTS* package

1   In SQL Server Enterprise Manager, switch to the StarterDTS package in DTS Designer.

2   Right-click an open area of the design sheet, and then click Package Properties.

3   On the Global Variables tab, locate the gsPackageName global variable in the Name column, type **UpdateSalesFacts** in the Value column, and then click OK.

4   On the Package menu, click Save As.

5   Type **UpdateSalesFacts** in the Description box, type **mypassword** in the Owner Password box, verify that Structured Storage File is selected in the Location list, type **C:\Microsoft Press\SQL DTS SBS\ DataMovementApplication\UpdateSalesFacts.dts** in the File Name box, and then click OK.

6   Type **mypassword** in the Password box, and then click OK.

7   Click OK to continue saving without a user password.

Now that you have created the basic structure for the *UpdateSalesFacts* sub-package, you are ready to add a step to insert data from a delimited text file into the *SalesStage* table.

Add new sales data to the *SalesFact* table by creating a Bulk Insert task in the *UpdateSalesFacts* subpackage

1   On the Task menu, click Bulk Insert Task.

2   Type **Load SalesStage Table** in the Description box, select SBS_OLAPConnection in the Existing Connection list, and then select "SBS_OLAP"."dbo"."SalesStage" in the Destination Table list.

3   Type **C:\Microsoft Press\SQL DTS SBS\DataMovementApplication\ NewSalesData.txt** in the Source Data File box.

4   Click Use Format File and then type **C:\Microsoft Press\SQL DTS SBS\DataMovementApplication\SalesData.fmt** in the Use Format File box.

5   Click OK to save this Bulk Insert task.

Now that you have created this Bulk Insert task to load new sales data into the *SalesStage* table from a delimited text file, you will add a *BatchID* column to the *SalesFact* table to store the *BatchID* value passed to the *UpdateSalesFacts* package by the *MasterUpdate* package.

Add the *BatchID* column to the *SalesFact* table to store *BatchID* values

1   Open SQL Query Analyzer and then connect to your local instance as a system administrator.

2   On the toolbar, click Load SQL Script.

3   In the Look In list, navigate to C:\Microsoft Press\SQL DTS SBS\Ch9\ChapterFiles, and then open the AddBatchIDColumn-ToSalesFactTable.sql script.

This script adds the *BatchID* column to the *SalesFact* table. This column will store the *BatchID* value for each row added to the *Sales-Fact* table by the *UpdateSalesFacts* subpackage.

4 Execute the AddBatchIDColumnToSalesFactTable.sql script to add this column.

Now that you have created the infrastructure to store the generated *BatchID* value with each row added to the *SalesFact* table, you are ready to add the step that adds data to the *SalesFact* table from the *SalesStage* table.

Add new sales data to the *SalesFact* table by adding a stored procedure to the SBS_OLAP database and an Execute SQL task to the *UpdateSalesFacts* subpackage

1 On the SQL Query Analyzer toolbar, click Load SQL Script.

2 In the Look In list, navigate to C:\Microsoft Press\SQL DTS SBS\Ch9\ChapterFiles and then double-click LoadSalesFactTable.sql.

This script creates a stored procedure that inserts rows into the *Sales-Fact* table based on data in the *SalesStage* table joined with dimension key values from the *ProductDim*, *CustomerDim*, and *TimeDim* tables. This script also inserts a row into the *AuditEvents* table to log the package completion and the number of rows inserted. The *INNER JOIN* statement will drop rows in the *SalesStage* table that do not have corresponding entries in the dimension tables from the rowset that is inserted into the *SalesStage* table. For example, the *TimeDim* table must contain values for January 1998, and the *ProductDim* table must contain information about new products sold during January 1998, before you add new sales data for the month of January 1998.

After you execute the *UpdateSalesFacts* package, you need to review the entries in the *AuditEvents* table to determine if any rows were dropped. You will add these row reporting steps later in this chapter. If you determine that rows were dropped, you can create a new batch that adds the missing values to the dimension tables and then adds only the rows that were dropped by the *JOIN* statement to the *Sales-Fact* table. You will create a step in this package to write the error rows to a *SalesError* table to make this task easier. In Chapter 10, you will walk through steps demonstrating how to do this.

```
SQL Query Analyzer - [Query - NETSYS1LPTP2.SBS_OLAP.NETSYS1LPTP2\...
File  Edit  Query  Tools  Window  Help

                                              SBS_OLAP

CREATE PROCEDURE dbo.LoadSalesFactTable
        @BatchID INT
        , @PackageName NVARCHAR(100)
AS
INSERT INTO dbo.SalesFact
        (ProductKey
        , CustomerKey
        , TimeKey
        , QuantitySales
        , AmountSales
        , BatchID)
    SELECT ProductDim.ProductKey
        , CustomerDim.CustomerKey
        , TimeDim.TimeKey
        , SalesStage.QuantitySales
        , SalesStage.AmountSales
        , @BatchID
    FROM dbo.TimeDim INNER JOIN dbo.ProductDim
        INNER JOIN dbo.CustomerDim
        INNER JOIN dbo.SalesStage
        ON CustomerDim.CustomerCode = SalesStage.CustomerCode
        ON ProductDim.ProductCode = SalesStage.ProductCode
        ON TimeDim.FullDateCode = SalesStage.OrderDate
INSERT INTO dbo.AuditEvents
        (BatchID
        , PackageName
        , StepName,
        AdditionalInformation
        , RowsComplete)
        VALUES
        (@BatchID
        , @PackageName
        , 'Load SalesFact Table'
        , 'Success'
        , @@Rowcount)

Query batch NETSYS1LPTP2 (8.0)   NETSYS1LPTP2\Carl (52)   SBS_OLAP   0:00:00   0 rows   Ln 1, Col 3
                                              Connections: 1
```

3   Execute the LoadSalesFactTable.sql script to add this stored procedure to the SBS_OLAP database.

4   Switch to the UpdateSalesFacts package in DTS Designer.

5   On the Task menu, click Execute SQL Task.

6   Type **Load SalesFact Table** in the Description box, select SBS_OLAPConnection in the Existing Connection list, and then type **EXEC dbo.LoadSalesFactTable ?, ?** in the SQL Statement box.

7   Click Parameters.

8   In the first row in the Input Global Variables list, select giBatchID.

9   In the second row in the Input Global Variables list, select gsPackageName and then click OK.

10   Click OK to save the Execute SQL Task.

Now that you have created the step that adds new rows from the *SalesStage* table to the *SalesFact* table, you will add dynamic configuration elements to the *UpdateSalesFacts* package.

Adding the Dynamic Configuration Elements to the *UpdateSalesFacts* Package

In the following procedures, you will add entries to the Config.ini initialization file specifying the location of the *UpdateSalesFacts* package, the name and location of the error log used by the *UpdateSalesFacts* package, and the name and location of the source and format files used by the *Load SalesStage Table* step in the *UpdateSalesFacts* package. You will then update the *Properties From INI File* step to use these new entries to update package and task properties. You will also update the *Properties From GVs* step to dynamically configure the maximum number of errors permitted by the *Load SalesStage Table* step.

Add dynamic configuration information to the Config.ini initialization file

1   Using Windows Explorer, navigate to C:\Microsoft Press\SQL DTS SBS\DataMovementApplication, and then double-click Config.ini.

2   Locate the [Subpackages] section, add a new line, and then type **UpdateSalesFacts=C:\Microsoft Press\SQL DTS SBS\ DataMovementApplication\UpdateSalesFacts.dts**.

This line adds the path that the *MasterUpdate* package will use to locate the *UpdateSalesFacts* package.

3   Locate the [ErrorHandlingFileNames] section, add a new line, and then type **UpdateSalesFactsPackage=C:\Microsoft Press\SQL DTS SBS\DataMovementApplication\UpdateSalesFactsPackageError-Log.txt**.

This line adds the path to the error file that the *UpdateSalesFacts* package will use for logging.

4   Create a new line at the end of the file, and then type **[NewSalesData]**.

5   Create a new line in the [NewSalesData] section, and then type **NewSalesData=C:\Microsoft Press\SQL DTS SBS\ DataMovementApplication\NewSalesData.txt**.

This line adds the path that the Bulk Insert task in the *UpdateSales-Facts* package will use to load new data.

6   Create a new line, and then type **FormatFile=C:\Microsoft Press\SQL DTS SBS\DataMovementApplication\SalesData.fmt**.

This line adds the path for the format file that the Bulk Insert task will use to interpret the data being added from the NewSalesData.txt file.

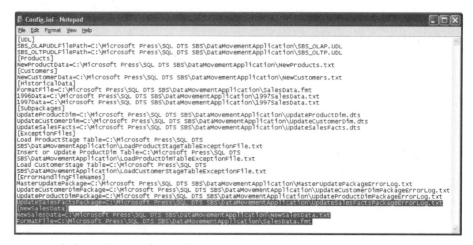

7   Save and close the Config.ini file.

Now that you have added the necessary information to the initialization file, you are ready to configure the *UpdateSalesFacts* package to read the new information in this initialization file by updating the *Properties From INI File* step.

Dynamically update task properties by updating the *Properties From INI File* step in the *UpdateSalesFacts* subpackage

1   Switch to the UpdateSalesFacts package in DTS Designer and then double-click the Properties From INI File step on the design sheet.

2   Click Add, and then select the Leave This Dialog Box Open After Adding A Setting check box.

3   Verify that UpdateSalesFacts is the focus in the left pane and then double-click LogFileName in the Property Name column in the right pane.

4   Select INI File in the Source list, type **C:\Microsoft Press\SQL DTS SBS\DataMovementApplication\Config.ini** in the File box, select ErrorHandlingFileNames in the Section list, select UpdateSales-FactsPackage in the Key list, and then click OK.

   You can now dynamically change the log file location by editing the Config.ini file before the package is executed.

5   In the left pane, expand Tasks and then click DTSTask_DTSBulkInsertTask_1.

6   In the right pane, double-click DataFile in the Property Name column.

7   Select INI File in the Source list, type **C:\Microsoft Press\SQL DTS SBS\DataMovementApplication\Config.ini** in the File box, select NewSalesData in the Section list, select NewSalesData in the Key list, and then click OK.

You can now dynamically change the name and location of the file used by this Bulk Insert task to add new data to the *SalesStage* table by editing the Config.ini file before the package is executed.

8   In the right pane, double-click FormatFile in the Property Name column.

9   Select INI File in the Source list, type **C:\Microsoft Press\SQL DTS SBS\DataMovementApplication\Config.ini** in the File box, select NewSalesData in the Section list, select FormatFile in the Key list, and then click OK.

You can now dynamically change the name and location of the format file by editing the Config.ini file before the package is executed.

10   Click Close and then click OK.

Now that you have configured these dynamic properties from the initialization file, you will configure the *Properties From GVs* task to use the *giMaxError-Count* global variable to set the *MaximumErrors* property for the Bulk Insert task.

Dynamically configure the *MaximumErrors* and the *BatchSize* properties for the *Load SalesStage Table* step in the *Update-SalesFacts* subpackage

1   On the design sheet, double-click the Properties From GVs step and then click Add.

2   Select the Leave This Dialog Box Open After Adding A Setting check box.

3   In the left pane, expand Tasks and then click DTSTask_DTSBulkInsertTask_1.

4   In the right pane, double-click BatchSize in the PropertyName column.

5   Select Global Variable in the Source list, select giBatchSize in the Variable list, and then click OK.

6   In the right pane, double-click MaximumErrors in the PropertyName column.

7 Select Global Variable in the Source list, select giMaxErrorCount in the Variable list, and then click OK.

8 Click Close and then click OK to save the modified Properties From GVs step.

> ▶ **Important**   The Bulk Insert task does not log error-causing rows. If you need to capture this information, you must use the Transform Data task to record error-causing rows to an exception file. However, writing errors to an exception file will slow down the data transfer. Ensuring a clean source file will yield the best performance.

Now that you have added the dynamic configuration elements to the Update-SalesFacts package, you will add branching steps.

Adding Branching Steps to the *UpdateSalesFacts* Package

In the following procedures, you will add a *Load SalesFact Table Bypass* step that will enable you to load data into the *SalesStage* table without also loading data from the *SalesStage* table into the *SalesFact* table each time you execute the *UpdateSalesFacts* subpackage. For example, you might want to load the *SalesStage* table weekly but load the *SalesFact* table only monthly. Incrementally loading the staging tables can save time and enable you to perform some error checking before you actually load the fact table and process the data into the Analysis Services cube. You will then add a *Delete Or Add Staging Data* step and a *Delete Staging Data* step that will enable you to delete staging data after you have verified that it has been successfully added to the *SalesFact* table. You will also modify the *Bypass Package* step to point to the *Delete Or Add Staging Data* step rather than the *Properties From GVs* step to enable the steps in this package to execute in the proper order.

Bypass the *Load SalesFact Table* step by creating an ActiveX Script task in the *UpdateSalesFacts* subpackage

1 On the Task menu, click ActiveX Script Task.

2 In the Description box, type **Bypass Load SalesFact Table** and then click Browse.

3 In the Look In list, navigate to C:\Microsoft Press\SQL DTS SBS\Ch9\ChapterFiles and then double-click BypassLoadSalesFactTable.bas.

This ActiveX script directs the execution of the *UpdateSalesFacts* package to the *LoadSalesFactTable* and *LogSalesFactTableError-Rows* steps or to the *LogLoadSalesFactTableBypass* step based on the value of the *gbBypassLoadSalesFactTable* global variable. By default, the *LoadSalesFactStep* and *LogSalesFactTableErrorRows* steps will execute in parallel.

4   Click OK to save this ActiveX Script task.

Now that you have created this branching step, you will create the global variable used in the branching step.

Add the global variable used by the *Bypass Load SalesFact Table* step in the *UpdateSalesFacts* subpackage

1   Right-click an open area on the design sheet and then click Package Properties.

2   On the Global Variables tab, type **gbBypassLoadSalesFactTable** in the Name column, select Boolean in the Type list, type **0** in the Value box, and then click OK.

The *Load SalesFact Table* step will execute each time the *Update-SalesFacts* package is executed unless the value of the *gbBypassLoad-SalesFactTable* global variable is changed to something other than 0.

Now that you have added this branching step, you are ready to add a delete staging data branching step to this package.

Add a delete phase to the *UpdateSalesFacts* package by adding an ActiveX Script task and an Execute SQL task and modifying the *Bypass Package* step

1   On the task menu, click ActiveX Script Task.

2   In the Description box, type **Delete or Add Staging Data** and then click Browse.

3   In the Look In list, navigate to C:\Microsoft Press\SQL DTS SBS\Ch9\ChapterFiles and then double-click DeleteOrAddStaging-Data.bas.

    This script is the same script used in the *UpdateProductDim* and *UpdateCustomerDim* packages because it performs the exact same function in this package.

4   Click OK to save this ActiveX Script task.

5   On the Task menu, click Execute SQL Task.

6   In the Description box, type **Delete Staging Data**, select SBS_OLAPConnection in the Existing Connection list, type **TRUNCATE TABLE dbo.SalesStage** in the SQL Statement box, and then click OK.

7   On the design sheet, delete the On Success constraint between the Bypass Package step and the Properties From GVs step and then double-click the Bypass Package step.

8   Change the phrase PropertiesFromGVs to **DeleteOrAddStagingData** each place it occurs in the ActiveX script and then click OK.

Now that you have added these branching steps to the *UpdateSalesFacts* package, you will add logging and error reporting steps to the package to enable you to easily determine the actions performed each time this package executes.

Adding Logging and Error Reporting Steps to the *UpdateSalesFacts* Package

In the following procedures, you will add logging and error reporting steps to create log entries in the *AuditEvents* table to record whether the delete or add staging data phase executed, the success or failure of the *Load SalesStage Table* step, whether the loading of the *SalesFact* table was bypassed, the success or failure of the *Load SalesFact Table* step, and the rows in the *SalesStage* table that were not successfully added to the *SalesFact* table.

Log whether the delete or add staging data phase executed by creating a Execute SQL task

1 On the Task menu, click Execute SQL Task.

2 In the Description box, type **Log Delete Branch Executed,** select SBS_OLAPAdditionalConnection in the existing connection list, and then click Browse.

3 Navigate to C:\Microsoft Press\SQL DTS SBS\Ch9\ChapterFiles in the Look In list and then double-click LogDeleteBranchExecuted.sql.

   This script inserts logging information into the *AuditEvents* table to document that the delete branch of the *UpdateSalesFacts* package executed. You will configure this step to execute after the completion of the *Delete Staging Data* step.

4 Click Parameters, select giBatchID in the Input Global Variables list to map this global variable to Parameter 1, select gsPackageName to map this global variable to Parameter 2, and then click OK.

5 Click OK to save this Execute SQL task.

You have created a step that will add a record to the *AuditEvents* table if the delete phase of this package executes. Next you will add the steps to record whether the *Load SalesStage Table* succeeds or fails.

Log the success or failure of the *Load SalesStage Table* step

1 Switch to SQL Query Analyzer and then click Load SQL Script on the toolbar.

   You will create a stored procedure that records the success or failure of the *Load SalesStage Table* step to the *AuditEvents* table along with a count of the number of rows in the *SalesStage* table.

2 In the Look In list, navigate to C:\Microsoft Press\SQL DTS SBS\Ch9\ChapterFiles, and then double-click LogLoadSalesStage-Table.sql.

   This script creates a stored procedure that enters a row in the *AuditEvents* table containing the *BatchID* value, the package name, the step name, the result of the package execution, and the number of rows in the *SalesStaging* table each time the stored procedure is called. The *BatchID*, package name, and execution result are passed to the stored procedure as input parameters. Entering the total number of rows in the *SalesStage* table into the *AuditEvents* table enables you to compare this value with the number of rows added to the *SalesFact* table by the *Load SalesFact Table* step, which you will add to this package. If you add data to the *SalesStage* table several times before you add these rows to the *SalesFact* table, you will receive a cumulative total of the rows in the *SalesFact* table, not the rows added by a particular iteration of the *Load SalesStage Table* step. If the number of rows added to the *SalesFact* table does not equal the number of rows in the *SalesStage* table, you have an error, which caused one or more rows to be dropped.

3   Execute the LogLoadSalesStageTable.sql script to add this stored procedure to the SBS_OLAP database.

4   Switch to the UpdateSalesFacts package in DTS Designer.

5   On the Task menu, click Execute SQL Task.

6   Type **Log Load SalesStage Table Success** in the Description box, select SBS_OLAPAdditionalConnection in the Existing Connection list, and then type **EXEC dbo.LogLoadSalesStageTable ?, ?, 'Success'** in the SQL Statement box.

7   Click Parameters, select giBatchID in the Input Global Variables list to map this global variable to Parameter 1, select gsPackageName to map this global variable to Parameter 2, and then click OK.

8   Click OK to save the Execute SQL Task.

9   On the Task menu, click Execute SQL Task.

10 Type **Log Load SalesStage Table Failure** in the Description box, select SBS_OLAPAdditionalConnection in the Existing Connection list, and then type **EXEC dbo.LogLoadSalesStageTable ?, ?, 'Failure'** in the SQL Statement box.

11 Click Parameters, select giBatchID in the Input Global Variables list to map this global variable to Parameter 1, select gsPackageName to map this global variable to Parameter 2, and then click OK.

12 Click OK to save the Execute SQL Task.

You have created the steps that will add a record to the *AuditEvents* table when the *Load SalesStage Table* step succeeds or fails. Next you will add a step that records whether the loading of new data into the *SalesFact* table is bypassed.

Log the bypassing of the *Load SalesFact Table* step

1 On the Task menu, click Execute SQL Task.

2 Type **Log Load SalesFact Table Step Bypass** in the Description box, select SBS_OLAPAdditionalConnection in the Existing Connection list, and then click Browse.

3 In the Look In list, navigate to C:\Microsoft Press\SQL DTS SBS\Ch9\ChapterFiles and then double-click LogLoadSalesFact-TableBypassed.sql.

This script inserts a row into the *AuditEvents* table if the *Load SalesFact Table* step is bypassed.

4 Click Parameters, select giBatchID in the Input Global Variables list to map this global variable to Parameter 1, select gsPackageName to map this global variable to Parameter 2, and then click OK.

5 Click OK to save the Execute SQL task.

You have created the step that records whether the loading of the new data into the *SalesFact* table is bypassed. Next you will add a step that records the success or failure of the *Load SalesFact Table* step.

Log the success or failure of the *Load SalesFact Table* step

1 Switch to SQL Query Analyzer and then click Load SQL Script on the toolbar.

You will create a stored procedure that records the success or failure of the *Load SalesFact Table* step to the *AuditEvents* table.

9

Completing the Application

2   In the Look In list, navigate to C:\Microsoft Press\SQL DTS SBS\Ch9\ChapterFiles and then double-click LogLoadSalesFact-Table.sql.

This script creates a stored procedure that enters a row in the *AuditEvents* table containing the *BatchID* value, the package name, the step name, and the result of the package execution each time the stored procedure is called. The *BatchID*, package name, and execution result are passed to the stored procedure as input parameters.

3   Execute the LogLoadSalesFactTable.sql script to add this stored procedure to the SBS_OLAP database.

4   Switch to the UpdateSalesFacts package in DTS Designer.

5   On the Task menu, click Execute SQL Task.

6   Type **Log Load SalesFact Table Success** in the Description box, select SBS_OLAPAdditionalConnection in the Existing Connection list, and then type **EXEC dbo.LogLoadSalesFactTable ?, ?, 'Success'** in the SQL Statement box.

7   Click Parameters, select giBatchID in the Input Global Variables list to map this global variable to Parameter 1, select gsPackageName to map this global variable to Parameter 2, and then click OK.

8   Click OK to save the Execute SQL Task.

9   On the Task menu, click Execute SQL Task.

10 Type **Log Load SalesFact Table Failure** in the Description box, select SBS_OLAPAdditionalConnection in the Existing Connection list, and then type **EXEC dbo.LogLoadSalesFactTable ?, ?, 'Failure'** in the SQL Statement box.

11 Click Parameters, select giBatchID in the Input Global Variables list to map this global variable to Parameter 1, select gsPackageName to map this global variable to Parameter 2, and then click OK.

12 Click OK to save the Execute SQL Task.

You have created the steps that will add a record to the *AuditEvents* table when the *Load SalesFact Table* step succeeds or fails. Next you will add a step that records rows that are not added from the *SalesStage* table to the *SalesFact* table to an error table.

Log error rows in the *SalesStage* table by creating the error table and a stored procedure and then creating an Execute SQL task

1   Switch to SQL Query Analyzer and then click Load SQL Script.

     You will begin by creating an error table that will store rows that could not be inserted into the *SalesFact* table from the *SalesStage* table because a corresponding row is missing on one of the dimension tables.

2   In the Look In list, navigate to C:\Microsoft Press\ SQL DTS SBS\Ch9\ChapterFiles and then double-click CreateSalesFactErrorRowsTable.sql.

     This script creates the *SalesFactErrorRows* table containing the details of each row that could not be inserted and the reason why the row could not be inserted.

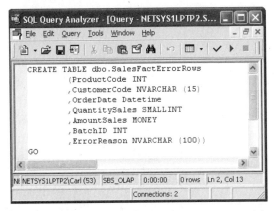

3   Execute the CreateSalesFactErrorRowsTable.sql script to add this table to the SBS_OLAP database.

4   On the SQL Query Analyzer toolbar, click Load SQL Script.

     You will create a stored procedure that will detect and insert error rows into the error table each time the stored procedure is executed.

5   In the Look In list, navigate to C:\Microsoft Press\SQL DTS SBS\Ch9\ChapterFiles and then double-click CreateSalesFactError-RowsSP.sql.

     This script creates the *SalesFactErrorRowsSP* stored procedure that queries the *SalesStage* table for rows without corresponding entries in the *ProductDim*, *CustomerDim*, and *TimeDim* dimension tables and inserts these rows in the *SalesFactErrorRows* table.

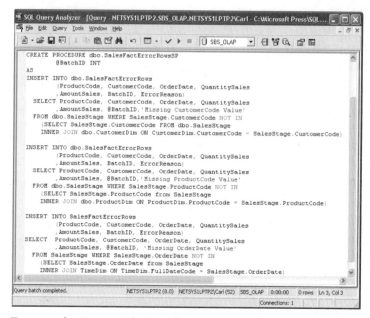

6   Execute the CreateSalesFactErrorRowsSP.sql script to add this stored procedure to the SBS_OLAP database.

7   Switch to the UpdateSalesFacts package in DTS Designer.

8   On the Task menu, click Execute SQL Task.

9   Type **Log SalesFact Table Error Rows** in the Description box, select SBS_OLAPAdditionalConnection in the Existing Connection list, and then type **EXEC dbo.SalesFactErrorRowsSP ?** in the SQL Statement box.

   You are using the *SBS_OLAPAdditionalConnection* connection object for this step because the *Load SalesFact Table* step, which will execute in parallel with this step, is using the *SBS_OLAPConnection* connection object.

10 Click Parameters, select giBatchID in the Input Global Variables list for Parameter 1, and then click OK.

11 Click OK to save the Execute SQL Task.

You have created the step that records rows dropped by the *INNER JOIN* statement into an error table. You are now ready to create user-friendly names for the new steps that you added to this package and ensure that the steps execute in the proper order by adding precedence constraints.

Configuring User-Friendly Names and Adding Precedence Constraints to Ensure That Steps Execute in the Proper Order

In the following procedures, you will configure user-friendly names for the steps referenced in the *Bypass Load SalesFact Table* step and then add precedence constraints to the steps you have added to the *UpdateSalesFacts* package to ensure that the steps execute in the proper order.

Change step names to user-friendly names in the *UpdateSales-Facts* subpackage

1   Right-click an open area of the design sheet and click Disconnected Edit.

2   In the left pane, expand Steps and then click DTSStep_DTSBulkInsertTask_1.

3   In the right pane, double-click Name in the Property Name column, change the name of this step to **LoadSalesStageTable,** and then click OK.

4   In the left pane, expand Steps and then click DTSStep_DTSExecuteSQLTask_1.

5   In the right pane, double-click Name in the Property Name column, change the name of this step to **LoadSalesFactTable,** and then click OK.

6   In the left pane, expand Steps and then click DTSStep_DTSActiveScriptTask_1.

7   In the right pane, double-click Name in the Property Name column, change the name of this step to **BypassLoadSalesFactTable,** and then click OK.

8   In the left pane, expand Steps and then click DTSStep_DTSActiveScriptTask_2.

9   In the right pane, double-click Name in the Property Name column, change the name of this step to **DeleteOrAddStagingData,** and then click OK.

10 In the left pane, expand Steps and then click DTSStep_DTSExecuteSQLTask_2.

11 In the right pane, double-click Name in the Property Name column, change the name of this step to **DeleteStagingData,** and then click OK.

12 In the left pane, expand Steps and then click DTSStep_DTSExecuteSQLTask_3.

13 In the right pane, double-click Name in the Property Name column, change the name of this step to **LogDeleteBranchExecuted,** and then click OK.

14 In the left pane, expand Steps and then click DTSStep_DTSExecuteSQLTask_4.

15 In the right pane, double-click Name in the Property Name column, change the name of this step to **LogLoadSalesStageTableSuccess,** and then click OK.

16 In the left pane, expand Steps and then click DTSStep_DTSExecuteSQLTask_5.

17 In the right pane, double-click Name in the Property Name column, change the name of this step to **LogLoadSalesStageTableFailure,** and then click OK.

18 In the left pane, expand Steps and then click DTSStep_DTSExecuteSQLTask_6.

19 In the right pane, double-click Name in the Property Name column, change the name of this step to **LogLoadSalesFactTableBypass,** and then click OK.

20 In the left pane, expand Steps and then click DTSStep_DTSExecuteSQLTask_7.

21 In the right pane, double-click Name in the Property Name column, change the name of this step to **LogLoadSalesFactTableSuccess,** and then click OK.

22 In the left pane, expand Steps and then click DTSStep_DTSExecuteSQLTask_8.

23 In the right pane, double-click Name in the Property Name column, change the name of this step to **LogLoadSalesFactTableFailure,** and then click OK.

24 In the left pane, expand Steps and then click DTSStep_DTSExecuteSQLTask_9.

25 In the right pane, double-click Name in the Property Name column, change the name of this step to **LogSalesFactTableErrorRows,** and then click OK.

26 Click Close.

You have given user-friendly names to the new steps that you added to the *UpdateSalesFacts* package. Now you are ready to add precedence constraints to ensure the package steps execute in the proper order.

Add precedence constraints to the *UpdateSalesFacts* subpackage

1 On the design sheet, arrange the steps according to their execution flow.

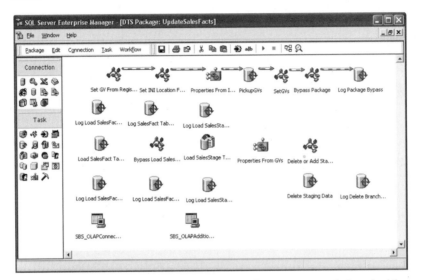

2 On the design sheet, click the Bypass Package step, and then hold down the Ctrl key and click the Delete Or Add Staging Data step.

3 On the Workflow menu, click On Success.

4 On the design sheet, click the Delete Or Add Staging Data step, and then hold down the Ctrl key and click the Delete Staging Data step.

5 On the Workflow menu, click On Success.

6 On the design sheet, click the Delete Staging Data step, and then hold down the Ctrl key and click the Log Delete Branch Executed step.

7 On the Workflow menu, click On Completion.

8 On the design sheet, click the Delete Or Add Staging Data step, and then hold down the Ctrl key and click the Properties From GVs step.

9 On the Workflow menu, click On Success.

10 On the design sheet, click the Properties From GVs step, and then hold down the Ctrl key and click the Load SalesStage Table step.

11 On the Workflow menu, click On Success.

12 On the design sheet, click the Load SalesStage Table step, and then hold down the Ctrl key and click the Log Load SalesStage Table Success step.

13 On the Workflow menu, click On Success.

14 On the design sheet, click the Load SalesStage Table step, and then hold down the Ctrl key and click the Log Load SalesStage Table Failure step.

15 On the Workflow menu, click On Failure.

16 On the design sheet, click the Load SalesStage Table step, and then hold down the Ctrl key and click the Bypass Load SalesFact Table step.

17 On the Workflow menu, click On Completion.

18 On the design sheet, click the Bypass Load SalesFact Table step, and then hold down the Ctrl key and click the Log Load SalesFact Table Bypass step.

19 On the Workflow menu, click On Success.

20 On the design sheet, click the Bypass Load SalesFact Table step, and then hold down the Ctrl key and click the Load SalesFact Table step.

21 On the Workflow menu, click On Success.

22 On the design sheet, click the Bypass Load SalesFact Table step, and then hold down the Ctrl key and click the Log SalesFact Table Error Rows step.

23 On the Workflow menu, click On Success.

24 On the design sheet, click the Load SalesFact Table step, and then hold down the Ctrl key and click the Log Load SalesFact Table Success step.

25 On the Workflow menu, click On Success.

26 On the design sheet, click the Load SalesFact Table step, and then hold down the Ctrl key and click the Log Load SalesFact Table Failure step.

27 On the Workflow menu, click On Failure.

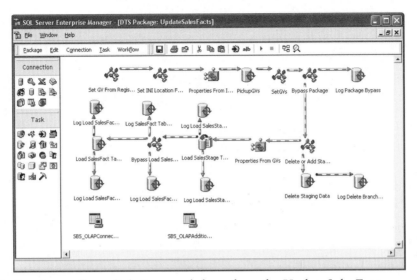

28 On the toolbar, click Save and then close the UpdateSalesFacts
package.

You have successfully created the *UpdateSalesFacts* package. Next you will add
a step to the *MasterUpdate* package to call this package.

Calling the *UpdateSalesFacts* Subpackage from the *MasterUpdate* Package

The *UpdateSalesFacts* package is designed to be called from the *MasterUpdate*
package after all the dimension update packages have completed. To accomplish this, you will first create an ActiveX Script placeholder task that will
execute after all the dimension update packages complete. The ActiveX Script
placement holder task will not actually perform any task; instead, it marks the
completion of all prior steps. After the ActiveX Script placeholder task executes, each fact table update task will execute in parallel. In our data movement
application prototype, only one fact table update package exists. However, in a
real-world application, you could add a number of additional fact table update
packages for additional Analysis Services cubes.

Add the placeholder step to the *MasterUpdate* package

1 In SQL Server Enterprise Manager, right-click Data Transformation
Services in your local instance.

2 Click Open Package and then open the most recent version of the
MasterUpdate package in the C:\Microsoft Press\SQL DTS SBS\
DataMovementApplication folder using a password of **mypassword**.

3   On the Task menu, click ActiveX Script Task.

4   In the Description box, type **Dimension Packages Complete** and then click OK.

5   On the design sheet, click the Call UpdateProductDim Subpackage step, and then hold down the Ctrl key and click the Dimension Packages Complete step.

6   On the Workflow menu, click On Completion.

7   On the design sheet, click the Call UpdateCustomerDim Subpackage step, and then hold down the Ctrl key and click the Dimension Packages Complete step.

8   On the Workflow menu, click On Completion.

Now that you have configured this placeholder task to mark the successful completion of all dimension update packages, you are ready to add a step to call the *UpdateSalesFacts* subpackage.

Add a step to the *MasterUpdate* package to call the *UpdateSalesFacts* subpackage

1   On the Task menu, click Execute Package Task.

2   Type **Call UpdateSalesFacts Subpackage** in the Description box, select Structured Storage File in the Location list, type **C:\Microsoft Press\SQL DTS SBS\DataMovementApplication\ UpdateSalesFacts.dts** in the File Name box, type **UpdateSalesFacts** in the Package Name box, and then type **mypassword** in the Password box.

3   Click the Outer Package Global Variables tab.

4   On the first line in the Variables box, select giBatchID in the Name list.

5   On the second line in the Variables box, select giConfigID in the Name list.

6   On the third line in the Variables box, select giMaxErrorCount in the Name list.

7   On the fourth line in the Variables box, select giBatchSize.

8   On the fifth line in the Variables box, select gbDeleteOrAdd and then click OK to save the Execute Package task.

9 On the design sheet, click the Dimension Packages Complete step, and then hold down the Ctrl key and then click the Call UpdateSales-Facts Subpackage step.

10 On the Workflow menu, click On Success.

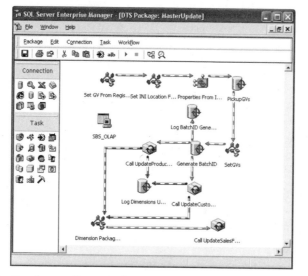

11 On the toolbar, click Save and then close the MasterUpdate package.

Now that you have configured the tasks required to update the *SalesFact* table and record its success or failure, you are ready to test the execution of the data movement application.

Testing the Data Movement Application with the *UpdateSalesFacts* Package

In the following procedure, you will execute the *LoadHistoricalData* package to delete all test data from the dimension tables. You will then execute the *MasterUpdate* package and its subpackages using the delete all configuration to delete all staging data from the staging tables. Finally, you will execute the *MasterUpdate* package and its subpackages using the default configuration and then query the *AuditEvents* table to determine the number of rows inserted into the *SalesFact* table from the *SalesStage* table by the *UpdateSalesFacts* package.

9

Completing the Application

Test the execution of the data movement application

1 In the SQL Server Enterprise Manager console tree, right-click Data Transformation Services in your local instance and then click Open Package.

2 Navigate to the C:\Microsoft Press\SQL DTS SBS\DataMovement-Application folder and then open the most recent version of the LoadHistoricalData package using a password of **mypassword**.

3 On the toolbar, click Execute.

Performing this step truncates all data in the dimension and fact tables, and then reloads the original historical data. By executing this task, it will be easier to observe the effect of executing the *Update-CustomerDim* and *UpdateProductDim* packages again, followed by the *UpdateSalesFacts* package because the test data that you have previously loaded into the dimension tables is deleted.

4 Click OK and then click Done.

5 Close the LoadHistoricalData package in DTS Designer and then switch to Windows Explorer.

6 Navigate to the C:\Microsoft Press\SQL DTS SBS\DataMovement-Application folder, and then double-click DeleteAllStagingData.cmd.

Performing this step eliminates all data in the staging tables to make it easier to observe the effect of executing the *UpdateCustomerDim* and *UpdateProductDim* packages again because the test data that you have previously loaded into the staging tables is deleted.

7 After the batch file completes, double-click MasterUpdateDefault-Configuration.cmd in the DataMovementApplication folder.

8 After the batch file completes its execution, switch to SQL Query Analyzer and click Clear Window on the toolbar.

9 In the query pane, type **SELECT * FROM SBS_OLAP.dbo.AuditEvents WHERE BatchID = 8 ORDER BY PackageName, ExecutionDate**, and then click Execute on the toolbar.

The delete branch of all three packages executed. The existing delete-all configuration called the delete branch of the *UpdateSalesFacts* package because the *gbDeleteOrAdd* global variable was passed from the *MasterUpdate* package when it called the *UpdateSalesFacts* package.

10 In the query pane, change the query to read **SELECT * FROM SBS_OLAP.dbo.AuditEvents WHERE BatchID = 9 ORDER BY PackageName, ExecutionDate,** and then click Execute on the toolbar.

The success or failure of the steps and packages in the data movement application are displayed. Notice that only 149 of the 152 rows of data in the *SalesStage* table were successfully copied to the *SalesFact* table.

11 On the toolbar, click Clear Window, type **SELECT * FROM SalesFactErrorRows** in the query pane, and then click Execute on the toolbar.

Notice that the *SalesFactErrorRows* table enables you to determine that these three sales on January 29, 1998, were not added to the *SalesFact* table because the *CustomerCode* for LACOR was not in the *CustomerDim* table. Once you correct this error by adding this customer to the *CustomerDim* table, you can use the sales data captured in the *SalesFactErrorRows* table as the source for a new batch that is added to the *SalesFact* table. You will perform this exercise in Chapter 10.

You have successfully added the *UpdateSalesFacts* package to the data movement application. The final step in creating the data movement application prototype is to add an Analysis Services Processing task to process the data that has been added to the SBS_OLAP database into an Analysis Services cube.

Creating the *SalesCubeProcessing* Subpackage

You can add the Analysis Services Processing task to a DTS package to process Analysis Services dimensions, cubes, and partitions from SQL Server dimension and fact tables. Processing a cube, dimension, or partition adds data to or replaces data in the object being processed using the data in the underlying relational database. You can define this task to perform full or incremental processing, or perform a complete data refresh. You can use an ActiveX Script task to dynamically specify the type of processing at run time based on a global variable value that modifies the *ProcessOption* property of the Analysis Services Processing task. For instance, if only new data is being added and the dimension structure of the cube is not changing, you might want to perform only an incremental processing of the cube or partition. For an example of such an ActiveX Script task, see *Changing Properties of an Analysis Services Processing Task* in SQL Server Books Online.

The Analysis Services Processing task is written using Microsoft Visual Basic 6. Because Visual Basic 6 does not support the free-threaded threading model, the Analysis Services Processing task must execute either on the main execution thread for a package or in a separate process space in which a new thread of execution is established using the Execute Process task. If the Analysis Services Processing task executes in a separate process space, several Analysis Services Processing tasks can execute in parallel. Choosing among processing options, executing multiple Analysis Services Processing tasks in parallel, and designing the data movement application to dynamically set different processing options at run time are beyond the scope of this book and this simple data movement application. For a complete example of a data movement solution that uses DTS to dynamically process Analysis Services objects based on the objects that require processing, and that processes objects in parallel using the Execute Process task, see the Microsoft SQL Server Accelerator for Business Intelligence, which can be downloaded at *http://www.microsoft.com/solutions/bi/*.

▶ **Note**   You must have administrator access to an Analysis Services instance to continue with the remaining procedures in this chapter. This instance can be on your local computer or on a remote computer. The following steps assume the Analysis Services is installed on your local computer. If it is not, restore the SQL DTS SQL.cab file to the remote computer, point the restored SQL DTS SBS database to the SBS_OLAP database on your local SQL Server instance, and then point the Analysis Services Processing task to the Analysis Services instance on the remote computer.

Restoring the Analysis Services Database and Adding an Analysis Services Processing Task

In the following procedures, you will begin by restoring an Analysis Services database from a .CAB file. This Analysis Services database contains the structure for the *Sales* cube, which is based on the schema you have been creating in the SBS_OLAP database. You will then create an Analysis Services Processing task in the *MasterUpdate* package to fully process the *Sales* cube, adding data from the SBS_OLAP database into *Sales* cube.

Restoring the SQL DTS SBS database to an Analysis Services instance

1   Click Start, point to All Programs, point to Microsoft SQL Server, point to Analysis Services, and then click Analysis Manager.

2   In the Analysis Manager console tree, expand Analysis Servers, and then click your Analysis Services instance to establish a connection to Analysis Services.

3   Right-click the Analysis Services instance in the console tree and click Restore Database.

4   In the Look In list, navigate to C:\Microsoft Press\SQL DTS SBS\Ch9\ChapterFiles, and then double-click SQL DTS SBS.CAB.

Restore Database

Server:	NETSYS1LPTP2
Database name:	SQL DTS SBS
File Information:	2 files; 12KB
Restore from:	C:\Microsoft Press\SQL DTS SBS\Ch9\ChapterFiles\SQL DTS SBS.CAB
Archive date:	6/24/2003 11:32:26 AM

[Restore]   [Cancel]   [Help]

5   In the Restore Database dialog box, click Restore, and then click Close when the Analysis Services database has been restored.

Restore Database Progress

2 of 2 files; 12KB of 12KB

Extracting database files from C:\Microsoft Press\SQL DTS SBS\Ch9\ChapterF
File: SBS_OLAP.src (0.0KB)
File: OLAPDB.REP (11KB)
Updating repository.
Updating DSO.
Validating roles.
Database successfully restored.

[Save Log ...]   [Close]   [Help]

6   Expand the SQL DTS SBS database, and then expand Data Sources.

7   Right-click SBS_OLAP and then click Edit to review the Data Link Properties.

The *Sales* cube and its dimensions in the SQL DTS SBS database are configured to connect to the SBS_OLAP database in the local SQL Server instance. Change the data link properties if you are using a remote Analysis Services instance to point to the appropriate SQL Server instance.

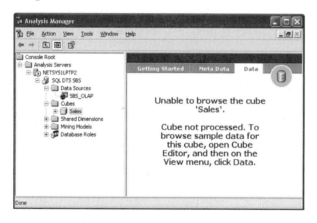

8   Click OK.

9   Expand Cubes in the console tree, click the Sales cube, and then click
the Data tab in the details pane.

Notice that you cannot browse the data in the *Sales* cube because it is
not processed.

Now that you restored the SQL DTS SBS database, you are ready to add an
Analysis Services Processing task to the *MasterUpdate* package and process the
Sales cube.

Processing the *Sales* cube by adding an Analysis Services Processing task to the *MasterUpdate* Package

1   Switch to SQL Server Enterprise Manager, and then right-click Data Transformation Services in your local instance.

2   Click Open Package and then open the most recent version of the MasterUpdate package in the C:\Microsoft Press\SQL DTS SBS\ DataMovementApplication folder using a password of **mypassword**.

3   On the Task menu, click Analysis Services Processing Task.

4   In the Name box, change the name of this task to **ProcessSalesCube** and change the Description of this task to **Process Sales Cube**.

    Notice that this task allows you to set both the task name and description when you create the task rather than just the description.

5   Select the Local Server check box.

    When you select this check box, this task will always try to connect to an Analysis Services instance on the computer on which the *MasterUpdate* package is executing. By selecting this check box, you will be able to migrate the data movement application from the development environment to the production environment without editing the *Process Sales Cube* step in the *MasterUpdate* package.

6   In the Select The Object To Process list, expand LOCALHOST, and then click SQL DTS SBS.

7   In the Select A Processing Option box, click Full Process, and then click OK.

8   Right-click an open area of the design sheet and click Disconnected Edit.

9   In the left pane, expand Steps and then click DTSStep_DTSOlapProcess.Task_1.

10   In the right pane, double-click Name in the Property Name column, change the name of this step to **ProcessSalesCube**, click OK, and then click Close.

Now that you have added the *Process Sales Cube* step to the *MasterUpdate* package, you will add a bypass step to enable you to execute the *MasterUpdate* package without processing the *Sales* cube.

Adding Step Bypass and Logging Steps

In the following procedures, you will add a step to enable you to bypass the *Process Sales Cube* step and then add a logging step to record in the *AuditEvents* table if the *Process Sales Cube* step is bypassed for a particular execution of the *MasterUpdate* package. You will also add logging steps to record the success or failure of the *Process Sales Cube* step.

Bypass the *Process Sales Cube* step by adding an ActiveX Script task

1   On the Task menu, click ActiveX Script Task, and then type **Bypass Process Sales Cube** in the Description box.

2   Click Browse, navigate to C:\Microsoft Press\SQL DTS SBS\Ch9\ChapterFiles, and then double-click BypassProcessSales-Cube.bas.

   This script is the very similar to the previous scripts you used to create branching tasks.

3   Click OK to save this ActiveX Script task.

4   On the design sheet, right-click an open area and then click Package Properties.

5   On the Global Variables tab, type **gbProcessBypass** in the Name column, select Boolean in the Type column, type 0 in the Value column, and then click OK.

6   Right-click an open area of the design sheet and click Disconnected Edit.

7   In the left pane, expand Steps and then click DTSStep_DTSActiveScriptTask_5.

8   In the right pane, double-click Name in the Property Name column, change the name of this step to **LogProcessSalesCubeBypass**, click OK, and then click Close.

Now that you have created the *Bypass Process Sales Cube* step and the associated global variable, you will add a step that logs the bypass of the *Process Sales Cube* step.

Log the bypass of the *Process Sales Cube* step by creating an Execute SQL task

1   On the Task menu, click Execute SQL Task, type **Log Process Sales Cube Bypass** in the Description box, and then click Browse.

2   In the Look In list, navigate to C:\Microsoft Press\SQL DTS SBS\Ch9\ChapterFiles, and then double-click LogProcessSalesCube-Bypassed.sql.

   This script inserts logging information into the *AuditEvents* table to document when the *Process Sales Cube* step is bypassed.

3   Click Parameters, select giBatchID in the Input Global Variables list, and then click OK.

4   Click OK to save this Execute SQL task.

You have created a step that will create a log entry in the *AuditEvents* table when the *Process Sales Cube* step is bypassed. Next you will create steps to log the success or failure of the *Process Sales Cube* step.

Log the success or failure of the *Process Sales Cube* step by adding Execute SQL tasks

1   On the Task menu, click Execute SQL Task.

2   Type **Log Process Sales Cube Success** in the Description box and then click Browse.

3   In the Look In list, navigate to C:\Microsoft Press\SQL DTS SBS\Ch9\ChapterFiles and then double-click LogProcessSalesCube-Success.sql.

4   Click Parameters, select giBatchID in the Input Global Variables list for Parameter 1, and then click OK.

5   Click OK to save the Execute SQL task.

6   On the Task menu, click Execute SQL Task.

7   Type **Log Process Sales Cube Failure** in the Description box and then click Browse.

8   In the Look In list, navigate to C:\Microsoft Press\SQL DTS SBS\Ch9\ChapterFiles and then double-click LogProcessSalesCube-Failure.sql.

9   Click Parameters, select giBatchID in the Input Global Variables list for Parameter 1, and then click OK.

10   Click OK to save the Execute SQL task.

Now that you have finished adding the *Sales* cube processing steps to this package, you will ensure that these steps execute in the proper order by adding precedence constraints.

Ensuring Execution Order and Testing the New Steps

In the following procedures, you will add precedence constraints to ensure that these new steps execute in the proper order. Next you will create a new configuration of global variables in the *PackageGVs* table that will enable you to execute the *Process Sales Cube* step in the *MasterUpdate* package while bypassing each of the subpackages. You will then create a new batch file and execute the *MasterUpdate* package to process the *Sales* cube. Finally, you will browse the *Sales* cube to verify that it was processed successfully.

Ensure execution order by adding precedence constraints

1   On the design sheet, arrange the steps according to their execution flow.

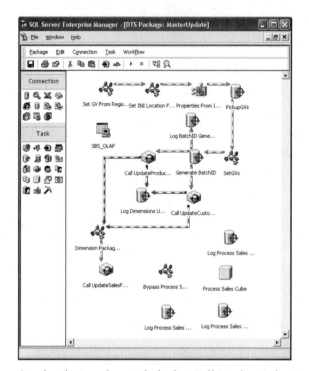

2   On the design sheet, click the Call UpdateSalesFacts step, and then hold down the Ctrl key and click the Bypass Process Sales Cube step.

3   On the Workflow menu, click On Completion.

4   On the design sheet, click the Bypass Process Sales Cube step, and then hold down the Ctrl key and click the Process Sales Cube step.

5   On the Workflow menu, click On Success.

6   On the design sheet, click the Bypass Process Sales Cube step, and then hold down the Ctrl key and click the Log Process Sales Cube Bypass step.

7   On the Workflow menu, click On Success.

8   On the design sheet, click the Process Sales Cube step, and then hold down the Ctrl key and click the Log Process Sales Cube Success step.

9   On the Workflow menu, click On Success.

10   On the design sheet, click the Process Sales Cube step, and then hold down the Ctrl key and click the Log Process Sales Cube Failure step.

11   On the Workflow menu, click On Failure.

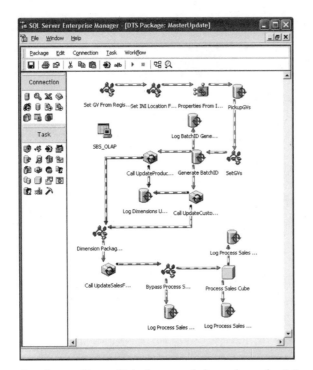

12 On the toolbar, click Save and then close the MasterUpdate package in DTS Designer.

13 Close SQL Server Enterprise Manager.

Now that you have created these precedence constraints, you will create a new configuration of global variables to enable you to execute the *Process Sales Cube* step in the *MasterUpdate* package while bypassing the steps in each of the subpackages.

Create a new configuration of global variables in the *PackageGVs* table and then create a new batch file

1 Switch to SQL Query Analyzer and then click New Query on the toolbar.

2 On the toolbar, click Load SQL Script, navigate to C:\Microsoft Press\SQL DTS SBS\Ch9\ChapterFiles, and then double-click Create-ProcessCubeConfigurations.sql

This script adds a record to the default configuration in the *PackageGVs* table, disabling the *Process Sales Cube* step. It then creates a new configuration in the *PackageGVs* table that bypasses each subpackage and executes the *Process Sales Cube* step in the *MasterUpdate* package.

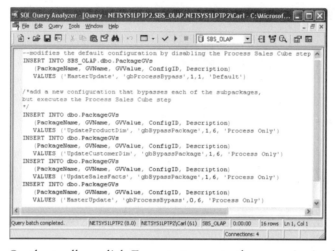

3   On the toolbar, click Execute to create these entries in the Pack-ageGVs table and then close this query in SQL Query Analyzer. Do not close SQL Query Analyzer.

4   Using Windows Explorer, navigate to the C:\Microsoft Press\SQL DTS SBS\DataMovementApplication folder, right-click Config2.cmd, and click Edit.

5   Change the value of the giConfigID parameter from 2 to 6 and then click Save As on the File menu.

6   Type ProcessOnly.cmd in the File Name box, select All Files in the Save As Type list, and then click Save. Close Notepad.

Now that you have created these configurations, you are ready to test the execution of the data movement application.

Test the execution of the data movement application

1   Using Windows Explorer, navigate to C:\Microsoft Press\SQL DTS SBS\DataMovementApplication and then double-click Process-Only.cmd.

2   After the ProcessOnly.cmd batch file completes its execution, switch to SQL Query Analyzer.

3   In the query window, change the query to read **SELECT * FROM SBS_OLAP.dbo.AuditEvents WHERE BatchID = 10 ORDER BY ExecutionDate** and then click Execute on the toolbar.

Notice that each of the subpackages were bypassed and then the *Process Sales Cube* step executed successfully.

4   Close SQL Query Analyzer, without saving any script changes, and then switch to Analysis Manager.

5   In the console tree, right-click Sales in the Cubes node and then click Refresh.

    The data that the Analysis Services Processing task loaded into the *Sales* cube is now visible for browsing.

6   Close Analysis Manager.

You have now successfully completed your prototype of a data movement application. In the next chapter, you will learn to use the data movement application to load monthly sales data into the Analysis Services cube and use the global variables and initialization file to control its execution without opening or editing any of the packages in the data movement application.

Chapter Summary

In this chapter you learned how to create a DTS package that you can use as a template for future packages. This template package enables you to quickly add to the data movement application additional packages that are configurable at run time using the same initialization file and global variables. You also learned how to add the remaining tasks to the data movement application to complete the prototype, including an Analysis Services Processing task to process an Analysis Services cube from within a DTS package.

Chapter

10

Operating the Data Movement Application

In this chapter, you will learn how to:

■ Load historical data

■ Use global variable and initialization file settings to load monthly data

■ Perform error checking, correct errors, and load corrected data

■ Create configurations to modify the execution of the data movement application

---

In this final chapter, you will operate the prototype of a data movement application to demonstrate its functionality and flexibility. You will begin by deleting the test data from the dimension, fact, staging, and auditing tables in the SBS_OLAP database and deleting all logs relating to the test data. You will then load the appropriate time records and historical data for calendar years 1996 and 1997 into the SBS_OLAP database and process that data into the *Sales* cube. Once the historical data is loaded, you will begin adding monthly sales data to the SBS_OLAP database and the *Sales* cube to exercise the capabilities of the data movement application. You will use the capabilities of the data movement application to load data from a non-default location, bypass tasks and packages for particular purposes based on configurations of global variables, verify and correct data load errors, and reload data that generated errors when it was originally loaded.

Resetting the Data Movement Application in the SBS_OLAP Database

In the following procedures, you will use the *TRUNCATE* statement to delete all test data from the dimension, fact, and auditing tables in the SBS_OLAP database, which will also reset the *IDENTITY* property for each table. You will then delete each log file in the C:\Microsoft Press\SQL DTS SBS\DataMovement-Application folder and delete the package logging data stored in Microsoft SQL Server. Finally, you will delete the delimited text files stored in the C:\Microsoft Press\SQL DTS SBS\DataMovementApplication folder that you used during the development of the data movement application.

▶ **Note**   If you skipped Chapter 9, execute the IfYouSkippedChapter9.cmd batch file in the C:\Microsoft Press\SQL DTS SBS\Ch10\SkippedChapterFiles folder before you begin these procedures. This batch file restores the SBS_OLTP and SBS_OLAP databases and copies the DTS packages that would have been created in Chapters 1 through 9 into the appropriate folders. It also records the location of the Config.ini initialization file in the Windows registry. If you do not want this batch file to overwrite any packages that you created in Chapters 1 through 9, you must move them or rename them before you execute this batch file. After executing this script you will also need to restore C:\Microsoft Press\SQL DTS SBS\Ch9\ChapterFiles\SQL DTS SBS.cab in Analysis Services. (See Chapter 9 for details.)

Reset the tables in the SBS_OLAP database

1   Open SQL Query Analyzer and then connect to your SQL Server instance as a system administrator.

2   On the toolbar, click Load SQL Script.

3   In the Look In box, navigate to C:\Microsoft Press\SQL DTS SBS\ Ch10\ChapterFiles and then double-click ResetTables.sql.

This script deletes all data from the dimension, fact, staging, and auditing tables in the SBS_OLAP database by using the *TRUNCATE TABLE* statement; this statement also resets the *IDENTITY* property on each of these tables to their initial *SEED* values (which in this case are 1). The *TRUNCATE TABLE* statement is used rather than the *DELETE* statement because it is faster, uses fewer system and transaction log resources, and resets the *IDENTITY* property. In order to execute the *TRUNCATE TABLE* statement, this script begins by dropping the foreign key constraints on the *SalesFact* table. It then recreates these constraints after the *TRUNCATE TABLE* statements have executed.

```
SQL Query Analyzer - [Query - NETSYS1LPTP2.SBS_OLAP.NETSYS1LPTP2...
File  Edit  Query  Tools  Window  Help

USE SBS_OLAP
GO
ALTER TABLE dbo.SalesFact DROP CONSTRAINT FK_SalesCustomer
ALTER TABLE dbo.SalesFact DROP CONSTRAINT FK_SalesProduct
ALTER TABLE dbo.SalesFact DROP CONSTRAINT FK_SalesTime
GO
TRUNCATE TABLE dbo.AuditEvents
TRUNCATE TABLE dbo.BatchIDValues
TRUNCATE TABLE dbo.SalesFact
TRUNCATE TABLE dbo.SalesFactErrorRows
TRUNCATE TABLE dbo.SalesStage
TRUNCATE TABLE dbo.TimeDim
TRUNCATE TABLE dbo.CustomerDim
TRUNCATE TABLE dbo.CustomerStage
TRUNCATE TABLE dbo.ProductDim
TRUNCATE TABLE dbo.ProductStage
GO
ALTER TABLE dbo.SalesFact ADD
    CONSTRAINT FK_SalesCustomer FOREIGN KEY
        (CustomerKey) REFERENCES dbo.CustomerDim (CustomerKey)
    ,CONSTRAINT FK_SalesProduct FOREIGN KEY
        (ProductKey) REFERENCES dbo.ProductDim (ProductKey)
    ,CONSTRAINT FK_SalesTime FOREIGN KEY
        (TimeKey) REFERENCES dbo.TimeDim (TimeKey)

Query batch NETSYS1LPTP2 (8.0)   NETSYS1LPTP2\Carl (52)   SBS_OLAP   0:00:00   0 rows   Ln 1, Col 1
                                                    Connections: 1
```

4   Execute the ResetTables.sql script.

Now that you have deleted the data in these tables and reset the *IDENTITY* properties, you will delete the delimited text files containing the test data and delete the text-based log files that the data movement application previously generated.

Delete delimited text files and text-based log files

1   Using Microsoft Windows Explorer, navigate to C:\Microsoft Press\SQL DTS SBS\DataMovementApplication.

> ▶ **Note**   If you skipped one or more of the previous chapters, some of the files listed below may not be present in the DataMovementApplication folder.

2   Delete the following files:
- 1996SalesData.txt
- 1997SalesData.txt
- LoadCustomerStageTableExceptionFile.txt
- LoadCustomerStageTableExceptionFile.txt.Dest
- LoadCustomerStageTableExceptionFile.txt.Source
- LoadHistoricalDataErrorLog.txt
- LoadProductDimTableExceptionFile.txt

- LoadProductStageTableExceptionFile.txt
- MasterUpdatePackageErrorLog.txt
- NewCustomers.txt
- NewProducts.txt
- NewSalesData.txt
- UpdateCustomerDimPackageErrorLog.txt
- UpdateProductDimPackageErrorLog.txt
- UpdateSalesFactsPackageErrorLog.txt
- UpdateTimeDimensionExecutionLog.txt

Now that you have deleted these text files, you will delete the logging information stored in SQL Server for the data movement application packages.

Deleting logging information stored in SQL Server

1   Open SQL Server Enterprise Manager.

2   Expand Microsoft SQL Servers, expand SQL Server Group, expand your SQL Server instance, and then expand Data Transformation Services.

3   Right-click Local Packages and then click Package Logs.

4   In the DTS Packages Available On The Server (LOCAL) list, select LoadHistoricalData.

5   Click Delete, click Delete All Logs For The Package: LoadHistorical-Data, and then click OK.

6   In the DTS Packages Available On The Server (LOCAL) list, select MasterUpdate.

7   Click Delete, click Delete All Logs For The Package: MasterUpdate, and then click OK.

8   In the DTS Packages Available On The Server (LOCAL) list, select UpdateCustomerDim.

9   Click Delete, click Delete All Logs For The Package: Update-CustomerDim, and then click OK.

10   In the DTS Packages Available On The Server (LOCAL) list, select UpdateProductDim.

11 Click Delete, click Delete All Logs For The Package: UpdateProduct-
Dim, and then click OK.

12 In the DTS Packages Available On The Server (LOCAL) list, select
UpdateSalesFacts.

13 Click Delete, click Delete All Logs For The Package: UpdateSales-
Facts, and then click OK.

14 Click Close.

Now that you have finished resetting the data movement application, you are
ready to load historical data into the SBS_OLAP database from the C:\Microsoft
Press\SQL DTS SBS\Ch10\ChapterFiles\Data folder and then process this data
into the *Sales* cube.

Loading Historical Data

Before you can successfully load the historical sales data for 1996 and 1997
into the *SalesFact* table in the SBS_OLAP database, you must add the appropriate time records to the time dimension table using the *PopulateTimeDimension*
package.

After the time records are added to the *TimeDim* table, you can use the *Load-
HistoricalData* package to load dimension data into the *ProductDim* and
CustomerDim tables from the SBS_OLTP database, and fact data into the
SalesFact table from delimited text files. The historical data that you will load is
located in the C:\Microsoft Press\SQL DTS SBS\Ch10\ChapterFiles\Data folder.
The *LoadHistoricalData* package is currently configured to load fact data from
the Sales1996.txt and Sales1997.txt files in the C:\Microsoft Press\SQL DTS SBS\
DataMovementApplication folder. You will edit the Config.ini file to point to
the *LoadHistoricalData* package to the SalesData1996.txt and SalesData1997.txt
files in the C:\Microsoft Press\SQL DTS SBS\Ch10\ChapterFiles\Data folder.
After you edit the Config.ini file, you will execute the *LoadHistoricalData*
package to load this historical data into the SBS_OLAP database, and then you
will execute the *MasterUpdate* package to process this data into the *Sales* cube.
Finally, you will verify that the historical data loaded successfully by viewing
the *AuditEvents* table and browsing the *Sales* cube using Analysis Manager.

Add Time dimension members by updating the UpdateTime-Dim.cmd file and then executing the *PopulateTimeDimension* package

1   Using Windows Explorer, navigate to C:\Microsoft Press\SQL DTS SBS\DataMovementApplication.

2   Right-click UpdateTimeDim.cmd and then click Edit.

3   Change the StartDate global variable value to **7/1/1996**.

4   Change the EndDate global variable value to **1/1/1998**.

5   Save the changes to the UpdateTimeDim.cmd batch file. Do not close the UpdateTimeDim.cmd file in Microsoft Notepad.

6   Switch to the DataMovementApplication folder in Windows Explorer, and then double-click UpdateTimeDim.cmd.

7   After this batch file completes its execution, double-click the Update-TimeDimensionExecutionLog.txt file in the DataMovementApplication folder to verify that the PopulateTimeDimension package executed successfully.

8   After reviewing the execution log, close the UpdateTimeDimension-ExecutionLog.txt file in Notepad.

Now that you have added time records to the time dimension table for the period covered by the historical data, you are ready to modify the Config.ini file to point to the historical data located in the C:\Microsoft Press\SQL DTS SBS\Ch10\ChapterFiles\Data folder.

Point the *LoadHistoricalData* package to new data files by modifying the Config.ini file

1   Switch to the DataMovementApplication folder using Windows Explorer, and then double-click Config.ini.

2   In the [HistoricalData] section, change the 1996Data key to **C:\Microsoft Press\SQL DTS SBS\Ch10\ChapterFiles\Data\ SalesData1996.txt**, and then change the 1997Data key to **C:\Microsoft Press\SQL DTS SBS\Ch10\ChapterFiles\Data\ SalesData1997.txt**.

3   Save the modified Config.ini file. Do not close the Config.ini file in Notepad.

You have just modified the Config.ini file to point to the new files, so you are ready to execute the *LoadHistoricalData* package.

Load the historical data by executing the *LoadHistoricalData* package using DTSRunUI

1   Click Start and then click Run.

2   In the Open box, type **DTSRunUI** and click OK.

You are using the DTSRunUI program because you have not created a batch file to run the *LoadHistoricalData* package. You do not need a batch file because you will run this package only once.

3   Select StructuredStorageFile in the Location list, type **C:\Microsoft Press\SQL DTS SBS\DataMovementApplication\ LoadHistoricalData.dts** in the File Name box, type **LoadHistoricalData** in the PackageName box, and then click Run.

4   Type **mypassword** in the Password box and then click OK.

5   Click OK.

The *ProductDim*, *CustomerDim*, and *SalesFact* tables were successfully loaded with historical data. The *SalesStage* table was used to stage the historical fact data before it was joined with dimension data from the three dimension tables and loaded into the *SalesFact* table.

6   Click Done and then click Cancel to close the DTS Run dialog box.

Now that you have loaded the historical data, you are ready to process that data into the *Sales* cube using the *MasterUpdate* package.

Process the *Sales* cube by executing the *MasterUpdate* Package and then review the *AuditEvents* table

1   Switch to the DataMovementApplication folder in Windows Explorer, and then double-click DeleteAllStagingData.cmd.

Executing the *MasterUpdate* package using the DeleteAllStaging-Data.cmd batch file executes the packages in the data movement application based on a *giConfigID* global variable value of 3. The global variables in the *PackageGVs* table associated with the *giConfigID* value of 3 specify that each subpackage execute its delete phase and that the *MasterUpdate* package process the *Sales* cube. Processing the *Sales* cube enables its data to be browsed. You must delete the data in each staging table before you load additional sales data to avoid duplicate data in the *Sales* cube.

2   After this batch file completes its execution, switch to SQL Query Analyzer and click Clear Window on the toolbar.

3   In the query pane, type **SELECT * FROM SBS_OLAP.dbo.AuditEvents ORDER BY ExecutionDate** and then click Execute on the toolbar.

Notice that the delete phases of the *UpdateCustomerDim*, *UpdateProductDim*, and *UpdateSalesFacts* subpackages executed, followed by the execution of the *ProcessSalesCube* task in the *MasterUpdate* package.

You have verified that the data in the staging tables was deleted and that the *Sales* cube was processed. Now you are ready to browse the *Sales* cube using Analysis Manager.

Browse the *Sales* cube in Analysis Manager

1   Click Start, point to All Programs, point to Microsoft SQL Server, point to Analysis Services, and then click Analysis Manager.

2   In the Analysis Manager console tree, expand Analysis Servers, expand your Analysis Services instance, expand SQL DTS SBS, expand Cubes, and then click Sales.

3   In the details pane, click the Data tab.

4   In the details pane, drag the Time dimension and drop it just above the Bill Country field in the Customer dimension.

Analysis Manager displays sales information sliced by the *Time* dimension. Notice that the *Sales* cube contains data only for 1996 and 1997.

5   Do not close Analysis Manager.

Now that you have verified that you can browse the *Sales* cube and that it contains only the appropriate historical data, you are ready to add new sales data for the month of January 1998.

Loading and Verifying Monthly Data

Before you can successfully load new sales data for January, you must add the appropriate time records to the *TimeDim* table, new product information (if any) to the *ProductDim* table, and new customer information (if any) to the *CustomerDim* table. You can add new time records for January 1998 by executing the *PopulateTimeDimension* package and passing appropriate global variable values to it by using the UpdateTimeDim.cmd batch file. The new sales information for January 1998 is stored in the SalesData199801.txt file located in the C:\Microsoft Press\SQL DTS SBS\Ch10\ChapterFiles\Data folder. You will edit the Config.ini file to point the *UpdateSalesFacts* package to this delimited text file. To demonstrate how to handle the error caused by a missing customer dimension member, you will not modify the Config.ini file to point the *UpdateCustomerDim* package to the new customer data stored in the NewCustData199801.txt file until after an error is generated. After you modify the Config.ini file, you will execute the *MasterUpdate* package using the MasterUpdateDefaultConfig.cmd batch file to load this new data, review the contents of the *AuditEvents* and the *SalesFactErrorRows* tables to determine the errors, and load a second batch that corrects for the errors that occur. Finally, you will process the *Sales* cube and then view the *Sales* cube in Analysis Manager to verify that the January data was added successfully.

Add new Time dimension members for January 1998 by modifying the UpdateTimeDim.cmd file and then executing the *PopulateTimeDimension* package

1   Switch to the UpdateTimeDim.cmd file in Notepad.

2   Change the StartDate global variable value to **1/1/1998** and then change the EndDate global variable value to **2/1/1998**.

3   Save the changes to the UpdateTimeDim.cmd batch file. Do not close this file in Notepad.

4   Switch to the DataMovementApplication folder in Windows Explorer, and then double-click UpdateTimeDim.cmd.

5   After this batch file completes its execution, switch to SQL Query Analyzer and then click New Query on the toolbar.

6   In the query pane, type **SELECT * FROM SBS_OLAP.dbo.TimeDim** and then click Execute on the toolbar.

   Verify that 580 rows appear in the results pane. It should contain a row for each date between July 1, 1996, and January 31, 1998.

7   Close the current query window without saving any changes, but do not close SQL Query Analyzer.

Now that you have added time records for January 1998 to the time dimension table, you are ready to modify the Config.ini file to point the *UpdateSalesFacts* subpackage to the delimited text file containing new sales data for January 1998.

Point the *UpdateSalesFacts* package to new sales data by modifying the Config.ini file

1   Switch to the Config.ini file in Notepad.

2   In the [NewSalesData] section, change the NewSalesData key to **C:\Microsoft Press\SQL DTS SBS\Ch10\ChapterFiles\Data\ SalesData199801.txt**.

3   Save the modified Config.ini file. Do not close the Config.ini file in Notepad.

You modified the Config.ini file, so you are ready to execute the *MasterUpdate* package using the MasterUpdateDefaultConfig.cmd batch file. Execution of this package loads the sales data for January 1998 into the *SalesFact* table in the SBS_OLAP database, but it does not process that data into the *Sales* cube. This allows you to check for, and correct, errors that might occur before processing the data into the *Sales* cube.

Execute the *MasterUpdate* package using the MasterUpdate-DefaultConfig.cmd file and then review the results

1   Switch to the DataMovementApplication folder in Windows Explorer and then double-click MasterUpdateDefaultConfig.cmd.

Executing the *MasterUpdate* package using the MasterUpdate.cmd batch file loads new sales data from the location specified in the Config.ini file into the SBS_OLAP database. No new product or customer data is loaded into the *ProductDim* and *CustomerDim* tables because the *ProductStage* and *CustomerStage* tables contain no data. No data is added to these tables during package execution because the keys in the Config.ini file for the *UpdateProductDim* and the *UpdateCustomerDim* packages do not point to valid delimited text files. However, the error caused by invalid delimited text files does not cause these packages to cease executing tasks because On Completion constraints are used after these steps rather than On Success constraints.

2   After this batch file completes its execution, switch to SQL Query Analyzer.

3   In the query pane, change the query to read **SELECT * FROM SBS_OLAP.dbo.AuditEvents WHERE BatchID = 2 ORDER BY ExecutionDate** and then click Execute on the toolbar.

The *LoadSalesStage* step added 152 new sales records to the *SalesStage* table, but the *LoadSalesFact* step added only 149 rows to the *SalesFact* table. Notice that the *UpdateProductDim* and *Update-CustomerDim* packages were unable to load any data from the delimited text files because the data files these packages attempted to load from did not exist. This failure is expected. Also, the *Sales* cube processing step was bypassed.

Now that you have added new sales data for January, you will view the data in the *SalesFactErrorRows* table to determine why three rows were not added to the *SalesFact* table. You will then correct the error and then add these error rows to the *SalesFact* table to ensure that the *Sales* cube will contain all sales data for January 1998.

Add missing dimension information and add the error rows to the *SalesStage* table and then to the *SalesFact* table

1   In SQL Query Analyzer, click New Query on the toolbar.

2   In the query pane, type **SELECT * FROM SBS_OLAP.dbo. SalesFactErrorRows** and click Execute on the toolbar.

The reason that three rows were not successfully inserted into the *SalesFact* table appears in the results pane. The *ErrorReason* column indicates that these rows were not inserted because the LACOR customer code was not present in the customer dimension table when the *UpdateSalesFacts* package attempted to insert sales data pertaining to this customer into the *SalesFact* table.

3   On the toolbar, click Clear Window, type **DELETE FROM SBS_OLAP.dbo.SalesStage WHERE CustomerCode != 'LACOR'** and then click Execute on the toolbar.

This script deletes the 149 rows of data in the *SalesStage* table that were successfully inserted into the *SalesFact* table. It leaves the three rows of new sales data in the *SalesStage* table that were not successfully inserted into the *SalesFact* table because the corresponding customer information was not added to the customer dimension table before the insert was attempted. The data movement application is designed so that it does not automatically delete data in the staging tables when the corresponding DTS package completes to enable you to easily resubmit error rows if necessary. Before you can resubmit these three error rows, you will point the *UpdateCustomerDim* package to the delimited text file containing the new data for the missing customer. The *UpdateCustomerDim* package will then load this information into the *CustomerDim* table.

4   On the toolbar, click Load SQL Script, click No, navigate to C:\Microsoft Press\SQL DTS SBS\Ch10\ChapterFiles, and then double-click ModifyDeleteConfigs.sql.

This script modifies configurations 3, 4, and 5 by configuring the *Process Sales Cube* step to be bypassed for each of these configurations. It also modifies configurations 4 and 5 by configuring the *UpdateSalesFacts* package to be bypassed for these configurations.

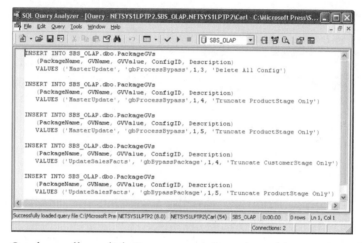

5   On the toolbar, click Execute and then close this query window. Do not close SQL Query Analyzer.

6   Switch to the DataMovementApplication folder in Windows Explorer, right-click DeleteAllStagingData.cmd and click Copy.

7   Right-click an open area in the DataMovementApplication folder and then click Paste.

8   Right-click Copy Of DeleteAllStagingData.cmd and then click Edit.

9   Change the value of the giConfigID global variable from 3 to **4**, and save this batch file as **DeleteProductStageData.cmd** (make sure you change the file type to All Files).

10   Change the value of the giConfigID global variable from 4 to **5**, save this batch file as **DeleteCustomerStageData.cmd** (make sure you change the file type to All Files), and then close this file in Notepad.

11   Switch to the DataMovementApplication folder in Windows Explorer, and then double-click DeleteProductStageData.cmd.

12   After this batch file completes its execution, double-click Delete-CustomerStageData.cmd.

13   After this batch file completes its execution, switch to SQL Query Analyzer and then click Clear Window on the toolbar.

14   In the query pane, type **SELECT * FROM SBS_OLAP.dbo.AuditEvents WHERE BatchID > 2 ORDER BY ExecutionDate** and then click Execute on the toolbar.

    Notice that the delete branch of the *UpdateProductDim* package executed as part of *BatchID* 3 and that the delete branch of the *UpdateCustomerDim* package executed as part of *BatchID* 4. The *UpdateSalesFact* package and the *Process Sales Cube* step was bypassed during each batch.

15 Switch to the Config.ini file in Notepad.

16 In the [Customers] section, change the NewCustomerData key to **C:\Microsoft Press\SQL DTS SBS\Ch10\ChapterFiles\Data\ NewCustData199801.txt.**

This text file contains the missing customer information for the new customer with a *CustomerCode* of LACOR.

17 In the [NewSalesData] section, change the NewSalesData key to **C:\Microsoft Press\SQL DTS SBS\Ch10\ChapterFiles\Data\ NoNewSalesData.txt.**

This step is required to avoid adding the new sales data for January a second time from the same text file. You could also modify the *UpdateSalesFacts* package to include a bypass step to bypass loading new data from a delimited text file whenever this functionality was required.

18 Save the modified Config.ini file. Do not close the Config.ini file in Notepad.

19 Switch to the DataMovementApplication folder in Windows Explorer, and then double-click MasterUpdateDefaultConfig.cmd.

The *UpdateCustomerDim* package adds new customer data to the *CustomerStage* table and then to the *CustomerDim* table. Thereafter, the *UpdateSalesFacts* table loads the three error rows remaining in the *SalesStage* table into the *SalesFacts* table.

20 After this batch file completes its execution, switch to SQL Query Analyzer.

21 In the query pane, modify the query to read **SELECT * FROM SBS_OLAP.dbo.AuditEvents WHERE BatchID = 5 ORDER BY ExecutionDate** and then click Execute on the toolbar.

One new row was added to the *CustomerStage* table by the *Update-CustomerDim* subpackage and three rows were added to the *Sales-Fact* table.

Now that you have verified that all January sales data was success-fully added to the *SalesFacts* table, you need to process the *Sales* cube.

22 Switch to the DataMovementApplication folder in Windows Explorer and then double-click ProcessOnly.cmd.

23 After this batch file completes its execution, switch to SQL Query Analyzer.

24 In the query pane, modify the query to read **SELECT * FROM SBS_OLAP.dbo.AuditEvents WHERE BatchID = 6 ORDER BY ExecutionDate** and then click Execute on the toolbar.

The *Sales* cube is successfully processed.

25 Switch to the DataMovementApplication folder in Windows Explorer and then double-click DeleteAllStagingData.cmd.

You must delete all staging data for January before you add new data for February.

Now that you have added all new sales data for January and processed the *Sales* cube, you are ready to browse the *Sales* cube to verify that the January data was added successfully.

Browse the *Sales* cube in Analysis Manager

1 Switch to Analysis Manager.

2 In the Analysis Manager console tree, right-click Sales and click Refresh.

3 In the details pane, drag the Time dimension and drop it just above the Bill Country field in the Customer dimension.

4 Expand 1998 and then expand Quarter 1 to display the sales information for January 1998.

5   In the Customer dimension list, click All Customer, expand All Customer, expand France, expand the region level, expand Versailles, and then click La Corne D'Abondance.

The sales made in January to the customer with the customer code of LACOR appear. The data movement application successfully added the error rows.

Now that you have verified that the *Sales* cube contains the January 1998 sales data, you will add data for February.

Add new Time dimension members for February 1998 by modifying the UpdateTimeDim.cmd file and then executing the *PopulateTimeDimension* package

1 Switch to the UpdateTimeDim.cmd file in Notepad.

2 Change the StartDate global variable value to **2/1/1998** and then change the EndDate global variable value to **3/1/1998**.

3 Save the changes to the UpdateTimeDim.cmd batch file and then close the UpdateTimeDim.cmd batch file in Notepad.

4 Switch to the DataMovementApplication folder in Windows Explorer, and then double-click UpdateTimeDim.cmd.

You have added time records for February 1998 to the *TimeDim* table. Now you are ready to modify the Config.ini file so that it will point the *Update-SalesFacts* subpackage to the delimited text file containing new sales data for February 1998.

Modify the Config.ini file

1 Switch to the Config.ini file in Notepad.

2 In the [NewSalesData] section, change the NewSalesData key to **C:\Microsoft Press\SQL DTS SBS\Ch10\ChapterFiles\Data\ SalesData199802.txt**.

3 In the [Customers] section, change the NewCustomerData key to **C:\Microsoft Press\SQL DTS SBS\Ch10\Data\ NoNewCustomerData.txt**.

   No new customer or product data is needed for February, and you do not want to add the LACOR customer again to the *CustomerDim* table because it would duplicate existing data in that table.

4 Save the modified Config.ini file and then close the Config.ini file in Notepad.

Now that you have modified the Config.ini file, you are ready to execute the *MasterUpdate* package using the MasterUpdateDefaultConfig.cmd batch file, which will load the sales data for February into the *SalesFact* table in the SBS_OLAP database.

Execute the *MasterUpdate* package, review the results, process the *Sales* cube, and delete staging data

1   Switch to the DataMovementApplication folder in Windows Explorer, and then double-click MasterUpdateDefaultConfig.cmd.

The February 1998 sales data is added to the *SalesStage* table and then joined with the dimension data and added to the *SalesFact* table. No new data is loaded into the *ProductDim* and *CustomerDim* tables because no data exists in the *ProductStage* and *CustomerStage* tables. No data is added to the *ProductStage* and *CustomerStage* tables during package execution because the keys in the Config.ini file for the *UpdateProductDim* and the *UpdateCustomerDim* packages do not point to valid delimited text files.

2   After this batch file completes its execution, switch to SQL Query Analyzer.

3   In the query pane, change the query to read **SELECT * FROM SBS_OLAP.dbo.AuditEvents WHERE BatchID = 8 ORDER BY ExecutionDate** and then click Execute on the toolbar.

The *LoadSalesStage* step added 122 new sales records to the *SalesStage* table, and the *LoadSalesFact* step added 122 rows to the *SalesFact* table. Since there are no new error rows, you are ready to process the *Sales* cube and delete all staging data.

4 Switch to the DataMovementApplication in Windows Explorer, and then double-click ProcessOnly.cmd.

5 After this batch file completes its execution, double-click DeleteAll-StagingData.cmd.

6 After this batch file completes, switch to SQL Query Analyzer.

7 In the query pane, change the query to read **SELECT * FROM SBS_OLAP.dbo.AuditEvents WHERE BatchID > 8 ORDER BY ExecutionDate** and then click Execute on the toolbar.

The Sales cube was processed during *BatchID* 9 and all staging data was deleted during *BatchID* 10.

8 Close SQL Query Analyzer without saving any queries.

You have processed the *Sales* cube, and you are ready to browse the *Sales* cube and add more sales data as it becomes available.

Browse the *Sales* cube in Analysis Manager

1 Switch to Analysis Manager.

2 In the Analysis Manager console tree, right-click Sales and then click Refresh.

3 In the details pane, drag the Time dimension and drop it just above the Bill Country field in the Customer Dimension.

4   Expand 1998 and then expand Quarter 1.

The sales information for January and February 1998 appears in the *Sales* cube.

You are now ready to add data for additional months and operate the data movement application on your own. Additional sales data for March, April, and May is located in the C:\Microsoft Press\SQL DTS SBS\Ch10\ChapterFiles\Data folder. Have fun!

Chapter Summary

In this chapter you learned how to operate the data movement application and manipulate how it executes by using an initialization file, global variables, and batch files. You were able to execute the packages in the data movement application exactly the way you wanted them to execute without having to open or edit any of the packages. As you work with this prototype of a data movement application, you will discover many ways in which you can improve upon its design. With the knowledge you have gained throughout the course of this book, you now have the skills to improve upon the design of this data movement application and build your own.

Index

Symbols and Numbers

A

B

G

H

I

About the Author

Carl Rabeler is an MCT, MCDBA, and MCSE. In conjunction with the Business Intelligence Practices group at Microsoft, Carl authored the technical documentation for the SQL Server Accelerator for Business Intelligence, the DTS Programming Practices Used in SQL Server Accelerator for Business Intelligence white paper, and the Microsoft Analysis Services Performance Guide white paper. Carl wrote the SQL Server High Availability Series, which is available via MSDN. He also wrote the Microsoft SQL Server 2000 System Administration MCSE Training Kit and the Academic Learning Series course based on that book. Before that, he was a subject matter expert for the Microsoft Official Courseware group from 1995 through 2000, working with both Microsoft SQL Server and Microsoft Exchange Server. Carl has also been an independent software consultant since 1989, developing hardware and software solutions for a variety of customers.

Get a **Free**
e-mail newsletter, updates,
special offers, links to related books,
and more when you

register online!

Register your Microsoft Press® title on our Web site and you'll get a FREE subscription to our e-mail newsletter, *Microsoft Press Book Connections.* You'll find out about newly released and upcoming books and learning tools, online events, software downloads, special offers and coupons for Microsoft Press customers, and information about major Microsoft® product releases. You can also read useful additional information about all the titles we publish, such as detailed book descriptions, tables of contents and indexes, sample chapters, links to related books and book series, author biographies, and reviews by other customers.

Registration is easy. Just visit this Web page and fill in your information:

http://www.microsoft.com/mspress/register

Microsoft®

- -

Proof of Purchase

Use this page as proof of purchase if participating in a promotion or rebate offer on this title. Proof of purchase must be used in conjunction with other proof(s) of payment such as your dated sales receipt—see offer details.

Microsoft® SQL Server™ 2000 DTS Step by Step
0-7356-1916-6

CUSTOMER NAME

Microsoft Press, PO Box 97017, Redmond, WA 98073-9830